Convictions

Convictions

by

DONALD COGGAN
Archbishop of Canterbury

WILLIAM B. EERDMANS PUBLISHING COMPANY
Grand Rapids, Michigan

Library of Congress Cataloging in Publication Data
Coggan, Frederick Donald, 1909–
    Convictions.

    1. Coggan, Frederick Donald, 1909–
2. Theology—Addresses, essays, lectures.
3. England—Biography. I. Title.
BX5199.C567A33 1976   230'.3   75-42458
ISBN 0-8028-3481-7
Printed in Great Britain

To the memory of my parents
and
in gratitude to my sisters, Norah and Beatrice,
who have helped me along the way.

Preface

IN THIS BOOK I have gathered together a number of lectures, sermons and addresses given during the thirteen and a half years in which I was Archbishop of York, and during my opening months as Archbishop of Canterbury.

The conditions under which they were given varied greatly— some abroad, some at home; some in great cathedrals, others in more humble buildings; some to big congregations, some to small. I have not gone to extremes to eliminate all repetition, for to have done so too rigorously might well have involved upsetting the balance of the addresses from which big omissions were made.

A glance at the contents of the book will show that a wide variety of subjects is dealt with. The treatment has often had to be slight, for some occasions only allowed a brief address. While this exposed the speaker to a charge of superficiality, the very outlinear nature of the treatment has this advantage. It invites the reader to do his own thinking and himself to fill in some of the gaps.

I hope that this collection, for all its faults, will serve both to illustrate what are some of the most important issues which have exercised my mind in recent years, and what have been—and are—some of the basic convictions by which my ministry is under-girded. I believe most of these issues will continue to concern us in the closing quarter of this momentous century.

Donald Cantuar:

Acknowledgments

THE AUTHOR AND publisher are grateful to those who have co-operated in making the material in this book available:

To Constable, Publishers, for permission to quote from *Authority in a Changing Society*, edited by C. O. Rhodes; to William Collins Sons & Co Ltd., Publishers, for permission to quote from "An Expostulation" by C. S. Lewis; to the Council of the Shaftesbury Society for permission to reproduce the Shaftesbury Lecture, given in October 1973; to the University of Western Australia Press for permission to reproduce the Lecture *The Relevance of the Bible for Today;* to the editor of the Leicester Cathedral Quarterly for permission to reproduce *Two Score Years —and Then?;* to the University of Exeter for permission to reproduce *Peter Green—Parish Priest.*

Contents

I TWO SCORE YEARS— AND THEN?

Retrospect and Prospect

THOSE OF YOU brought up on the Authorised Version or the Prayer Book Version of the Psalms will recognise the title of this lecture as having been suggested by the phrase of the Psalmist, "three score years and ten" (Psalm 90:10), man's allotted span, as it has come to be called. Others of you, more materially minded, may recall an advertisement which adorned our hoardings some years ago, put up by an insurance company which wanted to draw their clients' attention to the provision which they should make for the closing years of their lives. It read: "Three score years—and then?"

My title is, frankly, autobiographical. But, lest the adjective "autobiographical" should be interpreted in your thinking in terms purely personal or even self-centred, let me say at once that, though the framework of the lecture may be autobiographical, it will be so only in order to provide a structure on which to erect and set out certain thoughts, retrospective and prospective, about matters of far greater importance than any which might affect me alone.

It was two score years ago (to within a matter of days) that I was made deacon in St Paul's Cathedral, London, by Arthur Foley Winnington-Ingram, Bishop of London. That in itself is good enough excuse for retrospect. Within a matter of weeks (just over nine, in fact), I shall, God willing, be confirmed as Archbishop of Canterbury. That is good enough excuse for looking forward—or at least for trying to. I am at the parting of the way.

The Ashe Lecture given in Ashby de la Zouch Parish Church, 1st October, 1974.

Unlike Gaul which, we are assured on good authority, was divided into three parts, these forty years have been divided into five—three as a curate, seven as a professor, twelve as a theological principal, five and a half as a bishop and over thirteen as an archbishop. They have been years full of interest, as exhilarating in the variety of their work as they have been demanding in the calls they have made on thought and strength. Let me, in a few brief strokes, sketch each sphere of work, the better to see the background against which one has been able to detect the Spirit of God at work.

1. Islington, in North London, in the mid-thirties was no Garden of Eden. It was, in fact, an area which pretty accurately reflected the depression of a dismal decade. Its streets were drab and its tenement buildings noisy and ill-kept. The playing spaces of Highbury Fields were too far off for the children of that unangelic district round the Angel to get to very frequently. Their toes had a way of sticking out through their boots. Dad, as likely as not, was unemployed, and grandmum was living on an old-age pension of ten shillings a week. The Welfare State, to whose beneficence we have grown accustomed, was at that stage only a vision in the mind's eye of men like Keynes and Bevan. Conditions were grim, and called for all the cockney humour and resilience that could be mustered. And those hospitals! Miles of chocolate-painted corridors and, in the T.B. wards, windows open all day on both sides to admit the wind and fog; the blue-red noses of the patients and little else being visible above the sheets on the beds. A mother and father and ten youngsters, the baby cradled in a drawer, all of them in one upstairs flat—such were the conditions which obtained in 1934.

It was a strange world to which to come as the junior curate, the stranger, perhaps, because of the contrast it afforded with the work on which I had been engaged. Three years study at Cambridge (and what bliss those years afforded after the restrictions and the inhibitions of public school life!) had been followed by three years teaching of Semitic languages and literatures in the University of Manchester. It was a lively university in a lively city, where trams and tripe, philosophy and music, theology and science all seemed to prosper even if soot and fog abounded. The life was predominantly academic—that was how I earned my bread and butter; that was how I began to learn how to teach, learning more by the mistakes I doubtless made, than by any instruction in the art of teaching, for there was none. But as my late school years had been interspersed with visits to the slums of Hoxton, so my academic years at Manchester had seen many a sortie to the sordid areas of Manchester and the adjoining Salford. I came to Islington not without some experience of "the other side" of life. But Islington provided it at close quarters and with a more cruel intimacy.

Intimacy of contact with the people was not easy to achieve, but, once achieved, was precious. I used to notice, not without a measure of envy, the comfortable rapport which existed between the London City Missioner who was on the parish staff and the roughs who frequented his club in the crypt of the church. The kind of people to whom one sought to minister taught one to speak in simple language, and the kindly banter of the vicar who insisted that I addressed them on the Tell-el-Amarna tablets (was there ever such a lie?) served as a warning to put the great things of God in terms which could be understood by people who had little educational equipment (though they were often spiritual giants).

When the call to ordination came to this boy of sixteen, he could conceive of no greater destiny than that of being a parish priest in the sort of area to which, some nine years later, he went. It may well be that, in fact, there *is* no greater destiny than that. This is the very essence of the work of the clergy of the Church of England. But the years at Cambridge and then at Manchester (and the spell at Oxford reading theology) had made me look at the matter from another angle. *Quis custodiet custodes*? Might not the training of tomorrow's clergy be a work of greater influence than that of the parish priest? Could such gifts as God had given in the way of scholarship be best used in theological college work? It was such considerations as these which made one open, not without trembling, to the offer, when it came, of a post on the teaching staff of just such a college, and which led on to the spending of nineteen years in the cause of theological education.

2. The years at Wycliffe College, Toronto, were to prove years of great enrichment. My studies hitherto had lain mainly in the field of the Old Testament, of Hebrew and its cognate

languages Aramaic and Syriac. Now they centred mainly on
the New Testament, the teaching of Greek, the exposition of
Gospels and Epistles and of the Inter-Testament period to a lively
lot of men whose task it was to be the clergy of Canada's tomorrow.
But the work was not confined to study and lecture-room. There
was preaching a-plenty, and that not only in Toronto but in the
neighbouring towns and cities, harvest services in the fruit-laden
Niagara peninsular, summer services among the lakes and on Toronto Island, winter visits to Oshawa and Hamilton and Barrie
and a score of other towns. Then there were the journeys to
New Brunswick and Nova Scotia and Prince Edward Island, so
reminiscent of quiet homeland countryside; visits to the great
prairie towns whose vast grain towers rose like cathedrals
against the sky-line; and visits to the foot-hills of the Rockies,
and through and over them to the Pacific, to Vancouver and
Victoria. Canada was a mighty Dominion awaiting exploration
and abundantly rewarding the explorer.

Here, as one worked and travelled, one was introduced to an
aspect of the great Anglican Communion of which one had
known but little when serving in the Mother Country. Here, too,
one came to know some of the giants of the United Church
of Canada and, more distantly (for Vatican II was still far ahead),
of the Roman Catholic Church, especially in its strongholds of
Quebec and Montreal. Later journeys, in Africa and Asia and
Australia and elsewhere, were to widen the vision, but Canada
provided a good beginning.

Here, as I lectured and travelled and visited churches and
rectories (there are no vicarages in Canada), I saw the need of the
clergy for help in their work of preaching, and was able to do
something, through schools of preaching held at various centres,
to help some at least to see it not as a burden and a drudgery, but
as a "many-splendoured thing".

3.   But England called, an England in the throes of a desperate
war. The London College of Divinity, to whose principalship I
came just before the doodle-bugs began to fall, had been hard-hit
by war. It had no staff and its tiny residuum of students had been
transferred to another college. Decisions of great complexity as
to its future had to be made. Should it return to its old and battered
buildings at Highbury? Or should a new site be sought and new

buildings erected? Where should the right staff be found? What should be the dominant note which the college should sound? What kind of training was needed for men most of whom had seen service in the stern school of World War II and who were facing the challenge and the uncertainties of the forties and fifties of the twentieth century? These were questions not easy of solution, and their answers were only found by the mercy of God, the skill of a staff of high calibre and the support of a wife of wonderful devotion. The imagination and dash of Ralph Dean (later to become the second executive officer of the Anglican Communion), the provocatively stimulating lecturing of Douglas Webster (now canon of St Paul's), and the quiet and consistent godliness of Robert Hooper (later to become successively vicar of Midhurst, Lewes, and St John the Evangelist, Eastbourne) were only some of the gifts by which the Holy Spirit enriched the Church during that period and in that college.

They were testing years; but, as so often, testing years proved to be creative years. One learned to lean hard on the total adequacy of God.

4. The change from the principalship of a theological college to the oversight of a diocese was not, perhaps, as great as might be imagined. One's contact with the clergy, both in Canada and in England, had been deep, and one had been enabled to see at pretty close quarters the conditions under which they worked and the problems which they faced.

The winds which blew round York Minster on the feast of the Conversion of St Paul, 25th January, 1956, were cold, but the sight of a crowded minster was enough to cheer the man who came to be consecrated that day, and the prayers of the worshippers enough to steady him. The chief consecrator was Bishop Leslie Hunter of Sheffield, Archbishop Cyril Garbett having died less than a month before. Michael Ramsey, then at Durham, was about to follow him at York.

What better diocese could a new bishop go to than Bradford? It was—and is—unbelievably beautiful (most of it!), stretching up as far as Dent and Sedbergh and including "wuthering heights", which, while they can be forbidding and even frightening, can be exquisite in the charm of their colours and contours. It is, as English dioceses go, small, having been carved out as recently

as 1919 from the diocese of Ripon. I was to be only its third
bishop, A. W. T. Perowne and Alfred W. F. Blunt having been
my predecessors.

The diocese, I think it would be true to say, was in low water.
Alfred Blunt, scholar and man of God that he was, had outstayed
his strength, and things had run down. Much waited to be done
in terms of building of new churches, of encouragement of
clergy and laity, and so on. The cathedral, under the vigorous
leadership of its provost, John G. Tiarks (later to be Bishop of
Chelmsford), was being transformed from an ancient and dark
parish church five hundred years old to a light and beautiful
cathedral, fashioned after the design of Sir Edward Maufe. It
became a building worthy of being the mother church of a diocese.

The response and the warm-heartedness of the West Yorkshire
people would have heartened any man, and there was much to
encourage. But the stay was to prove short-lived.

5. With the resignation of Geoffrey Fisher from the arch-
bishopric of Canterbury in 1961 and Michael Ramsey's removal
to the primacy of All England, the see of York was left vacant.
The summons to succeed him at York came through the agency
of Harold Macmillan, after a preliminary talk with him at
Admiralty House (No 10 Downing Street was being repaired at
that time). It came, I recall, during a meeting of York Convocation, and my wife and I were staying at Bishopthorpe. It
was made over the telephone, just before I set off to make a
speech on the revision of the Catechism (of which task Archbishop
Fisher had put me in charge). It must, I think, have been a singularly bad speech that I made that morning, for my mind was
elsewhere!

Enthronement took place on 13th September, 1961, and proved
to be the prelude to over thirteen years of work of intense
interest and great variety. I have envisaged my work as archbishop
in terms of a series of widening circles. The smallest and most
intimate of these is the diocese of York, though this in itself is
no mean task. It would prove quite impossible if it were not for
the co-operation of a team, varied but closely knit, of three
suffragan bishops, three archdeacons, and twenty-seven rural
deans. The diocese, in addition to its historic and stately Minster,
has a wealth of churches, varying from such world-famous

buildings as Beverley Minster and Selby Abbey to great parish churches in the conurbations of Middlesbrough and Hull, and priceless gems, big and small, scattered in villages over the wolds. It is a high privilege for the archbishop to be able to do what in fact he was ordained and consecrated to do—to preach the Word and minister the Sacraments year in year out, and to institute his clergy to new charges, encouraging them in days when no priest's work is easy.

That is his first sphere of work. But beyond the diocese lies the province, consisting of fourteen dioceses, stretching up to the Scottish border and out to the little Isle of Man. Here he goes on visits of various kinds, generally to take part in some occasion of special significance to the diocese or district concerned.

The third circle which claims the archbishop's attention is wider in its outreach than diocese or province. It often finds its focus in London, where General Synod or some central committee calls for his presence. But often it is elsewhere—a school here or a university there, a gathering of clergy at a summer school or an assembly of a different kind looking for a word in season.

Beyond this sphere of influence lies the Anglican Communion, where other provinces and dioceses seem still to welcome the visit of an archbishop from England. What an immense variety of worship and work is to be found, from the Arctic to the Equator, in this brotherhood of episcopal Churches! And how enriched is the visitor when he returns home, and seeks to share with his own flock some of the treasures which he has found abroad!

The widest of all the circles is that of the world-wide Church as it seeks to minister to world-wide needs. As the barriers which have so long separated one branch of the Christian Church from another slowly lower, one can begin to see a little more clearly what the Lord of the Church meant when He said: "You are light to the world . . . You are salt . . ."

So two score years have slipped by—so swiftly! Perhaps as one scans them in retrospect, the most appropriate prayer is the Jesus prayer which forms so large a part in the devotion of the Eastern Orthodox Church: "Lord Jesus Christ, Son of God, have mercy on me a sinner".

But other reflections suggest themselves, and I offer some of them for you to ponder.

1. I am impressed by the *craving for God* which has manifested itself during these decades. This, from one point of view, is the more surprising when we consider the scientific sophistication of these years. During them, man has ventured out into space, taken his first timid steps on the moon, and started to explore the universe in person. Man has "come of age"—the phrase so beloved by Bonhoeffer has been taken up by a posse of theologians and expounded (though sometimes in ways of which he himself might well have disapproved). Why bother about God? Has not the time come when He can be discounted? Is not the very idea of Him a relic of a pre-scientific age?

Yet these are the very years in which we have witnessed a strange feeling after Him if haply men might find Him. Great numbers of our young people, sitting loose to, or even spurning, the orthodoxies of the established Churches, have felt the emptiness, the awful void, of an existence limited to what a materialistic creed can offer. They have sought for something deeper in the mysticism of the East, or for the experiences which can be induced by the use of drugs. They have refused—and how right they have been!—to restrict the use of the word "obscene" to the realm of the sexual, and, with a clarity of vision sometimes denied to their elders, have used the word of racism or of the despoliation of nature through an upsetting of the ecological balance or a defilement of the air or the sea. They may have no clearly defined doctrine of creation such as would satisfy a Christian theologian, but they have a clear perception of the blasphemy occasioned by an atomic bomb or by a Sharpeville.

And what about *Godspell* and *Jesus Christ Superstar*? These cannot be dismissed as mere blasphemies of the stage. That would indeed be a superficial judgment. Must they not rather be seen as a re-action to the question which refuses to be silenced in any age and—as is proving to be the case—least of all in this most scientific age: "Who *is* this Jesus?" The rise of the Jesus cults may seem to the orthodox to be a long stride away from the full-orbed trinitarianism of the Catholic faith. But he would be a foolish man who dismissed these movements as mere irruptions of the emotional. Why have they irrupted? This is no search for "pie in the sky when we die". The search for God is often most clamant where material conditions are most comfortable.

2. I note, secondly, *the resilience of the Christian faith.* It is true that, in the West, during these decades the winds have blown fierce and cold on the Churches. Numbers of adherents, of ordinands, of confirmees, of communicants have declined steeply. The authority of the Church, like that of the Bible and the creeds, has been a subject for questioning rather than for obedience. In Europe there has been recession; and in the United States of America, if this recession has been slower in making its appearance than it has here, it can scarcely be doubted that it is already under way. It may be that the recession is now being halted in the West and that a return has begun. We who are *in medias res* are hardly in a position to judge rightly.

But let us lift up our eyes and get a *world* view. No previous generation of Christians has ever been in a better position to do so. The mass media and the printed word especially, as well as world conferences, enable us to see how the total battle is going. Was Latourette right when he compared the progress of Christianity to the advance of the tide—recession and progress, recession and progress, but progress winning over recession? That picture of the learned Latourette has to be checked by the facts presented by the meteoric rise of world population, and especially in the countries of what we call the third world. In view of the figures of the demographers, we must not take the Latourette picture too optimistically.

But it is precisely in these countries which I have just mentioned that the growth of the Church is most rapid. The problem in many parts of Latin America and of Africa—to take only two areas—is not primarily how to make converts to Christianity. It is how to train and build up those who are pouring into the Christian Church at a rate which is proving embarrassing for its leaders.

God is not dead, for all that a brand of theologians has been telling us in recent years. God is not dead. Nor is His Church.

> For while the tired waves, vainly breaking,
> Seem here no painful inch to gain,
> Far back, through creeks and inlets making,
> Comes silent, flooding in, the main.
>
> (A. H. Clough)

3. I invite you to ponder, thirdly, *a return to the New Testament* during these two score years. You will note how I put this. Not "the *spread* of the New Testament", though I might well have touched on this, for these years have seen the birth and growth of the United Bible societies which have harnessed the scholarship and skills and devotion of the Bible societies of the world in the dissemination and understanding of the Bible. No: I refer to a "*return* to the New Testament".

In using this phrase, I am not shutting my eyes to the fact that a generation of New Testament scholars of the type of E. C. Hoskyns and Lionel Thornton (to mention but two) was followed by men who had to face questions raised by a Rudolf Bultmann there and a John Robinson here. I am simply noting the fact that, in decades during which fundamental questions of the deepest theological gravity about the New Testament were being raised and discussed, we have also been witnessing a return to the New Testament which is proving fruitful in the realm of the reunion of the Church. I think particularly of the matter of Anglican-Roman dialogue. Here we have been pressing back, behind the controversies of the centuries and especially of the Reformation period, to the beginnings, to the documents which bear to us the witness of the earliest generations of the faithful. As we have done so, we have begun to find a fundamental unity of belief which, for all the clouding of the intervening centuries, is borne witness to within the pages of Scripture. Evidence of such unity is to be found in the Agreed Statements on the Eucharist and on the Ministry issued by the Anglican-Roman Catholic International Commission in 1973. May this be but the beginning of a renewal of understanding such as we have not seen since the days of the Reformation.

4. I note lastly that, during these two decades, there has been a *revival of worship*. Within our own Anglican Communion, this has in part taken the form of the revision, sometimes conservative, sometimes more radical, of the services of the Church. No longer can one talk, as one could forty years ago, of "the incomparable liturgy" of *ecclesia anglicana* as binding together its constituent parts. A traveller throughout our communion is likely to find a very wide variety of forms of worship, though the Eucharist in its central part retains a universally recognisable form. Something

has been lost—not least in dignity and in the sense of the numinous, of the awe-full. But much has been gained, not least in the realisation that Christian worship is the worship, not only of "the man up there" in the sanctuary, but of the people of God as a whole. It is an activity, indeed the highest activity of which man is capable, in which all share—be it the girl who reads the epistle, the reader who preaches, or the priest who consecrates the elements.

But during these years the English Church has had the opportunity to benefit from and to enrich its worship by insights gained from other branches of the ecumenical Church. Who can watch an African, perhaps a first or second generation Christian, at worship without catching something of the joy which is so often lacking in the performance of the sober liturgies of the West? Have not the Pentecostals something to say to us about movement and the spontaneity of music and perhaps of dancing as an expression of the freedom which Christ brings to His worshippers? And do not the ancient liturgies of the Orthodox speak a word about resurrection and light to those of us who tend to stay our thoughts too long on one side of Calvary?

The worship of a truly ecumenical Church should be a livelier and a lovelier thing than that of a Church which has lived to itself for long and sometimes barren years. Intellect, emotion, and will should join hands in the sacrament of the Word and in the sacrament of the Body and Blood of Christ.

Yes, they have been rich years, these two score years.

"And then?" One is tempted to say with Amos: "I am no prophet nor the son of a prophet", and to leave it at that. The pace at which things are moving, within the Church and without, is so fast that he would be a very rash man who thought he could discern clearly the pattern of even a few years ahead. Prophecy would be rash. The expression of certain hopes might, however, be allowed. I offer you two such hopes even if only in skeleton form.

1. I hope that the Church will be true to its divine Master's commission to feed His flock. It is their task to feed the sheep—not to entertain the goats. Others can do that. It is their task to point men to *God*—only there will their thirst be satisfied. Others can provide the social services, but no government can lead men to God. This is not to disparage for one moment works of compassion done in the name of Christ, or to deny that we find Him

when we minister to His needy ones, for that is a basic tenet of the Gospel. What I assert is the truth of Christ's dictum that man cannot *live* on bread alone. He *must* have the Word of God. It is the primary privilege and responsibility of Christians to see that that Word is available for all, in a form they can understand and appreciate.

If what I have said about man's craving for God is right, then the members of Christ's Church must show the deepest sympathy and understanding to those who are seeking for the Bread of Life, however distorted the form of their plea.

I cannot now elaborate my views on the primacy of preaching as a means of grace, a continuation in time of God's work of redemption. I believe that it is a weak and enfeebled Church which has a low doctrine of the Word. But here I am thinking of something broader than the pulpit ministry by which men are fed. They are fed in more informal ways than that. They are fed when some hungry person opens up his need to a Christian man or woman, who is able, in humility and frankness, to tell them what the goodness of God has meant and at that moment means to them. This is feeding the flock of Christ. You do not need to be a professor of divinity to do that work. When St Paul was expounding the varieties of gifts with which the Spirit enriches his Church, he said that "to one is given through the Spirit the utterance of wisdom, and to another the utterance of knowledge . . ." (1 Cor. 12:8). Now if I need *knowledge*, I go to the good professor—his knowledge is indeed a gift of the Spirit. If I need *wisdom*, I may or may not go to the professor. That all depends on the kind of professor he is. For wisdom I may go to someone who has never read a book of theology and is never likely to, but who has lived long enough and near enough to God to be wise with the wisdom that comes from above. He (or she) can feed me. I need God. He or she may be the link, or perhaps *you*.

2. My second hope is that the Church in the next few years will recapture its joy. Should I be misunderstood if I said that in recent years we have had something of a surfeit of ecclesiastical breast beating? Of course, the Church has plenty to repent of, so let us repent, and do it thoroughly. But let us not go to the world as if we have nothing to be thankful for. God has worked

gloriously through His Church again and again, and is doing so today.

Is not the very resilience of the Church, of which I have been speaking, a cause for joy and exultation in the Holy Spirit? Is not the return to the New Testament, which I mentioned earlier, a sign of the activity of the re-creative Spirit, and therefore a cause for great joy? And is not the revival of worship another manifest sign of the operation in the Church of the Lord, the Life-giver?

It is time that those sections of the Church which have gone to the world suggesting that the proclamation of good news is rather unseemly and that all we can do is to ask the right questions, should re-read their New Testaments, and from them regain that note of confidence which is an authentic part of the Christian revelation. Too long has hope been the neglected member of the Pauline trio of faith, hope, and love.

When I speak of joy, I do not, of course, mean any back-slapping heartiness. Joy very often comes through pain, as birth comes through travail. Peace, the near-cousin of joy, is often found by running into the midst of the storm, not by avoiding it. Confidence and hope are found by grappling with problems, not by evading them. In the New Testament joy is no frothy thing. It is the result of faith in the crucified and risen Christ. "My soul magnifies the Lord, and my spirit rejoices in God my Saviour".

My hope and prayer for the Church of the last quarter of the twentieth century is that it will turn to the world a face that reflects something of Him "who, for the joy that was set before Him, endured the cross, despising the shame, and is seated at the right hand of the throne of God" (Heb. 12:2).

II GREAT OCCASIONS

Farewell Eucharist at York Minster

Love and Peace

2 Cor. 13:11 (RSV)
Finally, brethren, farewell. Mend your ways,
heed my appeal, agree with one another, live
in peace, and the God of love and peace will be
with you.

THE CHURCH IN Corinth had been a tough
proposition for St Paul. To found a Church at all in Corinth was
something of a triumph. "The Church of God in Corinth"
was, according to Bengel, "a joyful paradox". Vice, divisions,
defilement of flesh and spirit, Corinth had everything! No
wonder, then, that at the end of his second letter, St Paul's
farewell greeting had within it a note of rebuke: "mend your
ways, heed my appeal, agree with one another, live in peace".
All was not well. He bade them farewell with a heavy heart.

To you, my dear friends of the diocese of York, I say tonight,
"Farewell". It is not quite a final farewell, for I do not cease to be
your archbishop for another six weeks; but it is still very nearly a
final farewell.

There shall be no note of rebuke in what I say tonight. That
is not to say that the Church in this diocese is perfect. We have
still a very long way to go. There are areas where there is no
progress, where God's people show few of the fruits of the
York Minster, 24th October, 1974.

B

33

Spirit, where the first concern seems to be survival rather than mission. Such things can only make any shepherd of the flock anxious and concerned. But there are other areas where the life of the Spirit is strongly manifest, where the fruits of the Spirit grow plentifully, and where worship is joyful and witness powerful. Fortunate the man who has the diocese of York for his care, and its people for his friends! How grateful my wife and I are for all that you have given us during thirteen years and more of service among you!

I bypass, then, these words of implied rebuke in our text, and I fasten on the promise with which it ends: *"The God of love and peace will be with you".*

Let us hold that title of God up to the light, as we might hold up some precious jewel to see its full glory. Those two words, *love* and *peace*, sum up pretty accurately the two main themes of this glorious service.

1.   *Love.* It was the precentor's suggestion that the Gospel for tonight should be that passage which is read at the consecration of bishops and never ceases to move me deeply, the passage in which Jesus and Peter confront one another. Risen Christ and penitent Peter face to face! What can you do with a man who, at your hour of direst need, lets you down not once nor twice but thrice, who swears he never knew you, and underlines the denial with a curse? Dismiss him? Have done with him? Disown him? That would be *our* way. But it was not Christ's. He asked one question only, and that repeated as many times as the denial had been made. "Simon, son of John, do you love Me?" That is the root, the nub, the essence of the matter.

God's love had surrounded Simon, son of John, from before his birth, through his call and during the years of discipleship. And religion, after all, is at its deepest a love affair between the great Lover (who is God) and the beloved (who is you). The love of God did not cease towards Simon when he denied God's Son. God loves us *in* our sin, and *through* our sin, and goes on loving us, looking for a response. And when there is some spark of response, however feeble, life begins, and hope springs up, and service is made possible. "Lord, You know everything; You know that I love You."

We often tend to over-complicate religion and make it more

difficult than it need be. When this note of responding love, of grateful indebtedness, is missing from our religion, the fire and the joy go from it.

Listen to this seventeenth century German writer:

> Thee will I love, my strength, my tower,
> Thee will I love, my joy, my crown,
> Thee will I love with all my power
> In all my works, and Thee alone,
> Thee will I love, till sacred fire
> Fills my whole soul with pure desire.
>
> Uphold me in the doubtful race
> Nor suffer me again to stray;
> Strengthen my feet with steady pace
> Still to press forward in thy way:
> That all my powers, with all their might
> In Thy sole glory may unite.

That is real Christianity—the response of utter gratitude to almost unbelievable love!

2. *Peace.* What do I mean when I say (as I shall do in a few moments) "the peace of the Lord be always with you"? What am I praying for you? And what will you be praying for me when you reply: "And with thy spirit"?

I am praying for the *tranquillity of mind which arises from reconciliation with God.* I am asking that you will have no controversy about anything with God; and that, if you have, you will lay down the arms of your rebellion tonight before you come to receive the Sacrament. What joy there will be in heaven—and in York Minster—when you do that!

I am praying that *complete harmony will exist in your relationships with one another,* a deep care and concern for the welfare of those whose lives you touch. I am thinking of our families, where relationships are at their deepest and most intimate, and where love is best thought of as courtesy in little things. I am thinking of our parochial church councils, where differences of opinion and outlook *can* become creative, where tensions *can* make music rather than discord. I am thinking of our deanery synods and our diocesan synod, where we wrestle with problems which sometimes seem almost overwhelming, but where we find strength in worship, in the thrust and parry of debate, and in the fun of laughing together! And it is all done out of love for Christ our Lord.

Yes, the peace of reconciliation with God and of harmony with one another.

But isn't this all a bit unrealistic in a world which is torn by strife? Isn't it selfish to be talking about tranquillity of mind when there is Ireland across a narrow sea, war rumbling on in Vietnam, bombs exploding in London, and violence erupting at our football matches? What right has a Christian to talk about peace in *that* context?

He has *every* right. Indeed, he must so talk. At our baptism we were signed with the sign of the Cross in token that we would not be ashamed to confess the faith of Christ crucified and fight under his banner. And our confirmation was empowering and "ordaining" to that end. The churchman who is not *at war*, actively battling against God's enemies and man's, had better ask himself whether he is a Christian at all. *But*—and this is the point—he cannot effectively battle unless the peace of God within him is a reality. If he is in a wrong relationship with God or with others, his sword is blunted in his hand—or thrust out of it! But if he knows the peace of sins forgiven, if his feet are shod with the Gospel of *peace*, then he can go into battle unconcerned about himself, with the peace of God garrisoning heart and mind, and all his undivided strength engaged in the battle with the world, the flesh and the devil. Did not his Master go to His own last great conflict with sin and death, at peace? He is recorded as having said to His men: "Peace I leave with you. A peace that is my own I give to you". He knew. He knows.

We have talked about the love of God and the peace of God. But our text speaks of the God of love and of peace. The truth is you cannot have the gifts without the Giver. And the marvel of the Gospel is that the Giver gives Himself to us—constantly, unreservedly—in the Sacrament to which so soon we shall come truly and earnestly repenting of our sins and being in love and charity with our neighbours; in those daily times of prayer and quiet without which life is arid and discipleship dies; in those acts of service done in the name of the Servant Lord, Jesus Christ.

So I commend you to God, the great Giver, and to the word of His grace which is able to build you up.

"Live in peace, and the God of love and peace will be with you".

Canterbury Enthronement

Realism and Confidence

St John 16:33
In the world you shall have tribulation. But be of good cheer, I have overcome the world.

I SEE IN these words of my text two things:—
(i) The *realism* of Jesus. "Tribulation". He was on His way to the Cross. His followers would tread in the steps of the Crucified.
(ii) The *confidence* of Jesus. "Be of good cheer. I have overcome the world. The victory is Mine."
The touch of the Evangelist in recording these words is sure. There is realism and confidence; suffering and victory; Calvary and Easter. He got it right.

That picture comes to us from the first century. Let me take you from the first to the third.

Listen to this from St Cyprian, writing to a man by the name of Donatus:—

This seems a cheerful world, Donatus, when I view it from this fair garden, under the shadow of these vines. But if I climbed some great mountain and looked out over the wide lands, you know very well what I would see. Brigands on the high road, pirates on the seas, in the amphitheatres men murdered to please the applauding crowds, under all roofs misery and selfishness. It is really a bad world, Donatus, an incredibly bad world. Yet in the midst of it I have found a quiet and

Sermon at the Enthronement in Canterbury Cathedral, 24th January, 1975.

holy people. They have discovered a joy which is a thousand times better than any pleasure of this sinful life. They are despised and persecuted, but they care not. They have overcome the world. These people, Donatus, are the Christians . . . and I am one of them.

Now let me take you from the third to the twentieth century, and to that last quarter of it in which we live and are called to bear our witness to our Lord. The parallels with the conditions of the first and third centuries are close—tribulation; violence; a materialism which shuts its eyes to extremities of wealth and poverty existing side by side; the abandonment of old gods and a pathetic inability to replace them with anything adequate for the needs of modern man; fear on every side; and because iniquity abounds, the love of many growing cold.

Under these conditions, what is the Church to say to the world in its fear, its agony, its wistfulness? I believe that the emphases of Jesus as recorded by St John are precisely those which are most needed today—*realism* and *confidence*.

1. *Realism.* Let the Church face the fact—and face it totally unblinkered—that it is in for a time of tribulation. If we are fools enough, for Christ's sake, to follow Him, then we must face tribulation and even crucifixion. And there must be no whining when that comes, no complaining when the winds are contrary; no crying to the world, for the sake of popularity, "peace, peace, when there is no peace"; no "healing of the wounds of My people lightly"! Our radical sickness calls for a radical cure—and that can only come by way of the Cross. Did that secretary write more wisely than she knew when, by an error of typing, she referred to my *enthornment* instead of my *enthronement*?

2. *Confidence.* When the Christian speaks of confidence, he does not mean a kind of starry-eyed optimism based on a theory of human progress and perfectibility. Rather, he means hope based on the resurrection-victory of Jesus.

In recent years this confidence has been strangely lacking in certain parts of the Church. We have passed through—and indeed are still passing through—a period in which loss of nerve has marked the attitude of too many of us. God knows the Church

has enough, and more than enough, to repent of, as I have said
on other occasions. But repentance is not a masochistic breast-
beating which scarcely conceals a death-wish! Repentance is a
positive thing, a life-attitude of turning one's back on what is
sinful and worthless, and turning one's face towards the living
God.

It is time that we said, unitedly and joyfully, to all who will
listen: "We are not interested in the possibility of defeat. Our
confidence is in the risen Lord, who said 'On this rock I will
build my Church and the gates of hell shall not prevail against it'.
We know something of the power of the Holy Spirit. We are
open to learn more of Him. We await the surprises of tomorrow.

Crises? Yes, we see them all around us. We know that the word
means judgment, and we can discern the judgment of God at
work in the history of our time. But for us, crisis speaks of
opportunity.

> Then, welcome each rebuff
> That turns earth's smoothness rough,
> Each sting that bids nor sit nor stand
> But go!

In the power of the risen Christ and with the stimulation of the
Holy Spirit, we *will* go—in confidence and joy.

Against that background of realism and confidence, I touch on
two matters—the first addressed primarily to the Church of
England and the Anglican Communion (though it undoubtedly
affects Churches beyond her bounds); the second addressed to all
who name the Name of Christ.

1. *One of the greatest needs of the Church at this moment is a
steady increase in the number of those coming forward to ordination.* Not
for one moment must we lower the standard of those who apply
for training. To do so would be to court disaster. But for too long
the numbers of those seeking ordination in the Church of England
(as in other Churches) have been declining. Such a decline is like
a haemorrhage in the human body. Recently we have seen a
change, an upturn in the numbers. But this will need to increase,
and to continue to increase over a long period, if we are to make
up losses and right our manpower situation.

By all means let us engage in experiments in forms of ministry. Let us train auxiliary clergy. But let us not delude ourselves into thinking that this kind of thing will solve all our problems. It will not. We must have a steady supply of parish priests who will give themselves wholly to this one thing—the thoughtful ministry of the Word, the awesome ministry of the Sacraments, the visiting of the homes of the people, the ceaseless ministry of intercession, the equipping of the laity for their witness.

Let us then say to our young men: "There is no finer life than that of a parish priest. Covet this calling. Train for it. Pour your best into it. Glory in it. Count yourself thrice-blessed if you hear God calling you to it."

Of course we shall have to pay for the training and maintenance of these men. We can no longer rely on dead men's money—nor toy with stewardship—nor fail to tithe our income in a business-like fashion. The truth is that when confidence revives, when love of God waxes warm, when faith burns bright, financial problems begin to solve themselves.

Why do I fasten on the need for recruits to the ordained ministry, on such an occasion as this? I do so precisely because I believe in the ministry of the laity. That is only apparently contradictory, for it is in fact saying that the main work of Christ's Church will be done by the witness of the faithful laity. If however that witness is to be intelligent and infectious, it will demand an adequate supply of full-time, well-equipped, highly qualified clergy whose primary task will be to train the front-line troops for their warfare.

2.   My second word is addressed to all who name the Name of Christ. It can be summed up in one sentence: "*We must grow till our arms get right round the world*". When you put your arms round somebody, you tell him that you love him. It is a sacramental act. The world desperately needs loving, and it will have to be done sacramentally by outward and visible signs of the inward grace of God's love.

Such an embrace will be costly. It will involve the abandonment of much that we have hitherto taken for granted. Our *divisions* will have to go—does not this very week of Christian unity remind us to ask ourselves how we can preach reconciliation if we ourselves are not wholly reconciled? Our *possessions* will have to go, and that includes many of those buildings of small historic value which do little more than consume our money and our energies. Our *selfishness* will have to go, for much of the global village in which we live is deprived of those necessities without which no human being can fully live—food, literacy, education, freedom, knowledge of the Christian way. Round such deprived millions our arms must go, and for that we must grow. Our most powerful arms will be the arms of prayer.

It is significant that the man who spoke those words "We must grow till our arms get right round the world" was General Booth of the Salvation Army. He was a man like Pope John, whose arms were stretched out wide to embrace the world—and a very costly stretching it was. But these two men, so different from one another in so many ways, were at one in this, that they were disciples of One whose arms were stretched out wide, on a cross, and whose hands were pierced, pierced by and pierced for the sin of the world. "By whose stripes we are healed."

I want these words which I have spoken to reach your hearts, to remain in your minds, to nerve your wills, and to ring round the world. Let me repeat them to you with emphasis.

The *realism* of Jesus. "In the world you shall have tribulation". The Church militant expects wounds, for it follows a wounded Lord.

The *confidence* of Jesus. "I have overcome the world". We are on the victory side of Calvary. We are children of the resurrection. We are sons of the Holy Spirit.

So:—

> Forth in the peace of Christ we go;
> Christ to the world with joy we bring;
> Christ in our minds, Christ on our lips,
> Christ in our hearts, the world's true King.

Westminster Abbey Welcome

Life *is* Christ!

Phil. 1:21
To me life is Christ.

THE FEAST OF the Conversion of St Paul is a day of special significance to me. It was nineteen years ago today that I was consecrated a bishop in the Church of God. Had I been free to choose any day in the Christian year for my consecration, I could not have chosen one which would have been more congenial to me than this. For from my young manhood onwards, St Paul has been a formative influence in my life.

This year, on the eve of the day on which we celebrate his wonderful conversion, I was enthroned as Archbishop of Canterbury. Now, on the evening of the day itself, we have met to join in a great act of worship in this Abbey.

May I say how much the presence of leaders and representatives from other parts of the Anglican Communion and of sister Churches from all over the world means to me and to the Church which I represent. We were supported and strengthened by the presence of many of you in Canterbury Cathedral yesterday. We are thankful for the presence of all of you here tonight. We pray God's blessing on the worship you offer in the triune Name and on the work that you do in God's service.

Many of you I know already and esteem as brothers in Christ. Many more I hope to meet either in your own countries or in this. In this week of Christian unity, I greet you in the words

Westminster Abbey, 25th January, 1975.

of St Paul: "If . . . our common life in Christ yields anything to stir the heart, any loving consolation, any sharing of the Spirit, any warmth of affection or compassion, fill up my cup of happiness by thinking and feeling alike, with the same love for one another, the same turn of mind, and a common care for unity" (Phil. 2:1–2).

I take my text tonight from this same Epistle to the Philippians, five monosyllables from chapter one, verse 21: "*to me life is Christ*".

The letters of St Paul confront us with a strange phenomenon. Unlike most other letters, there is about them an element of timelessness, a relevance to man and his destiny and his predicament which seems quite independent of the particular century or age in which they are read. They come to us from an era in some ways very unlike our own, an era whose men had not begun to think in the sort of scientific categories to which we are accustomed. And yet their message, rightly understood, is as fresh as this morning's newspaper, and far more likely to provide a clue to the problems there set out than the editorials written about them!

How can this be? What is the reason for the perennial freshness and relevance of these first-century letters? Let me suggest certain factors which may begin to give us an answer.

I note, *first*, the *range of the apostle's thought*. He takes the cosmos for his canvas, and the world for his parish. He is concerned with the whole cosmic process and with its redemption in Christ. Nothing less than that would do as a stage on which to set the drama of deliverance wrought by the incarnate, crucified, risen Lord. The sheer range of the apostle's thought, the majestic vision of a universe "freed from the shackles of mortality" and entering "upon the liberty and splendour of the children of God"—this is big enough for any age and any race and any thinking.

"He doth bestride the world like a Colossus"—and bestrides it to conquer it for Christ.

Secondly, I note that *he grapples firmly with man's basic problems*. He wrestles—if I may steal a Johannine phrase to illustrate a

Pauline theme—with "sin, righteousness and judgment". After all, the things that matter, that *really* matter in the long run, go deeper than economic questions, however pressing such questions may be. Can a man like me be right with God? Dare I look up into the Face of God—and laugh with joy? Can a man such as myself become holy? A miracle would be needed; but is the miracle possible? Can I become "a member of Christ, the child of God, and an inheritor of the Kingdom of heaven"? Is there a place for one like me within the redeemed community?

These are the fundamental, basic questions which really matter. By these things men live—or die. And these precisely are the issues which are basic in the Pauline letters. The apostle's language may at times be technical and need interpretation, but he were a foolish man who did not share the apostle's wrestling, and, as he shared, watch him point the way to life everlasting.

Thirdly, I note *his consistent ethical awareness*. Here is no vague theory-monger. His thoughts reach to heaven, but his feet are firmly on the ground. He has no room for pious language, if there is no love; he has no place for tongues, if the Body of Christ is not built up; he has no time for religious talk, if there is not the fruit of the Spirit—love, joy, peace . . .

As I read his letters and picture him standing tonight in some prominent place in London, outside the Abbey, in Hyde Park or wherever, I think I can see him growing increasingly impatient with talk about a charter of *rights*, and bringing us back, with inexorable logic, to the need, rather, for a charter of *duties*. The man who is at home in the sphere of justification and sanctification and redemption is equally at home dealing with problems of dishonesty, impurity or ill-temper. The marks of a lovely character issue as naturally from his great and fundamental doctrines as does fruit from a healthy tree or a rose from a well-pruned bush.

Fourthly, and most important of all, I note *his total indebtedness to Christ*. His ruling concept is that of being "in Christ". All the rest of what is most central in his writings—redemption, salvation etc.—is subsumed in this. "If any man be *in Christ*, there is a new creation". In short, and in glorious simplicity, "to me, life *is* Christ".

Here is a man who has discovered, to his eternal surprise and joy, the total adequacy of Christ—for this life, and for the next. For, when a man is incorporated into the Body of Christ, united with Christ in death and resurrection, even "death is gain"! If Christ, as St Paul firmly believed, was the key to the interpretation of the total cosmic process, he was also the key to the apostle's own greatest problem—himself!

His experience of Christ—strong, vivid, personal—was necessarily ecclesiastical experience. For to be "in Christ" was to be in His Body—with all that that entailed of joy and grief, of pain and toil, of battle and wounds. Well did St Paul know the truth of what Archbishop Garbett was to write many centuries later: "The Church is an army on the march in a hostile country, and not a rest camp for the tired". He contended against the principalities and powers, against the world rulers of this present darkness, against the spiritual hosts of wickedness—and he contended unto blood.

There are many other reasons for the perennial freshness and relevance of these Pauline letters, but these must suffice for tonight. Are not the points which I have made precisely those which are most needed in a perplexed and disillusioned age? And are they not precisely those which the Church should constantly be handling, with joy and confidence and awe?

Nothing less than a world-view will do for a Church entrusted with the Gospel of Christ. If the whole creation is the scene of God's renewing activity in Christ, His Church must not rest content till every nation and people and tongue has at least had the opportunity to learn of its Redeemer and become subject to its King. World mission is the necessary corollary of the divine love as manifested in Christ.

We may well ask: Is this the prime passion of the Church of the nineteen-seventies? If not, is that Church being true to the apostolic message? I think *not*. The Church's task is not done till every tongue has confessed that Jesus is Lord, to the glory of God the Father. If that be so, the younger Churches will no doubt need the continued help of the Churches of the West. But, equally, the older Churches will need missionaries from Africa and Asia and Latin America, to share with them the many-coloured wisdom of God. Mission must be thought of, not only in world terms, but in terms of interchange, a sharing of gifts and of insights, "till we all attain to the unity of the faith and of the knowledge of the Son of God, to mature manhood, to the measure of the stature of the fullness of Christ".

As St Paul grapples firmly with man's basic problems, so must the Church today. That Church, if it is to be true to its very nature, must be deeply concerned with social problems—drains, and drugs, and disasters of all kinds. But it must never allow itself to become little more than an arm of the social services. It deals with "sin, and righteousness, and judgment". Firmly rooted in time, its message transcends time, and prepares men for eternity. Its commerce is with the things of the spirit—with forgiveness and holiness and eternal life and the powers of the world to come.

If the Church's witness to the world is to be bright and unsullied, it will, like St Paul, be constantly and consistently aware that no doctrine is worth much unless it has an ethical outcome in life. Many of us have longed, for decades, to see a revival of interest in the person and work of the Holy Spirit. In recent years we have seen just that. We are seeing that disturbance of the Spirit which is the mark of Him whose ways are the ways of fire and of wind. He has brought—he is bringing—freedom and joy and peace. There is a song in the land where too long there has been silence or groaning. Only let us remember, the Spirit of whom we speak and whose presence we feel is the Spirit of Jesus; and if the marks of Jesus—His love and compassion and endurance and unity and grace—are lacking in us His disciples, we must question the reality of the experience we claim.

All this brings me to the last point of which I spoke in connection with St Paul. I bade you note "his total indebtedness to Christ". "To me", he could say, "life *is* Christ". Charles Raven, that fascinating scientist-theologian who loved to ponder and expound the writings of St Paul as he in turn had pondered and expounded the meaning of Jesus, wrote of Christ: "He takes us, and fills us with a life not our own, a life which is beyond sorrow and romance. He takes us, and in His grip we live abundantly, sharing for a moment the activity of His overwhelming love."

"He takes us, and in His grip we live abundantly." That is it. There is little more need be said.

There is justification.

There is holiness.

There is unity.

There is life.

Bradford Cathedral Jubilee

A Cathedral in Our Midst

2 Cor. 4:18
The things which are seen are temporal:
the things which are unseen are eternal.

IT IS GOOD to be back in the Cathedral where, nearly fourteen years ago, I was enthroned as third bishop of the diocese; back in the cathedral where, a few years ago, we celebrated five hundred years of its use as a parish church; back in the cathedral whose enlargement and beautifying we watched almost stone by stone in the late fifties. And now today we celebrate half a century of use of the old parish church as the cathedral and mother church of one of the more recently formed of our English dioceses. It is indeed good to be back.

I value the opportunity of speaking to this big congregation. Part of it consists of regular worshippers, for Bradford Cathedral has always been, and still is, a parish church. But part of it, naturally and rightly, consists of people who rarely, if ever, worship here. They have come as this is a great day in the life of this city and they hold within the city's life some office of importance. It may well be that there is a good deal of perplexity as to what place a cathedral occupies in the life of modern England, not least in a highly industrialised city such as our city of Bradford.

There are still some who think of cathedrals in terms of Trollope, *Barchester Towers*, Mrs Proudie, etc., or even of Derek Nimmo and the T.V. programme, *All Gas and Gaiters*!

Bradford Cathedral, 25th November, 1967.

49

Perhaps, if one hunted far enough, one could find relics of that kind of thing even today. Others, better informed and more knowledgeable, expect to find in the modern English cathedral standards of liturgical worship and of sacred music which cannot be surpassed—think, for example, of St Paul's or Westminster Abbey or York Minster. Others realise that, from many points of view, this century has seen the revival of cathedral life, vigour and usefulness—Coventry newly built, a place of lively worship and experimentation, of social concern, of evangelistic outreach; Guildford in its glory, surrounded by and making an impact on the new university: Liverpool, Manchester, Bradford, centres of activity at the very heart of great Northern cities, and mother churches to which the parishes and organisations of the diocese love to come, like children to their parents' home.

To some, no doubt, a cathedral and all it stands for is a colossal irrelevancy, a huge waste of money and manpower, a hangover from the medieval ages into the age of technology and of the dominance of the physical sciences. There are no doubt some here tonight who think in such terms, and are present only because they conceive it to be their duty to represent their institution by personally attending. Since this is Bradford and in Bradford we know how to hit hard and speak the truth in love, I say frankly that I believe such a view to be fundamentally wrong. That said, it is up to me to go on and make clear what any cathedral church stands for in our generation; what it says to our generation.

A cathedral stands for *excellence*—for unimpeachable standards. This is especially true, of course, in the sphere of architecture, of art, of stained glass, of music, of beautiful worship. Nothing less than the best will do here. When priest and people together "do the Eucharist", they do it as perfectly as they know how—to the glory of God from whom all beauty derives, and as a kind of standard by which all their work, in warehouse, office, shop, or college is measured. Standards slip. Sloppiness can so easily invade worship. Cathedrals should stand as a kind of bulwark against the insidious temptation to be content with less than the best in the sacred and in the so-called secular.

A cathedral speaks of *the presence of God* in the midst of His people. I rejoice that Bradford's mother church is not out at Heaton or in any of the suburbs, but right in the middle of the industries and offices of the people—surrounded by warehouses and shops and post-office. This fact—and it is true of so many of our cathedrals—says to me: "God is not divorced from life. Jesus was born in the out-house of an inn, was found by country folk, shepherds busy at their work; He laboured in a shop, preached in His home-town, died just outside the city where He had ministered." The Christ of Bethlehem and Calvary speaks of a God whose heart and mind and will were disclosed, *made known*, in the midst of His people. He is not far from any one of us.

A cathedral stands as *a warning*. By its very presence in our midst, it warns us of the futility of a life whose dimensions are limited by this life only, which responds only to what can be seen and heard. "The things that are seen are temporal; the things which are unseen are eternal." You cannot take your bank-balance with you when this little life is through, nor your reputation, nor your status. A life which has no touch with the Eternal is a poor and anaemic thing. A cathedral in our midst, whether we enter it frequently or not, says to us: "The man who lives without regular worship is not living as God intends him to live." A prayer-less life is an existence devoid of the dimensions for which God made it. Such a man can have only a worm's-eye view of the universe. Beware the barrenness of a Christ-less life!

In short, a cathedral is a place for *meeting with* God. Such a meeting brings peace in the midst of stress—gives a sense of proportion when we tend to get our values and our priorities wrong. Such a meeting means that we are enabled, in the words of William Temple,

> to quicken our conscience by God's holiness
> to nourish our mind by His truth
> to purify our imagination by His beauty
> to open our heart to His love, and
> to surrender our will to His purpose.

This is no luxury for the devout. This is a necessity for all. It is preparation for sacrifice and for battle—and only those who so engage in battle can really be said to *live*.

If this be true, Bradford Cathedral has a great task ahead of it in the coming years. If this be true, there will be great searchings of heart among many who come to this service as to just one of a series of engagements and have found instead an exposition of truth which can leave no hearer unaffected.

"The things that are seen are temporal; the things which are unseen are eternal."

It is a word from beyond which must not go unheeded.

General Synod
Presidential Address

True Patriotism

IF I TAKE as my subject today the theme of Church and nation, I do so not to provide members of General Synod with an essay on Church and State, establishment and disestablishment, etc., but, rather, to invite you to engage with me in a brief biblical study of what membership of his nation means to a man of God. So I put my theme in the form of a question: *What does membership of his nation, what does patriotism mean to a Christian? What does it entail for him?*

Patriotism is no "in-word" today. Its unpopularity is due partly to the fact that it has been misused. If by patriotism we mean: "My country, right or wrong", then clearly that view is to be rejected on all counts. That is a travesty of its true meaning.

If by that word we mean: "My country first, its wealth and demands first, to the neglect of the needs of other nations including those of the third world", then again we have a travesty of its true meaning. Such an interpretation would indeed be folly in a shrinking world, a world whose member nations daily become more and more inter-dependent for their full development. Only a global view makes any sense today.

If, however, we turn to the Bible, we find that its outstanding figures—in both Testaments—were patriots in the deepest and truest sense of that word. A brief study of them may provide us with certain clues as to what Christian patriotism should mean today.

1. The figure of *Moses*, as depicted for us in the dramatic story

4th February, 1975.

of Exodus 32, is a noble one. The people of Israel had apostatised, and Aaron had been their leader in apostasy. Moses's anger blazes as he descends from the mount of revelation, and he casts the tables from his hands and they shatter. Then, his fury spent, he turns to prayer.

The prayer is one of intercession and compassion for the people's sin: "Oh, this people have sinned a great sin, and have made them gods of gold". He pleads for their forgiveness. But, if the sin is such that there can be no forgiveness, then, such is his love for the people, he would be prepared for his own name to be blotted out of God's book of life. This, surely, is the deepest form of patriotism, expressing itself in costly and self-sacrificing prayer.

The New Testament counterpart of that story is found in St Paul's Epistle to the Romans where he pleads for his own people who have turned their backs on God's revelation of Himself. "I could even pray to be outcast from Christ myself for the sake of my brothers, my natural kinsfolk . . . My deepest desire and my prayer to God is for their salvation" (9:1 and 10:1).

2. Of the prophets, Hosea stands out as the patriot *par excellence*. The depth of his home tragedy, involving desertion by his wife, gave him insights into the nature of God, insights denied to others lacking experience of such suffering. His yearning for the return of his wife whom he dearly loved led him to see that God yearned for the return of His bride, His adulterous nation who had left Him for gods that were no gods.

The passion of a broken heart breathes through the disjointed sentences of this tragic book—a book whose author sees God now as a broken-hearted husband, now as a father holding out his hands to a child taking its first tottering steps.

Did any of the prophets see deeper into the heart of God than this broken-hearted patriot, Hosea?

3. But, of course, the greatest of the Hebrew patriots was Jesus, Son of Mary, Jesus, Son of God. We have only to watch Him, as St Luke depicts Him (19:41), breaking down in grief as He looks over His beloved Jerusalem, and, with set face, going to the capital there to lay down His life for her people, to see religious patriotism at its deepest and costliest. "If thou hadst known, even thou, at least in this thy day, the things which belong

unto thy peace!" "O Jerusalem, Jerusalem, which killest the prophets and stonest them that are sent unto thee: how often would I have gathered thy children together, as a hen doth gather her brood under her wings, and ye would not!" (13:34)

What can we learn from this outline study of those great patriots which might be of value to us Christians in our relation to our own nation in this her hour of lost-ness?

I suggest three things.

1. Patriotism to a Christian means prayer, constant, deep and costly—

> To bear Thy people on their hearts,
> And love the souls which Thou dost love.

If those words have a primary application to the priest in relation to his people, they have an equally valid application to every Christian in his relation to the nation of which he is a part.

This prayer may occasionally find expression in days of special prayer called at times of special national significance or danger. But it finds better expression in that constant prayer which may emerge from a thoughtful reading of the daily paper or from listening to the radio news bulletin. It is a prayer which is constantly asking questions—what is God seeking to say to my nation through the present state of affairs? What part have I, and the community of which I am a member, in doing the will of God in this emergency?

2. This kind of patriotism may well involve the Christian in criticism of his nation and of its governmental policies. But such criticism cannot be given, as it were, from outside. We are part and parcel of our nation, in its glory and in its shame. Our very loyalty to our nation may have to express itself in terms of criticism, as we bring to bear on it the particular insights which God has given to us His children.

If I give as examples two things of which I have been speaking much lately, I do so without apology, for I believe they need constant reiteration.

(a) *The essential sin of our nation is that it has inverted the divine order.* If we do this, putting self first, others next, and God last (if indeed any room is left for Him at all), we become idolaters. We assent to the creed of greed. We grasp. We get. We acquire. But we cease to *be* what God designed us to be.

(b) *If, as a nation, we become obsessed with our rights, then we inevitably come under judgment.* I spoke recently in Westminster Abbey, of the need of this nation not so much for a charter of rights—we have heard much of that—as for a charter of *duties*. When we begin once again to put our accent on that, health will begin to seep back into the veins of our nation. But not till then.

3. *One thing bound together that great trio of whom we have been thinking this morning—Moses, Hosea, Jesus. It was a certain agony inseparable from a deep patriotism.* These men spoke from within their nation. They were part and parcel of it, with two of them conscious that they shared in the sinfulness of the nation whose ways they felt called by God to denounce. Out of such an agony they spoke, not in their own name, but in the name of Him who sent them.

Perhaps this is England's greatest need today—a band of men and women whose patriotism goes so deep that it leads them to pray, to criticise, to agonise; and out of that prayer, that criticism, that agony, to bear their witness, in season and out of season, to the truth of God as it has been revealed to them in Christ.

Dedication in Liverpool Cathedral

Holy Ground

Exodus 3:5
Put off thy shoes from off thy feet, for the place whereon thou standest is holy ground.

WHAT A VISTA has passed before us in each phase of this great service! As we have entered into it, we have watched the growth of the cathedral once again—the birth of the idea in 1901, the dedication of the Lady Chapel in 1910, the consecration in 1924, the central space in 1941, the first bay in 1961—today, with great rejoicing, the appropriation and dedication of the second bay and the launching of the plan for the third bay and the west front. All this—or practically all of it—has taken place within the life-time of many present here today. It is small wonder that the note of thanksgiving and praise has rung out again and again!

The members of the Committee have shown a sense of realism in their decision to cut down on the design of 1962, in the face of rapidly rising costs. They know that we, who have this work at heart, are engaged in a race against time, for every year that passes sees costs soar. They have acted with wisdom and foresight in setting before us an objective that is crystal clear both as to the amount of money and the time involved, that is that we must find half a million pounds and we must finish the work in seven years. That task, big as it undoubtedly is, should not be beyond us, if we go to it with a will.

As your archbishop and as patron of your Appeal Committee, I wish you well as you launch your "Finish the Cathedral" Appeal.

Appropriation and Dedication of second bay of the nave, 4th May, 1968.

Remember Drake and his "continuing to the end until it be thoroughly finished". Remember a greater than Drake "who for the joy that was set before Him *endured* . . ."

Let there be no hesitation, no vacillation. Keep right on to the end!

It may be that, when the history of this generation comes to be written within its proper perspective, we shall see that, from some points of view, it has been the great age of our English cathedrals. I think not only of the building of Liverpool, of Guildford, of Coventry—so different from one another and yet in their varying ways so glorious—or of the rescuing of York Minster from the fate which so nearly overwhelmed it. Those four achievements alone, in a small country and in a period marked by two great wars, point to a striving on the part of our people after the best in architecture, in sculpture, in glass, in art, in aesthetics, in technology. Giles Gilbert Scott, Edward Maufe, Basil Spence, John Piper, Carl Edwards, Harry Stammers—these and a score of others are names which will live long after our little day. These men and similar have helped us to fasten our attention on the creation of things of enduring beauty to the glory of God, and in so doing they have done something in weaning us from lapsing into the sordid and the second-rate. For that—and for them—thanks be to God!

I believe that history may see this century as the great century of our cathedrals from another, and even more important, point of view. In a new way, many of our cathedrals have really become the mother churches of their dioceses, the spiritual nerve-centres of their life. They are, of course, the seat of their bishops, the scene of their ordinations and other episcopal acts. But they are also the places of worship in which, in great numbers and on great occasions, the diocesan family can gather in truly representative fashion. Further, they are places of pilgrimage and so, if rightly used, of evangelism, places where, through eye-gate and ear-gate, the mighty acts of God in Christ can be brought home to men. Again, they are fitting places for liturgical experimentation, for the promotion of religious drama, for the setting forth of new forms of music and art in the service of Almighty God.

Bishop George Bell's name will always be revered for what he did at Canterbury and Chichester. Liverpool is proving not backward in following in his pioneering steps. In his enthronement address, Bell said: "Whether it be music or painting or drama, sculpture or architecture or any other form of art, there is an instinctive sympathy between all of these and the worship of God." How right he was, and how gloriously many of our cathedrals are demonstrating that sympathy!

I go further. Coventry Cathedral is set firmly in the very midst of an industrial city. Guildford Cathedral finds itself in the centre of a new university pulsating with young life. Liverpool Cathedral dominates, and in dominating stands to serve, one of the greatest trading centres of the world. All these speak to us of God in His majesty *in the midst of* His people; of the intertwining of religion and life, of sanctuary and market place. "Emmanuel—God with us" is the proclamation of these cathedrals. They warn us of the fatuity, if not blasphemy, of a so-called religion which is in fact unrelated to life, which is a mere formality, which cries out "Lord, Lord", and does not carry into effect the orders which the Lord gives His people. And at the same time they speak to us of the need of quiet in the midst of activity, of worship before activity, of withdrawal with God before advance in His name, of the set of the will in quiet meditation and prayer before the rush of business and the claims of society.

"Put off thy shoes from off thy feet, Moses, for the place whereon thou standest is holy ground." *Then* "I will send thee, and I will be with thee." It is an ancient story. But it is an ever-modern truth, which each new generation must learn. Each new generation—yes, and each individual man and woman, must learn it anew. So must you. So must I.

For these never-changing truths this great cathedral stands, unflinching, immovable.

By these truths, please God, we will stand, down the years, until we see, face to face, Him whom now, unseen, we worship and adore.

Presentation of NEB Old Testament in Westminster Abbey

A New Translation

I Tim. 4:13 (NEB)
Devote your attention to the public reading of the Scriptures.

Two PICTURES FILL my mind tonight. The first is the picture of this great congregation, gathered in Westminster Abbey for a very special purpose, and reaching out to millions of people throughout the world who are deeply interested in that which brings us together. The second picture is that of a senior man engaged in writing a letter to a junior, back in the closing decades of the first century. On the face of it, one would not think that there was any connection between these two pictures. They are so different. On one hand there is the dignified beauty of this ancient Abbey, the vast outreach of the Christian Church across the world, the use of the mass media in bringing our actions here into the homes of peoples of all nations. On the other hand, we see two early disciples getting to grips with the problems confronting tiny scattered communities of Christians in the Graeco-Roman world—how they should continue, spread, behave, worship. There *is* however a connection, and it is a close one. It has to do with a book, or, rather, a collection of books.

Let me explain.

We are here to celebrate the completion of a great enterprise in the world of ecumenical co-operation, of scholarship, of publishing, and, I believe, of evangelistic outreach. In 1961 we

16th March, 1970.

met in this place to present to the Heads of the Churches the New
Testament in its new translation. Tonight we meet for a similar
purpose, but the gift we offer is that of the Old Testament and of
the Apocrypha (together with the New English Bible New
Testament in a very slightly revised form). As in 1961, so in 1970,
the translation is a wholly new one, for the work is not a revision
of former translations. The translators have been able to avail
themselves of, and to incorporate in their work, a wealth of
scholarship which, in the nature of the case, was not to hand in
the days of Bede or Wycliffe, or Tyndale, or Coverdale, or in the
days when the King James' version of 1611 or the Revised Version
of the late nineteenth century was produced.

Revision of the Scriptures is a never-ending task. We do not
pretend to give the world a final edition as it were of the Bible in
the English tongue. There can be no final edition. Scholarship
advances. Language and idiom change. What we present is the
best that British scholarship of the twentieth century can offer.
It is unworthy, no doubt; for what man, or what group of men,
can ever be worthy of translating such a book as the Bible? But it
is the best we can do. We offer it humbly and gratefully in return
for the privilege of sharing in the work.

Those of us who, like myself, have served on the Joint Committee on the New Translation of the Bible have carried the least
of the burdens associated with this enterprise. The members of the
four translation and literary panels have endured the heat of the
day or, rather, of the long years—twenty and more. Invidious
though it may be to mention names, it would be totally ungrateful
to omit the name of the director, Dr C. H. Dodd, who, against
the background of his profound Biblical scholarship, has guided
the project with a sure and steady hand. We owe more to him
than can ever be adequately acknowledged. With him we link
the name of Sir Godfrey Driver, whose father in 1874 joined the
team which produced the Revised Version. Thus father and son
have spanned nearly a century in the work of Biblical translation.
With the names of Dodd and Driver we link too that of Professor
McHardy, whose responsibilities have included the supervision
of the translation of the Apocrypha and a large share of the general
oversight of the whole work especially in its closing stages.

The labour involved in the book presented to the Churches

tonight has been immense. Was it worth it? Many will no doubt ask this question. "We have the New Testament", they might say; "why not leave it at that, with perhaps a cursory glance when necessary at Old Testament or Apocrypha in any translation that may be to hand?"

For the beginning of an answer, I go back to the second picture I sketched for you and to the text I gave you. The senior man, concerned for the welfare of the infant Churches, writes to the junior: "Devote your attention to the public reading of the Scriptures", that is to say of the Old Testament (for the New was only then in process of being written and had not yet "congealed" into a clearly defined Canon). "If the Church is to be strong, if it is to stand its ground," he would say, "it must listen to what the Old Testament has to say. It would be the height of folly to abandon it or to neglect it." Thus it was that the early Church went to the world with a book in its hand, and that book was the Old Testament. True, those thirty-nine books were soon to be joined by the twenty-seven of the New Testament, with (as it were in the background) the books of the Apocrypha—books which, as Article VI has it, "the Church doth read for example of life and instruction of manners . . .". But the Church viewed the Old Testament as an integral part of its Holy Scriptures and resisted the tenets of those who, like Marcion in the second century, would have thrown it overboard.

Was the Church right to adopt this attitude? I believe it was. If, as we hold, Christianity is an historic religion, grounded in certain events which took place in the Near East at specific times and places, and focussed in the Person of Jesus of Nazareth, the Word made flesh, then there can be few things of greater importance than to know what it was that led up to those events, and what formed the background of that Person. It is this which the Old Testament provides for us.

But it does more. As we watch the great figures of the Old Testament pass before us, we see men and women who were not content with a superficial view of life and society—"let us eat and drink, for tomorrow we die"—but noble souls (*and* some not so noble!) who were prepared to wrestle with the great issues of life and death, of justice and love, of God's goodness and the frightful problems thrown up by man's sin and folly. "Wrestle", I said. Have you ever heard of a man more *im*patient than Job? Read the book that bears his name and you will see a man, sorely tested, trying to work out a theodicy, a justification of the ways of God with men, that would not do despite to his intelligence and would at least fit some of the facts. No, we have *not* heard of the patience of Job—that was one of the mistranslations of the old version of 1611. We have "heard how Job stood firm". The New English Bible is right here.

Job was only one of a galaxy of men whose writings and stories make up the documents of the Old Testament, well-nigh all of them perplexed by the conundrums which life threw at them. They believed that at the heart of the universe was a God of justice—some would have said a God of love. And around them was a world of incredible beauty and miracle—"the heavens declare the glory of God". But they were also surrounded by monstrous manifestations of wrong—war, sickness, and the weak going to the wall. How make sense of that? Out of such a situation came the doctrine, scarcely hinted at in the Old Testament, of life after death, of judgment to come, of heaven and hell. Out of it there also grew something even more momentous. There emerged a Figure—was it an historic person?—was it an idealised figure?—was it a nation or the godly part of a nation?—a Figure of One who Himself "bore our sufferings . . . endured our torments . . . was pierced for our transgressions . . . and by whose scourging we are healed". This suffering Servant of the Lord, the prophet could see (even if dimly), would take our sufferings and make something of them, would take the minus of our agony and out of it make a plus. Is not a plus the sign of the Cross?

On this Jesus modelled His ministry. Out of the struggles of men of old, out of their wrestlings with man's deepest perplexities, there emerged a figure which Jesus was not ashamed to take, to assume as His own, to vivify. In a very real sense, the writers of the Old Testament had "prepared a road for the Lord through the wilderness", had "cleared a highway across the desert for our God". We might go so far as to say that it was only because God had in former times spoken to our forefathers in fragmentary and varied fashion through the prophets that He was able, at last, to speak to us as He did in His Son. Men saw in Him. and especially in the events of Passion week and Holy Week, the supreme manifestation of God's character, the God Who, faithful to His word and the very nature of His being, "so loved the world that He gave His only Son".

"It was no envoy, no angel, but he himself that delivered them; he himself ransomed them by his love and pity, lifted them up and carried them . . ." The words are Old Testament words; the translation is our new one. The truth is eternal; the relevance personal. Luther was right when he saw in the Bible the cradle that bore to us the Babe of Bethlehem, who is the Christ of Calvary and the eternal Word of God. We do not worship the Bible. We are not bibliolaters. But we thank God for it, Old Testament as well as New, as being that which bears to us Him who is the Life and the Light of the world. Through that library of books, now complete in its new translation, we hear afresh the voice of the Spirit, saying to the Churches and to us as individuals: "God has spoken. See that you do not refuse to hear the voice that speaks."

Shakespeare
Quatercentenary Service

Man of the People

St John 2:25
He knew what was in man.

THIS IS NOT the occasion for a panegyric on
William Shakespeare. The passing of four centuries since he was
born in this town has only served to show how great he was and
how well justified is the estimate which a modern critic gives of
him: "he remains the unchallenged champion in the whole field
of English literature". There are others far better qualified than
I to sing his praises. But that is hardly the object of a sermon in
this house of God where Shakespeare was baptised and where,
fifty-two years later almost to the day, his body was carried in for
burial.

The question I ask today is this. *Whence did Shakespeare derive
his extraordinary insight into human nature?* What is the bearing of
that question and its answer on English life—or, to set it in a wider
context in a shrinking world—on human life, today?

That such insight was his is obvious to those who know his
works. "It happens very rarely in the history of literature that a
craftsman who has acquired perfect control of his medium and a
masterly ease in handling the techniques and conventions of his
day is also a universal genius of the highest order, combining with
his technical proficiency a unique ability to render experience in
poetic language and an uncanny intuitive understanding of
human psychology". So writes David Daiches. That is well put,
though we may ask whether the adjective "intuitive" ("an

Stratford-on-Avon, 26th April, 1964.

intuitive understanding of human psychology") perhaps begs the
question.

There were, I believe, several things which combined to give
him that understanding.

He was a man of the people. Though his father, John, was a
citizen prominent in the life of the town, he never learned to write
(or so Professor Rowse would have us believe), nor is there
evidence that William's wife could read. William came from
good, solid, English middle-class stock, but as life went on he
mixed with all classes. The friendship of his patron, the Earl of
Southampton, and of his circle of influential friends, must have
greatly broadened him. He had every opportunity of knowing
men—men of the country in and around this town; men of the
city—he was a craftsman, a man of the theatre as well as a play-
wright; men in court circles—and what a galaxy surrounded the
queen—Cecil and Bacon and Matthew Parker and Robert Dudley,
men who in any generation would make a lasting mark on history.

He had his opportunities and he seized them. Lacking—so it
would seem—a university education in the formal sense, he roved
the world with observant eye, noting the foibles of frail men and
women, reading rapidly, avidly; absorbing what he read, adapting, transmuting, reshaping, refining, improving. It has been well
said that his characters "grew out of the soil of life". He observed,
he watched, "aware of everything and with a great capacity for
suffering and charity".

All that must be said. But to leave it at that would be to by-
pass perhaps the most important clue in the answering of our
question. No one could claim that Shakespeare was a consistently
or deeply religious man. His private life left much to be desired.
His ideas of death seem sub-Christian when seen in the light shed
on it by the New Testament. For him death is "a sleep and a
forgetting". It is the great unknown—

> For who could bear the whips and scorns of time . . .
> But that the dread of something after death . . .
> puzzles the will,
> And makes us rather bear those ills we have
> Than fly to others that we know not of?

Or, more depressingly:

    No longer mourn for me when I am dead
    Than you shall hear the surly sullen bell
    Give warning to the world that I am fled
    From this vile world, with vilest worms to dwell.

All this contrasts glaringly with the New Testament concept of "departing and being with Christ which is far better"; of being "like Him and seeing Him as He is"!

But for all that, Shakespeare was a man who had drunk deeply at the wells of Holy Scripture. The Bible (in the Bishops' and Genevan versions), the Book of Common Prayer (of 1559), and the works of Ovid were the three books by which the developing mind of Shakespeare as boy and young man was nourished, and the first two were more formative than the third. We can see the little boy, the adolescent, the young man, singing the psalms, saying the prayers, listening to the Bible stories, absorbing its values, comparing them with life around him. How he loves his colourful biblical figures—Cain and Jephthah and Samson and Solomon and Job and Judas and Peter and Pilate. . . !

But it is more than a mere knowledge of the facts and personalities of the Bible which has coloured the work of Shakespeare. Listen to this:—

    What a piece of work is a man! How infinite in faculties!
    . . . in action, how like an angel! in apprehension, how
    like a god! the beauty of the world, and the paragon of
    animals!

Whence did he derive this? From observation of human nature? In part, no doubt. But it is based on the biblical insight of the eighth Psalm, quoted and developed in the Epistle to the Hebrews.

Or recall this from *Measure for Measure*:

                Alas, alas!
    Why, all the souls that were, were forfeit once;
    And He that might the vantage best have took
    Found out the remedy.

How often must Shakespeare have pondered the massive Pauline scheme of redemption for these lines to appear in this argument with such apparent effortlessness!

There is then more to it than mere *intuition* when we come to ponder Shakespeare's expertise in the human passions, or his knowledge of the human heart. There are profound biblical insights lying behind, for example, the awful nihilism of Macbeth and his obsession with an unexamined ambition to do what he knows to be wrong. Shakespeare has touched, not only the stuff that men are made of. He has touched the mind of God as it is reflected in Holy Scripture.

We have asked the question "Whence did Shakespeare derive his insight into human nature?" We are at least on the way to an answer to that question. And in finding that answer we begin to see the bearing of both question and answer on human life today. Perhaps the greatest danger to our civilisation is contentment with the superficial. That is particularly true in the case of the *have* nations (I use the phrase in contrast to those nations whose people live largely in poverty and degradation). Our danger is so to concentrate on the verbs to *have* and to *acquire* that we neglect the verbs to *be* and to *live*. As a matter of fact, poverty and affluence involve men and nations in similar dangers. The man (or the nation) forced to wrestle with problems of want—be it in the realm of commodities or of medicine or of education—is tempted to think that, given plenty, all his problems will be solved. *Have* enough, *acquire* enough, and he will *be* all right. He will know what it is to *live*. That is on the one hand. On the other, the man (or the nation) who has reached a state of affluence—our own nation is a case in point—is tempted to think that he has all that he needs. He *has* money. He has *acquired* the benefits of a Welfare State, a pension scheme, an adequate system of insurance, a motor car, a television set, all the gadgets thought necessary for a man of position in the 1960s. And that—so he is led to believe—is all he needs. But in believing that, he fails to ask the fundamental questions about himself, his *being* and his *life*. What is he? Where does he come from? Whither is he bound? Why is he here at all? The man who does not ask these questions is in danger of living like the brutes that perish. Nor are there lacking signs that our so-called highly developed civilisations are lapsing in that direction.

Here is a peril of the greatest magnitude—a national peril, a personal peril. Insidious in the way it silently steals upon us all, we find ourselves, almost before we realise it, under the domination of a way of life which uses the wrong verbs and asks the wrong questions; which stresses things and neglects persons; which strains to possess, and troubles not to live.

Is there any antidote to such an imminent danger? I think there is.

I have said that behind much of Shakespeare's deepest work lie the profound insights of the biblical revelation. I believe we neglect these at our peril. I believe that in these lies the antidote to our danger.

That we have moved away from them there can be little doubt. The thought-forms of the Bible do not come easily to men of the twentieth century. We no longer think in terms of a three-storey universe. We are "conditioned" to think scientifically, and we use the word "science" in the restricted sense of the physical sciences, forgetting its wider implications. And so, because we find biblical thought-forms difficult, we tend to abandon biblical insights—to our immeasurable loss.

But, it may be asked, would not a return to the insights of the Bible be a step back rather than forward? I do not think so, for it is the function of the Bible to bring us face to face with Jesus Christ, and He is the great Contemporary of every man of every age. "Jesus Christ is the same yesterday, today, and for ever." I do not believe that, whatever a man has acquired, be it of wealth or even of culture, he has learned to live until he has faced Him, His claims, His demands and His infinite grace.

Many of you will have read the Newsom Report on Education ("Half our Future"). Not the least valuable part of that fine seventh chapter (devoted to "Spiritual and Moral Development") is its insight into the fact that it is not enough to teach youngsters Bible stories, or the geography and customs of Palestine, and to leave it at that. Nor is moral instruction enough. To leave it at that is to engage on "evading tactics". Christianity must be shown to be relevant to life, to have something to say to the problems which confront any thinking adolescent. The teacher must, in other words, help him to see something of those profound biblical insights of which I have spoken in reference to the works of Shakespeare.

It was said of One infinitely greater than Shakespeare: "He knew what was in man." That knowledge He derived in part from mixing with common people. He came of humble stock Himself and was at home with tax-gatherers and sinners. And yet, with perfect ease He could mix with religious and civil leaders, and could stand unbowed before a Pilate and a Herod. He saw the poverty of the rich, the shabbiness of the over-dressed. "He knew what was in man."

But there was more to it than that. His mind, like Shakespeare's, was fed on Holy Scripture (only He had but the Old Testament, while Shakespeare had the New as well). He pondered, from His youth up, on the holiness of God, His sternness and His love, His demands and His succour as adumbrated in the Jewish revelation.

Even that was not all. He lived close to God. When a man knows God, he knows God's creatures too. This is as true as its converse—that when a man loses contact with God, he is in danger of having a superficial judgment of men. But we must go even further—we believe that He who, as man, knew what was in man, as very God moved among men, revealing, rescuing, redeeming.

It is the first function of Scripture to bring us face to face with Him, for it is in His light that we see light and that we enter life as God means it to be lived.

Let, then, this quatercentenary celebration be to us not merely an occasion for commemorating the birth of a great Englishman. Let it be a summons to ponder the source from which he derived his deepest insights. In returning to that source, we shall find ourselves facing Him Who knew—and knows—what is in man and is ever ready to meet him in forgiveness and in grace.

Florence Nightingale Memorial Service

Personal Work

St John 17:19
For their sake I consecrate myself.

WHY CHOOSE AN archbishop to give the address at a service like this? What does he know about the work of a nurse? (For that matter, what does a nurse know about the work of an archbishop?) Would it not have been better to get the Matron of a Hospital as preacher tonight?

Yes—I think it might. I am a great believer in having a woman as a preacher on certain occasions, when she knows her Lord and can speak clearly in His Name. But I have been asked to do this and I am thankful to have this opportunity of speaking to you on this occasion.

Perhaps I know a bit more about your splendid calling than you might imagine. My younger daughter is a doctor, working in the field of gynaecology and obstetrics. I have been wonderfully served by nurses on the very rare occasions when I have been a patient. And, as a matter of fact, your job and mine have a great deal in common.

Let me explain.

It is often thought that the main part of an archbishop's work is done in public—in the glare of television lights and with cameras clicking all round. Some of it *is* like that. He has the privilege of addressing great gatherings, like this one, for instance. But much of his time and energy goes into work which never gets any publicity, and never catches the public eye. I think this "private" work is some of the most important he ever does. I am

Westminster Abbey, 9th May, 1968.

thinking not only of the letters he writes—he does many hundreds of these a year—but of his work with individuals which occupies many hours every week. People come to him, sometimes in trouble, often in perplexity, perhaps in need of guidance. If he knows his job, he listens. He tries never to appear to be flurried or in a hurry. He helps them to weigh up their questions. Sometimes he has to press rather hard, and it hurts. Sometimes he can bring healing. It is close and intimate work. It is costly work, and sometimes leaves him a bit drained. But the very intimacy of the work is what makes it so wonderfully worthwhile. And if he can, in the course of the talk, point his friend to the only One who can really make men whole in every part of their being, then he has done a job beyond all price. He may do it by means of a few words simply spoken. He may do it just by what he is. He may do it in both ways.

In describing my job I have in fact been describing yours. People come within your reach just because they are in trouble. Often it is primarily physical trouble—they have had a motor accident or a fall. Often, behind the physical trouble, is some less tangible but no less real difficulty—there is a mind diseased or a spirit burdened, and under the burden they have broken. The doctor does what he can; so does the specialist; so does the man in the lab. It is a team effort. But the person who sees most of the patient, spends longest with him, gets closest to his needs, is, I imagine, the nurse. Often, the pressure of work is such that she is tempted to get flurried. But she does her best to keep cool, and to bring quiet attention and so to open up the way to healing. Often, perhaps in the night, she is able to say a word that will bring comfort and strength when no one else is near to do this. Sometimes, if she knows and serves the Lord Christ, she can put in a simple word which will point the patient to Him. It is a great ministry, this service of expert and loving care carried out in ward or lab. or administrator's office. It can only be fulfilled when we resist the temptation to see the person we are ministering to as a "bod", and see him for what he is, a *person* in his own right, a person infinitely precious to God, made in His image though often estranged from Him, a person who can only be made whole through the ministry of other *persons*. Your work—and mine—is *personal* work, or it is nothing at all.

That was in fact the way that *Jesus* went to work. I know He was a great preacher—and that was a wonderful part of His ministry, though it looks as if the crowds whom He drew at the beginning of His work fell away when they saw the cross looming up. But much of His work—*most* of it, so the Gospels suggest—was done on a person to person basis. I watch Him at work with the paralysed man, tracing the root of his paralysis to some sin which had not been forgiven (perhaps a wrong relationship which had never been put right). I see Him bringing sight to eyes which had long been dim, and clear speech to a man whose hearing and speaking apparatus seemed all blocked up. I hear Him putting penetrating questions which themselves seemed to get to the root of the problems: "What do you want Me to do for you?" "Do you desire to be made whole?" It was in ways of this kind that He set about healing men and women.

In the difficult business of character-making, how long and hard He wrestled with Simon Peter, to make him whole, to change the shifty, morally cowardly volcano of a man into a man whose powers were harnessed and controlled and therefore usable! But He did it, and made Simon into Peter, apostle, preacher, martyr. How patiently He worked with Philip who was so slow to come to understand Him! And how sympathetically He entered into Thomas's doubts and rescued him from the disaster of a life of unbelief! He *made* those twelve men—or, rather, eleven of them (for one would not stand for the rigour of the making and fell by the way). And He did the same for the women, a Mary Magdalene here, a woman from King Herod's court there, a poor broken thing by the well in Samaria on another occasion.

It was not easy work. It meant lining up His will with that of His Father in heaven. It meant the discipline of prayer, sometimes while others were asleep. It meant, if I may come back to my text, *consecrating* Himself for their sakes. That is to say, He dedicated Himself as an offering to God for them. It meant, in the end, death on a cross, where He bore their sins and carried their sorrows—and ours, too, for that matter. For all down the years, when men have seen that Figure on the cross, they have found release and wholeness of personality.

Your work and mine, each in our different spheres, is *personal* work. So was our Lord's. The effectiveness of *His* work was due to the fact that He lived a life in constant touch with God, drawing on His power, acting as a channel for His love. His was a *dedicated* life and ministry—full of peace in spite of the surging crowds, full of joy in spite of the approaching cross. As people came into touch with Him, they found something of His wholeness, His health, His holiness, seeping into them.

If we are to be of full use to God in ministering to His people, it will only be when we have dedicated ourselves to Him for their sake. That calls for decisive action. We don't drift into this. Every day the act is renewed. We can put it to Him like this:

> Just as I am, thine own to be,
> Lord of all life, who lovest me,
> To consecrate myself to Thee,
> O Jesus Christ, I come.

That is the kind of prayer to which He always responds—the prayer of dedication, of consecration. From the praying of it flows a ministry *for* us and a blessing *through* us. That is all we can ask.

Christmas Day
in York Minster

The Dayspring

St Luke 1:78
The tender mercy of our God, whereby the
dayspring from on high has visited us.

DARKNESS HOLDS VERY few terrors for the average
Englishman. At the turn of a switch, darkness becomes light.
We live in a world of electricity and bulbs and batteries, and we
take it all for granted—at least, until there is a "cut", or a blackout
such we endured in World War II.

But for Easterners like the men of the Bible, and indeed for
many an African and Asian today, darkness is linked with fear—
fear of the unseen and the unknown. Put your foot down in the
dark, and you may tread on a snake. Go on a journey in the dark,
and you may fall into the hands of a marauding band. Darkness
is the time for the thief and the scoundrel.

Small wonder, then, that the Bible is full of allusions to the
perils of night and to the dangers of darkness. Death itself is referred to as "the valley of the shadow", or, more correctly, "the
darkest valley". By contrast, goodness and light seem always to
go together. Christ is "the true Light coming into the world",
and Christians are called "children of light" and are charged to
"put on the armour of light". It is an image easily understood by
an Easterner and even by us sophisticated mechanically-minded
Europeans.

The text takes up the theme very sensitively. "The tender
1970.

mercy of our God, whereby the dayspring from on high has visited us". Zechariah, father of John Baptist, is represented as uttering a prophecy as he looks on his infant son. He sees him as the Lord's forerunner, preparing the way of the Christ, for an event of supreme importance has happened. How can he describe it? It is like a glorious sunrise. I do not mean the kind of timid, fog-dimmed thing which—if we are lucky—we see after breakfast on English winter mornings. I mean the bold blazing thing which the Jew sees in Israel—a tip of golden-red on the horizon before, almost in a trice, the darkness is dissipated, the cold of the night is gone, and the dayspring from on high has visited him. Gone is the chilliness of his fragile tent. Gone is the apprehension of the night. Gone is the fear of beast and thief.

This is the meaning of the Incarnation—of Christmas—for the Christian. What once for him was dark and fearsome is no longer so. *Death*—that dark valley—has been illuminated, for Christ has brought life and immortality to light by his Gospel. The future—hitherto the sphere of the unknown and therefore feared—can hold no horrors, for the God and Father of our Lord Jesus Christ holds the key to it. We walk into it in the companionship of Him who is the Light of the world and our Light. And even *disaster*—for the unbeliever an unalleviated terror—is illumined by the One who can turn darkness into light and make a cross a sign of conquest.

This is the essence of Christmas. The crib is the place of God's tender mercy. He has come to visit us in great humility—and we are glad!

But to leave it there would be wholly wrong. There are areas of life still dark, because Christ's light has not penetrated them. There are homes in this diocese of ours where the inmates have no idea of what Christmas is all about.

I took part, some months ago, in a popular television programme. In a local authority children's home, one recently-admitted little girl wanted to know who I was and what I did. "Listen", they said to her, "he's going to tell us about Jesus." I read a passage from the New Testament in which Christ was mentioned two or three times. The little girl was horrified and gave a gasp of disapproval. To her "Christ" was only a swear word. When I had finished, she said, with a look of disdain, "He never said nowt about Jesus."

It was *dark* there, wasn't it? Why had she been brought up with no dayspring, no sunrise? In *Christian* England? Is there anybody like that within a mile of you?

Further afield, "deep darkness broodeth yet". Black fears white, and white fears black—hence prison without proper trial, and the fear of speeding up the end of apartheid. Communist fears capitalist, and capitalist communist—hence the expenditure of vast sums of money on armaments, while people cry out for lack of food for the belly and literacy for the mind. Employer fears employee, and employee employer—hence illicit strikes with all the misery they bring in their wake.

I know no answer to this darkness short of a spread of the light of Christ. When that dayspring visits us, fear begins to depart. When I see that negro as a brother in Christ; when the communist glimpses the revelation of God in Christ and the capitalist leaves his greed at the foot of the cross; when the employer gives a fair wage and the employee gives an honest day's work precisely because both see themselves as members of God's family and recipients of His tender mercy; then the darkness will begin to disappear, fear will go, and confidence be born.

This is too big a theme for Christmas morning. Ponder it, before you return to the round of your daily work again. See how intimately the truth of it impinges on our own life and witness. "A Christian is not truly a Christian until he is 'a Christianiser'", wrote Cardinal Suenens. That is to say, if the dayspring from on high has visited you, it is incumbent on you to share its light, else you will lose it. The very darkness of the world—of our own England—is a summons to witness and to light-bearing, that those who still sit in darkness and in the shadow of death may welcome the dayspring who is Christ the Lord and have their feet guided into the way of peace.

What better Christmas greeting can I give to you than this— that you and yours may increasingly rejoice in the Light that shines on us from Bethlehem, and that more and more your feet may be guided into the way of peace?

Easter Day
in York Minster

Life

St John 14:19
Because I live, you too will live.

THERE IS A widespread doubt in the minds of men
as to whether there is anything beyond this little life. Bertrand
Russell, who died a few weeks ago, put it bluntly: "I believe that
when I die, I rot", he said. Barbara Wootton (Baroness Wootton
of Abinger), who occupies a prominent place in the House of
Lords and who has done much for the reformation of the laws
which govern our society, has given us her "autobiographical
reflections" in a book entitled *In a World I Never Made*. In this
book, she concludes "that death is to be equated with the extinc-
tion of human consciousness and is correctly defined as an ir-
reversible coma". She works out her philosophy of life in a
framework confined within what she calls "the brief flash that
illumines the interval between birth and death". There are, of
course, millions of atheists and agnostics who hold similar views.

Within the Churches, too, among people who would strongly
resent not being called Christians, there are many who are very
dubious whether there is a "beyond" at all, and if there is, what
the grounds are for believing in it. It is to such especially that I
would address myself this Easter morning.

At the heart of the Christian Faith is the belief that Christ is
risen. We agree with St Paul when he wrote: "If Christ was not
raised, then our Gospel is null and void, and so is your faith."
1970.

78

There is room for difference of opinion as to what precisely is meant by the resurrection of Jesus, and as to the exact meaning of the "resurrection body" in which He appeared to His disciples. But this at least we mean when we say that Christ is risen: After He was done to death and buried, He was seen and recognised and spoken with on a number of occasions by a variety of people. Further, when His bodily presence had been withdrawn, His disciples did not think of Him as "gone" (except from their physical sight). He was with them "nearer than breathing, closer than hands and feet". He was not a memory, to which they fondly looked back. He was a Presence, a Person, to whom they prayed and with whom they daily communicated, whose coming they awaited, whose will they sought to obey, whose service they loved to fulfil. *At the least*, that was what the resurrection of Christ meant to the early disciples. And it is what it has meant to millions down the years, and still means today. They would agree with the reply given by a Christian to a man who affirmed that God was dead. The Christian said: "Strange! I was talking with Him this morning".

St John reports our Lord as saying to His disciples just prior to the crucifixion: "Because I live, you too will live." I take that to mean two things:—

First, it means that because Christ rose and is alive for ever, those who are united to Christ will live with Him when this little life is done. In fact, in many ways this life is preparatory school experience and training for that. If in this life a union has been established between a man and Christ, the physical incident of death will not break that union. If, baptised into Christ and strengthened with His Body and Blood, a man lives a life of discipleship and of increasing devotion to Him, he will scarcely notice death. It will be the gateway to closer union, fuller service, deeper love, and richer likeness to the One he has loved while on earth.

The Christian bases this expectation and hope and faith not on some idea of spring following winter, and the "death" of an acorn giving way to the "life" of an oak tree (suggestive as these analogies may be), but on the conviction expressed in the text: "Because I live, you too will live." And by that faith, and in that hope, the Christian is content to live and to die. With Christian, in *Pilgrim's Progress*, he can say as he crosses the river: "I feel the bottom, and it is good."

Secondly, the words "Because I live, you too will live" have a present meaning as well as a future one. When the New Testament speaks of eternal life, it speaks of a present reality as well as of a future hope. The first disciples found this promise come true immediately after the resurrection and for the rest of their earthly lives. St John says that, on the first Easter evening, when least they were expecting Him, the risen Lord appeared to them and performed a deeply symbolic act. He breathed on them and said: "Take Holy Spirit. Receive the life which is not yours by nature and which God alone can give. Breathe in deeply. Let God's Life fill you here and now." And in obedience, as they were prepared to receive, the new life was given—the coward heart made brave, the impure clean, and the doubting strong. Take Holy Spirit!

When in South Africa, my wife and I went to visit a couple of whom I have been vividly reminded as I have been considering the meaning of these words. The man had been a soldier and had also held a post of some importance in the insurance world. For most of his life he had had little if any Christian faith, and little if any time for religion. Then he had some heart trouble which occasioned a visit to the doctor. The doctor, who also had little time for religion, asked his patient if he were a man of faith. On receiving a negative reply, he said: "You might care to look at this" and thrust into his hand a copy of Thomas à Kempis *On the Imitation of Christ*. My friend leafed through it, and the Spirit of God touched him. Do not ask me exactly how it happened. "The wind blows where it wills; you hear the sound of it, but you do not know where it comes from, or where it is going. So with everyone who is born from Spirit". That happened ten years ago. Today that man will tell you that up to then, up to the day when God spoke and he responded, it seems he had scarcely lived. During this last decade he has known the meaning of the words: "Because I live, you too will live." He does. And he will. He told me, simply and straightforwardly, what the words "in union with Christ" had come to mean to him, especially in recent months.

The conditions for the enjoyment of this new life, this eternal life, are essentially simple, though the results of its possession go deep and are far reaching. "Anyone who loves Me," St John reports Jesus as saying, "anyone who loves Me will heed what I say; then My Father will love him, and we will come and make our dwelling with him." That union means life—full life in the here and now; life that shall endless be.

That is the essential meaning of Easter, and in that deepest of all senses I wish you in Christ our Lord "a happy Easter".

"Anyone who loves Me will heed what I say."

"Because I live, you too will live."

Whit Sunday
in York Minster

The Life-Giver

Acts 2:2
Suddenly there came ... a noise like that of a
strong driving wind which filled the whole
house ...

IT IS A strange thing —the wind. It is invisible, yet so
powerful. I watch it at work from my study window at Bishopthorpe, where the sailing boats go by and often get becalmed.
Then there is a movement, and the sail is caught by the unseen
wind, and away goes the boat. A lovely, powerful thing, the wind.

It is a refreshing thing, too. The air in some building is stale
and foetid. You open the window. You let the breeze blow
through, and all is sweet and fresh again.

It can, of course, be a terrifying thing, too. A tornado is simply
wind at work, stripping the trees, lifting the roofs, breaking down
the shelters, changing all the established patterns.

When the biblical writers wanted to speak of the unseen God
at work in society or in the Church or in individuals, they had, of
course, to use picture language. They seized on the metaphor of
wind. In fact, in both the main biblical languages, the word for
"spirit" and the word for "wind" are the same. "The *wind* blows
where it wills; you hear the sound of it, but you do not know
where it comes from, or where it is going", can equally well be
translated "the *Spirit* blows where it wills ..."

After our Lord's crucifixion and resurrection and ascension,

1972.

82

the disciples found themselves dis-spirited. Can you wonder? He, Jesus, had been the inspiration of their lives, breathing into very ordinary men and women something of His own Spirit, refreshing, driving, and sometimes destroying. It was terrifying sometimes, but infinitely exciting. And now He was gone—or so it seemed. But He had told them to wait. That is always a wise thing to do when you have had a body-blow. So they waited, silently, expectantly.

They were not disappointed. It came. Or, rather, He came, whose coming was like the wind, unseen, refreshing, powerful, driving, destructive of old patterns, constructive of new. Pentecost had arrived. The Church was reborn. And so a group of inward-looking, dis-spirited men and women became the nucleus of a Church which was to drive its way through from Jerusalem to Rome, up through Europe to a primitive little island called Britain, and then even to the uttermost parts of the earth with a power which (as I saw in Africa last month) is winning tens of thousands to Christ and His Church every year.

During the major part of this century, the Church has been engrossed (I almost said pre-occupied) with the doctrine of the Church—its nature, its unity, its mission, its message. From the historic conference at Edinburgh in 1910, through the great ecumenical conferences in which some of us have taken part up to and including the one at Uppsala in 1968, we have had our heads down, working away at these problems. And our work has not been unproductive by any means. In spite of disappointments and set-backs grievous to be borne, we have made big advances, and there are greater to come in the realm of unity, joint worship and work. But I think it likely that God is seeking to draw the attention of His Church to a matter which is even more basic than the matter of the Church itself. I mean the Spirit, without whom the Church is dead; the Spirit who, as the Creed has it, is "the Lord, the life-giver".

Are we willing to hear what God is trying to say to His people, to us in England, encrusted as we are by our long traditions and our set ways, by our natural conservatism and by the caution of the centuries? Are we willing to listen to the wind?

Let me give you some examples of what I have in mind, as I put them in question form.

What are we to do about the "Jesus people" movement?

Dismiss it, as the vulgarity of American-inspired adolescents? That is the easiest thing to do. But suppose that, in spite of its lack of concern with things like Church order, things which mean so much to us; suppose that it were true that, through this movement, the wind of the Spirit were blowing where it wills; and suppose we failed to listen to the wind? What then?

What of that other movement, broadly called charismatic, which has already invaded this country and is penetrating significantly the Roman Catholic Church as well as the Free Churches and our own? What are we to say about this? The easiest thing to do is again to ignore it, or even to dismiss it with a contemptuous aside about speaking in tongues. I am personally not deeply interested in this particular phenomenon in the movement, though it is an undoubted characteristic of New Testament Christianity. I think it matters little today compared with the ethical fruits of the Spirit, such as love and joy and peace and self-control. But I *am* interested in unholy men being made holy, and joyless women being filled with joy. I am interested in lives re-made, and this is undoubtedly happening through the charismatic movement. Is this, I ask, the Spirit blowing where He wills? Suppose we failed to listen to the wind? What then?

Again, a friend of mine, an Englishman of learning, has written a large book, published by the Oxford University Press, called *Schism and Renewal in Africa.* This is a study of the independent Churches which are springing up like mushrooms in Africa in numbers almost unbelievably large. Their growth is both tragic and comic. If you find their number and variety alarming, ask yourself who it was who imported the scandal of our divisions into Africa. It was we Westerners! We can hardly be surprised if fissiparation, begun by us, is increased by them. These Churches, with so many things which are totally unlike what we know in England—their joyful informality which contrasts with our English stiffness, their use of women in the Church which contrasts with our timidity in this field, their African patterns of worship which remind us that Christianity was not born in the West—these Churches are producing new Christians at a phenomenal rate. We may not, indeed we do not like their theological and liturgical irregularities. We can find plenty of features to which we will object. But supposing that God were trying to say something through them to us set, staid Anglicans; and suppose we failed to listen to the wind? What then?

Let me take another example, this time from much nearer home and from territory much more familiar to most of us. A friend of mine died in 1972. He was Dr E. V. Rieu, editor and translator of best-selling paper-back classics. "An agnostic for half his life," it said in a long obituary notice in *The Times*, "he became an Anglican at the age of sixty, made a new translation of *The Four Gospels*, and was a member of the joint Churches Committee for the new translation of the Bible." The anonymous writer of the obituary let us into the secret of this spiritual Odyssey. When one of Rieu's sons heard that his father was to undertake, single-handed, a translation of the Gospels, he said: "It will be very interesting to see what father makes of the Gospels. It will be still more interesting to see what the Gospels make of father." In fact, they made of the agnostic a committed Christian. Or, rather, the Spirit used Holy Scripture, as He so often has done down the centuries, to effect a life transformation. "The Spirit blows where it wills . . ." But supposing that God were trying to speak to *us* as he did to E. V. Rieu, through the medium of the Bible, and we failed to listen to the wind? What then?

The truth is, of course, that, as Augustine said, God, while He is "always at rest" is also "always at work". The wind of His Spirit never ceases to blow. Sometimes it is a gale, like these great movements of which I have spoken; a tornado, a hurricane, demanding attention from those who have ears to hear, who think, who ponder, who weigh up facts. Sometimes it is a still small voice, touching conscience, assaulting will, demanding response from individuals. All that then matters is that we set our sail to catch the wind; that we see there is nothing to block the coming of the Spirit, no disobedience to thwart His power or obstruct His operation. All that matters is that, like Saul of Tarsus on the Damascus Road, we be "not disobedient to the heavenly vision", nor deaf to the wind of the Spirit.

Given that, the mighty Spirit of God will find in us, as He found in the first disciples at Pentecost, men and women through whom His grace and power can come to others, using us as agents of His holiness in society.

There can be no greater destiny for anyone than that.

Harvest Thanksgiving in York Minster

The Responsibility of Man

Psalm 8:6–8
Thou makest him master over all thy creatures;
thou hast put everything under his feet:
all sheep and oxen, all the wild beasts,
the birds in the air and the fish in the sea,
and all that moves along the paths of ocean.

I IMAGINE THAT this order of service was drawn up by our late dean, Dr Eric Milner-White.[1] It bears the stamp of his skilled craftsmanship. The note of thanksgiving rings throughout it. And when, in living memory, have we had more cause for thankfulness than in the autumn of this wonderful year, when sunny week has followed sunny week in warm and golden succession? He would have to be a man of some resourcefulness who could find much to grumble about this year!

You will have noticed, however, that at one point in the service, into the theme of jubilation there slipped a note of judgment; into the theme of thanksgiving there came a note of almost sombre thoughtfulness. "Beloved," said the Minister as he received the loaf, "do not forget that the judgment of God is upon us, for any misuse of our stewardship, for any neglect of our land, for all waste and adulteration of our food, and for all injustice in its distribution that we can prevent." Was our late dean wrong in introducing that sombre note? Ought he to have

4th October, 1974.

[1]Some of the themes in this sermon are further elaborated in *The Ethics of Scientific Farming* and *Some Christian Convictions for the Twentieth Century*.

left this unsaid, and let us go on our way unmindful of these things? It would have been easier for us if he had left us to sing the well-known harvest hymns, to take part in a picturesque pageant, to watch a drama enacted, and so to go on our way for another year. Easier, yes. But *wrong*. For the dean assumed, rightly, that the Minster would be filled with men and women who were prepared to *think*, not just to have their ears tickled or their aesthetic taste titillated. He assumed that, in those whose lives were closely linked with the soil, there burned, even if in varying degrees, a sense of responsibility. I assume that too. It is, indeed, with the matter of *responsibility* that I wish to deal.

We have all heard of areas of fertile land reduced to dust-bowls because the owners have treated their land irresponsibly. Determined to extract the last ounce of yield, to make the highest possible profit, they have over-fertilised and over-cultivated it, and called down upon themselves the curse, the nemesis, which, in the long run, attaches to all irresponsible uses of the resources of nature. This is in some ways a more tragic abuse of nature than that neglect of it which allows briars and thorns to come up and to proliferate. It is what our service called a "misuse of our stewardship".

But the service also spoke of "injustice in the distribution" of food. What had the dean in mind? I imagine he was thinking of the situation which obtains all over the world today whereby one half of the world lives in plenty and the other half in poverty, poverty varying from mild forms of under-nourishment to downright starvation. This glaringly anomalous state of affairs ought to shock us into action. But *what* action?

Let me suggest three things that we can do:—

1. We can generously support those agencies like Inter-Church Aid and Oxfam which exist to relieve human suffering and to make up deficient diets in parts of the world less fortunate than our own.

2. We can extend the use of the weapons of science in bringing their discoveries to bear on the vast problem of food cultivation and production in a world whose population increases by sixty million every year. If, as I believe, the Holy Spirit is behind the discovery of all new truth and of its beneficial application to life, then the scientist engaged on this task should see himself in the

role of a collaborator with God in the alleviation of human misery due to inadequacy of diet.

3. We can spurn the blandishments of those politicians, of whatever party, who promise us a higher level of living while doing comparatively little about improving the lot of the "have not" nations. It is a temptation, particularly at election times, for the politician to say: "You have it pretty good. Put us into power, or keep us in power, and we will see that you have it better." The Christian answer is surely this: "We are not very interested in having it better (except in certain comparatively minor areas of our national life where clearly injustice still persists). We *are* interested in voting for a party which will openly challenge us to consider need on a world scale and to pay heavily for the alleviation of that need; which will encourage scientists—not least agricultural scientists—to do their work in and for the "have not" nations; which will challenge us to the exercise of responsibility on a national scale on broadly Christian lines."

In such ways as these we can, in however small a degree, make our contribution to the diminution of human misery throughout the world.

I noticed, however, that the service spoke not only of injustice in distribution of goods, but of "adulteration of our food" as a cause for the judgment of God. The phrase is a striking one, and touches on an issue of vast importance which must exercise the minds of all thinking people. Modern man, as I have already said, is faced by a meteoric rise in population—and people must be fed. But modern man also has skills unknown to and undreamed of by his grandparents or even his parents. The use of chemicals, the practice of factory farming, and so on, put into our hands responsibilities of almost terrifying dimensions. It will not do to bury our heads in the sand, to look back to the old days, and to fail to use to the full methods of production which science has made available to us. That would be to be traitors to our fellow men. But we must not shut our eyes to the fact that the weapons of modern science are full of danger.

There is, for example, the danger of cruelty to animals inherent in factory farming. Cruelty does not necessarily follow the use of these methods, but the temptation to allow bad conditions in the interests of quick and easy profit is very great indeed, and the suffering involved needs little imagination. I am glad to read that the National Farmers' Union is holding an enquiry into intensive livestock farming methods, and that work began recently in Dorset and Somerset.

There is the danger to human health consequent on the use of chemicals after inadequate field trials. Such a phrase as "provisional commercial clearance as having low mammalian toxicity" needs very careful scrutiny. What is meant by "provisional"? and what by "low mammalian toxicity"? Where immediate profit is the aim, profit which gives insufficient attention to the effects of chemicals or radiation on nature and on man, we have a use of science which can only be labelled as dangerous, irresponsible and immoral.

What is the Christian contribution to this matter? The issues involved are highly technical, and I would not dream of going into details of a sphere about which I am necessarily ignorant. But thoughtful scientists and farmers have a right to look to the Church for certain lines of moral guidance. I offer the following comments:—

1. *We accept the findings of science with thankfulness.* God is the God of all truth, whether that truth be concerned with the atom, chemicals, insemination, or the incarnation. We accept the findings as coming from God for the service of His creation.

2. *We recognise that in all of us motives operate which must be controlled and sometimes denied.* Avarice, an appetite for quick returns, is a passion which needs stern handling. Give rein to it, and animals will suffer, the fields will suffer, and it may well be that man will suffer—in his body and even in his genetic processes. Avarice aligned to science is a combination potent for ill. The public must not be used as guinea-pigs for ill-tested experimentation.

3. *We are world-citizens.* By this I mean that we are not only members of a local community here in Yorkshire; or even of the English nation; or even of the British Commonwealth of Nations. We are members of a world whose most distant members are now very close to us, whom our Lord has taught us to regard as brothers and sisters *if they are in need.* To think in narrower terms than that is to indulge in selfishness which in biblical terms is

equated with idolatry. The measure of our responsibility is the need of our world.

At the beginning of this sermon, I quoted a text. You may have forgotten it by now. As a matter of fact, I believe I have been expounding it in what I have already said: "Thou makest him master over all thy creatures: thou hast put everything under his feet: all sheep and oxen, all the wild beasts, the birds in the air and the fish in the sea, and all that moves along the paths of ocean." God has given man dominion. He can think and discover. Therefore he can manipulate and use. It is right that he should. But *God* has given that power to man. Therefore he is responsible for the use he makes of it. He is supreme over nature, but he is accountable to the God before whose judgment seat we all shall one day stand. His use of the resources of nature—be they chemical or animal—is a divine charge.

I believe that it is only when a man becomes a Christian disciple, bowing in worship before the God who is Creator and Redeemer, living in obedience to the dictates of the Spirit of Truth, pondering the meaning of responsibility to his fellows for whom Christ died, to the animal creation and to all nature, it is only *then* that he can develop into the kind of being God made him to be. It is only *then* that he can use to the full the powers that God has put within his grasp.

It is to that full and glad discipleship that I bid you—some for the first time, some to go further on a road already part explored.

Along that road mankind—you, I—will find the fulfilment of our destiny.

III GREAT THEMES

Social and Religious Issues

Some Christian Convictions for the Twentieth Century

THE MOST FAMOUS of the portraits of the Archbishops of York which hang in our drawing room in Bishopthorpe is that by Orpen of Archbishop Cosmo Gordon Lang (1908–28). It is a brilliant piece of work, though some would say a cruel one. Lang himself described it as "proud, pompous, and prelatical"—a remark which caused Hensley Henson to ask the Archbishop to which of these epithets he took exception! There he sits, robed, serene, his eyes apparently following the visitor as he enters the room and takes his stand beneath the picture. But once the visitor has managed to disengage himself from that penetrating glance, he notices that there is far more to the picture than the portrait of the man who is, as it were, the centre-piece. There is the background. Suitably subdued, it consists almost entirely of folds of red and green velvet. Subdued, yes; but immensely important. The setting matters much.

I stand today in the notable succession of those who since 1917 have given the Shaftesbury Lectures. As I look at the titles of these Lectures, I am made aware of the fact that most of them deal, pretty intimately, with human beings. The titles indicate as much —"Reverence the Child", "The Progress of Child Welfare", "The Shaftesbury Society and the Cripple", "A Christian Concept of Education", and, most recently, "The Handicapped in the Community", and so on. The "painters" of these lectures have, rightly, focused their attention on the central figure, the human being in need of the sort of aid which the Shaftesbury Society exists to provide. Today, however, I will seek to fill in the background, in

27th Shaftesbury Lecture, October 1973.

93

the belief that, if we are to see the human being truly and to help
him effectively, we must take very careful note of the conditions
in which he is set; we shall not get *him* right in our thinking if we
do not study his *environment*.

Man and his environment are inseparable. I shall say much
to you today about "man", but in doing so I shall not refer to
any special division of *homo sapiens* (children, cripples, deaf, or
whatever), but to the race of which you and I and "all God's
children" are part.

We shall touch today on many problems which affect our
race—population explosion, pollution, conservation, ecological
balance, abortion, and so on. We shall do so in the realisation that
these matters have in recent years come into the forefront of the
thinking not only of the scientists but of the man in the street—
popularised greatly by the activities of such men as the Duke of
Edinburgh and by the setting aside of special periods such as
European Conservation Year for their consideration. This is all
to the good. We do well to be anxious about our world and about
our race—as I shall shortly show. The prospects sketched by those
who know what they are talking about in these areas are often
frightening. The alarm bell should be rung: the danger lights
should be flashed.

I shall, then, spend a few moments in pointing out the shoals
on which, all too easily, the human ship could be wrecked; and
if, in doing so, I cover ground all too familiar, I ask you to accept
that it is merely an introduction (but a necessary introduction)
to the more basic, background questions the discussion of which
will constitute the larger part of this lecture.

The questions I wish to pose run along these lines: Has the
Christian any particular contribution to make to the debate?
When he speaks on these issues, is he simply jumping on a
popular band-wagon and adding his voice to the voices of other
do-gooders? Or can he do something valuable in providing a
basis of thinking so solid that it will provide a foundation which
will ensure a discussion on right lines and at least keep our eyes
fixed in the right direction as we peer into the future and seek to
find solutions? Has the Christian any convictions—theological,
doctrinal convictions if you like—about nature, God and man
which are relevant to the debate? I would put it even more
pointedly than that. I would ask: Has the Christian anything to

say apart from which the wrong questions may be asked and the solutions prove to be wide of the mark?

I believe he has. But that must wait meantime.

What are the sort of problems that I have in mind? I mention two:

1. *The population explosion*
I will not bore you with figures. I will simply remind you that, between now and the end of this century, it seems pretty certain that the population of the world will double, unless there be some colossal natural disaster or an outbreak of atomic war to stop it. The best way to grasp what is happening is to look at the sort of graph which Barbara Ward and René Dubos give on page 42 of their book *Only one Earth: The Care and Maintenance of a Small Planet* (Pelican Books, 1972). When we consider the demands made by such growth of population on food supplies alone, and when we remember that it is in the hungriest nations of the world (Asia, Africa, Latin America) that the growth is fastest, we begin to ask searching questions about the negative aspects of the Pope's encyclical *Humanae Vitae*, and the relevance *for today* of the command to "be fruitful and multiply" (Genesis 1: 28).

I said I would not bore you with figures. I won't. But I will give you some which will startle you. In 1968, so the Population Reference Bureau said, there were 225 births per minute, and 93 deaths. That means that *then*, world population rose by 132 per minute. The rate of increase is much higher now. What bearing has this on problems of intercourse, birth control, abortion, food production, euthanasia, literacy, education?

2. *The pollution problem*
Three elements can be polluted: the *earth*, by de-afforestation, over-use of the land, chemical fertilisers, radio-active fall-out, noise, etc. The *air*, by radio-active gases, industrial pollution, planes, and noise. The *water*, by industrial waste, sewage effluent, oil leakage, over-fishing. We need to remind ourselves that the ocean is a vast septic tank, with no plug to let anything out. Every ounce hitherto dumped or channelled into the sea, from the very morning of time until the modern age of general industrialisation, has accumulated in one form or another inside

the same land-locked sea, the lowest section of our biosphere and the only one with no outlet for refuse. "The ocean has none of the infinitude we give it in our dreams" (Ward and Dubos, *op. cit.*, p. 272).

Facts such as these highlight the problems of ecology. (I pause for a moment to define that much used and not always understood word. Ecology has been defined as: "the study of the relationship of living things in their physical environment". Or again: "The mutual relations between organisms and environment". Or, slightly more fully, according to the *Oxford English Dictionary*: "the study of spacial distribution of a population in reference to material and social causes and effects".) Mankind has an unbelievably wonderful house in which to live. There are signs that he is not a very good house-keeper. Ecological balance can terribly easily be upset, and, once upset, who knows whether it can be righted? For example, if you kill a lake, as many are in fact being killed, can you make it live again? And even if you can, at what cost? Nature is a strange mixture of mighty majesty and extreme fragility. Its balance can easily be unhinged.

That great human being, Yehudi Menuhin, in an essay entitled "If I were Eighteen" (printed in *Theme and Variations*, p. 105 ff.) asks this question and makes these searching comments:

How many (of our urban population) have a clear idea about our relationship to and dependence upon the earth, our responsibility to ourselves and our children and our children's children? For we must realise that we cannot take out of anything more than we put into it if we wish continuity of existence, nor can we always take out in one form and put in in another. Particularly must we respect the cycle of life, which if interrupted at any point by the substitution of a synthetic or inert substance for a living one, inevitably breaks down, bringing disease and death to all living things.

If you want examples of the kind of things which Menuhin is thinking of, let your mind range over dead rivers, over smog, over dust-bowls, over Calcutta.

I referred to these problems of pollution in my harvest sermon in York Minster some ten years ago in 1963. What we have experienced since then is frightening. It is now possible to pollute the *universe*, and man has actually begun to do this by means of moon-shots. No longer is the earth a self-contained, closed unit. We have learnt to break out of it, and to take with us in our journeys into space the pollution which is a part of us and of our native environment. Our successors will have to take this very seriously.

More immediately relevant is the vast problem of *mind*-pollution through pornography and the mass media. This has sufficiently been brought to the attention of the public by the publication of the report of the Longford Committee to allow of a mere reference here. I myself believe that, just as good literature and good art raise and ennoble character, so bad literature and bad art degrade it. It is a matter for thankfulness that Mr Robert Carr, who was Home Secretary when the Longford Report was published, showed signs of taking more seriously than did his predecessor, Mr Maudling, the grave problem of *mind*-pollution, especially among the young. Are there not greater evils than a carefully regulated measure of censorship? Is it not better to erect the fence of protection at the top of the abyss than to provide the ambulance of an increasingly expensive penal system at the bottom of it?

Let me declare my basic conviction: I believe that there are, within what I would call the Judaic-Christian revelation, certain insights into these problems which point in the direction of their solution. I believe too that we neglect these insights at our own peril and at the peril of the race of which we are a part. I believe that it is urgent that we spread these insights with all the powers at our command.

The following are of primary importance:

1. The earth is the Lord's

So the Psalmist maintained (24:1). It is not primarily man's, still less the landlord's! There is a secondary sense in which the earth belongs to man. The Psalmist puts it like this: "All the whole heavens are the Lord's: the earth He hath given to the children of men" (115:16). That is to say that man is put in trust with the earth by the Creator. This is the main thrust of the teaching contained in the Genesis stories of creation.

Here God is depicted as deeply concerned not only with man but with the earth in which he is set, and with the relationship

D

between the two. Creation is good and to be rejoiced in. The earth is good and is to be worked at. Man is to "subdue it" and to "rule over" fish, birds, and every living thing (Gen. 1:28). He is in charge, *put* in charge by the Creator-God. He is responsible to Him for the use that he makes of the earth and its contents. He is, in the words of Psalm 8 (vv. 5 ff.), little less than a god, crowned with glory and honour, master over all God's creatures, with everything put under his feet. But this is not so that he may exploit, nor that he may give rein to his innate craving for profit, but that he may make responsible use of nature for the glory of God (see especially vv. 1 & 9).

2. *The nature of man*

Man is at once part of nature (part of the evolutionary process, if you will) and above nature. He is literally answerable to God, as we have just seen and as I have stressed on other occasions. He is also God's vice-gerent. In a sense, he is outside nature, dominating it. But, at the same time, he is within nature, finding his fulfilment only in so far as he is in harmony with it. He is to "dress and keep" the garden, not to destroy it or abuse it. His dignity lies in the very fact of his accountability, for it is something which he does not share with the animals, though in so many other respects he is one with them (in his appetites, in the reproductive process, etc). If he is to find fulfilment, he will only do so as he treats with utmost seriousness the doctrine of stewardship.

It is essential to begin to grasp the biblical concept of man, what he is in the intention of God, what he is in actual history, what he can become if he is restored and forgiven—essential if we are to get things right in the complicated state of affairs in which modern man finds himself. When the Genesis story insists that man was made in the image of God, it is seeking to say that, unlike the birds and the animals, man was endowed with powers to think, to reason, to ponder, to wonder, to know his Maker and to respond in love to Him. Endowed with free-will, he had the capacity to be a "man for others". This is the picture of the opening chapters of Genesis. But one has only to read as far as chapter 4 to come to a story of jealousy, of anger, of selfishness, and of murder. Cain murders Abel his brother. Aggressiveness takes over, competitiveness holds the field, and it is not long before blood is shed. It is from such causes that resentments and wars, the rape of the earth and the pollution of our resources spring. Man's bliss is broken, his peace is shattered.

The concept of "peace" in the Bible is far more extensive in its outreach, far deeper in its meaning than that word in English often implies. Peace to us who have seen two wars in as many generations means the absence of war—just that. But when a Hebrew spoke of peace he had in mind something comprehensive and positive, comprising all that he meant by "good". "Peace", says Pedersen (*Israel* I–II, p. 311 ff.) "designates the fact of being whole", "consists in complete harmony", "expresses every form of happiness and free expansion". So, when Jesus said to the woman who was a sinner, "Your faith has saved you; go in peace", He was authoritatively bidding her leave the restrictions and inhibitions of her old life and move out into a new experience of freedom and fullness of life.

"Salvation" and "peace" are two concepts very close to one another; they flow into one another. Salvation in the biblical vocabulary means life at the highest level of experience. The word is familiar to us in the proper name Joshua (Hebrew) and Jesus (Greek). It derives from a root which means "to be spacious". Thus Joshua lived up to the meaning of his name when he delivered his people from their enemies, got them out of a tight corner into liberty. Thus a greater than Joshua, son of Nun, Jesus, son of Mary, delivers His people from the confinements, the inhibitions, the complexes of sin. He brings "peace", total welfare. He *is* our peace (Eph. 2:14).

Here the whole doctrine of man is heightened and glorified by the doctrine of the Incarnation, the doctrine of the Son of God who was also Son of Man, not shrinking from calling men His brothers (Heb. 2:11), sharing the same flesh and blood with them (v. 14), made like them in every way (v. 17). So God has sanctified His world through the Incarnation of Christ. So He has ennobled human nature. Christianity does not run away from the material. It sees God working within it and through it. The material is sacred. Nature, including human nature, must be regarded as such. It must never be violated.

When, therefore, man handles nature, he must bear in mind not only technical considerations, but moral ones, based on his belief in God as Creator, Christ as the incarnate Son of Man, and man as a being reaching his fulfilment in so far, and only in so far, as he acts responsibly to God. If he arrogates to himself the function of creator, then he commits blasphemy, and lays himself open to the consequences of the abuse of nature—such as we see around us today. If he spoils God's creation and disaster ensues, he must not blame God.

Professor C. F. D. Moule sums up the matter well. He writes: "Restoration and liberation come when man assumes his proper position in ecology, not contracting out of his responsibilities and giving up the use of nature, but using it responsibly and according to the will of God" (*Man and Nature in the New Testament*, p. 14).

Man reaches his highest act of responsible use of nature when he becomes a pro-creator. In the acts of intercourse and birth, a man and a woman act on behalf of (*pro*) the Creator, in bringing new life into being. The Lord of life uses them as pro-creators to continue and extend his life-giving processes. The bearing of this insight into the real nature of things on the problems connected with abortion is apparent. It should be borne in mind particularly when any revision of the Abortion Act of 1967 is envisaged. The present situation leads to an appalling trivialisation of the act of pro-creation. New lives are conceived with the knowledge that, on almost any trumpery excuse, they can be snuffed out, at various stages of foetal development.

I need not give you figures to alert you to the facts as they are. You know them well. What is perhaps not so frequently realised is the appalling task which revolts many nurses who have to deal with the after-effects of abortions, and the equally appalling problems of conscience with which doctors have to wrestle (I remind you that I am the father of a gynaecologist). There is that in the sensitive consciences of medical men and women—both those who acknowledge a Christian allegiance and those who do not—which revolts at the cheapening of life and the denial of the kind of outlook which lies behind all I am saying, and which is tied up with a loose approach to abortion.

Some very hard thinking and courageous acting will be called for in this field.

3. *The theology of enough*

To say that we live in a technological age is to utter a truism. To say that we live in a rapacious age, or in a prodigal age, is to make a statement more deserving of thought. For this is, in fact, the case. Ours is a rapacious society. Only lately (is it too late?) have we become "aware that the exploitation and pollution of the world's resources constitutes an even more serious threat to human society than the old exploitation of men by men" (Bruce Allsopp: *Ecological Morality*, p. 8). We are too "civilised" to exploit men by engaging in the slave-trade. But we do not seem to be civilised enough to realise that the materialistic rapacity of modern technological man leads to the spoliation of nature and will, if continued, lead to disaster for our race. "It has taken millions of years to create our environment and we are expending it prodigally knowing, if we stop to think, that what we use could not be replaced within any time-span which is meaningful in relation to the whole of human history" (B. Allsopp, op. cit., p. 30).

Let us face the issues as they really are. Pollution is to a great extent the end result of simple greed. Take one example. We take oil out of the earth and transport it in the cheapest possible way in huge and vulnerable tankers, often with untrained crews, from one country (which wants the maximum financial benefit from the oil) via the ships of another country (which wants the maximum profit from the transport) to a third country (which cares little what happens to it on the way, so long as it is there to burn up). We are rapacious. We must get the last ounce, or the last inch, out of everything. But the Old Testament law-givers saw that to adopt that attitude was to court disaster. Sabbatical years were to be observed, for men, for beasts, for the earth; years of Jubilee were to be kept; the corners of the field were to be left so that the poor might glean; planting and re-planting was to be engaged in where the earth was bare (see, for example, Lev. 19:9–10; Deut. 24:19–22; Lev. 25:1–7). "Don't squeeze the last ounce out of nature's bounty. Don't snatch. Don't grab" — the message comes loud and clear even in the pages of the Old Testament, but it often falls on deaf ears nineteen centuries after the giving of the revelation of the New.

Was it not Gandhi who said that there is *enough in our world for man's need but not enough for man's greed?* An over-simplification, perhaps; but the point is worth taking. This, however, is not the current philosophy of our day.

At the Church Leaders' Conference held at Selly Oak in September 1972, one of the Commissions devoted itself to the subject of men's stewardship of God's world. It considered such subjects as those which are engaging our attention now and the immorality of the existence of a privileged élite while at the bottom of the social pyramid were millions of fellow human-beings stunted by malnutrition, scratching a bare living in filthy, workless cities and disintegrating countryside. "Man," the Commission declared, "through his thoughtlessness, greed and presumption, reflected in his misuse of science and resources, has done violence to the harmonies and balances of nature. *By his substitution of size for value he has distorted, as with a cancer, the natural and healthy proportions of nature. The situation demands repentance, expressed in a radical re-orientation of human attitudes towards nature, man and God.*"

"The theology of enough"—this is the phrase which Christians have evolved who have been pondering these things. There is needed a revolt—and who better to initiate and foster it than the Christian disciple?—a revolt against the violence which rapacity breeds, against the creed of giantism ("the bigger the thing, be it organisation or motor car or profit, the better"), against the *prodigality of a society which puts profit before people, and which is prepared to rape and violate nature provided that luxury is promoted. This is obscenity; we are at last learning not to restrict the use of that word to a sexual context.* It is obscene to pollute the earth, the air, the water. It is obscene to allow twenty per cent of the world's people to own eighty per cent of its capital resources. It is obscene to give the verb to grasp, to acquire, to possess, precedence over the verb to be.

The writer of the Book of Proverbs tilted at such an attitude. He wrote (30:15–16):

> The leech has two daughters;
> "Give", says one and "Give", says the other.
> Three things there are which will never be satisfied,
> Four which never say "Enough!"
> The grave and a barren womb,
> A land thirsty for water,
> And fire that never says "Enough!"

Satire? It certainly is! It stings and hurts and probes. And don't we need it!

The biblical principle behind "the theology of enough" springs from belief in a God who declares "his almighty *power* most chiefly in showing *mercy* and *pity*" (Collect of the Eleventh Sunday after Trinity). This, surely, is where our values have gone wrong. We think power consists in a plethora of goods, never mind how they are come by. Jesus said that the *meek*, those of a gentle spirit, were the ones who should have the earth for their possession (St Matthew 5:5). We are now beginning to see that this, so far from being mere poetic hyperbole, is literal truth. Disobey that truth and you will have the earth alright. But it will be a dustbowl. It is a lesson desperately hard for a sophisticated generation to learn. William Wilberforce learnt it in his own day and in the circumstances of his own life. He gave away so much that he lived his closing years in comparative poverty, having sold his little estate and gone to live alternately with his two parson sons. "A man can be as happy without a fortune as with one," he said. He had learnt to travel light.

If it is hard for an individual to learn this lesson, that the verb to be matters incomparably more than the verb to have, it is infinitely harder for an acquisitive, rapacious, and prodigal society to do so. But can there be much question that, until mankind does begin to learn that lesson, the hopes for its future are very small? And on whom is it more incumbent to learn that lesson and to teach it than on the followers of Him who "made himself nothing, assuming the nature of a slave" (Phil. 2:7)?

One of the shortest of the books of the Apocrypha is "The Song of the Three". It is an addition in the Greek version of Daniel (between 3:23 and 3:24) and purports to record the prayer of Azariah (Abednego) and the song of the three men in the furnace of fire. This song is headed in the New English Bible "The Praises of Creation" (vv. 28–68). We know it, in a shortened form, as the *Benedicite*. A cynic has said that

> the *Benedicite*
> is a nicety
> to relieve
> the tedium (Te Deum).

It is much more than that. It is a paean of praise in which the whole creation, animate and inanimate, is called on to

> "bless the Lord;
> sing his praise and exalt him for ever".

The version in the Apocrypha is much fuller than that in the Book of Common Prayer and is worth a careful reading. The whole creation is invoked—heavens, sun, moon and stars; the elements, rain, winds, snow; nature, mountains, seas, springs; animals, fish and birds; and men, priests, laymen, holy and humble of heart—"bless the Lord; sing his praise and exalt him for ever."

We must not dismiss this splendid poem as merely a poet's fancy—only *men* can bless the Lord. Dare we say this? I think not. Who has not been in a well-tended garden on a spring day, or in an English countryside in the autumn, and has not felt that, in a very real sense, that bit of nature is blessing the Lord and singing his praise? And conversely, who has not viewed some scene of desolation, some area blasted by man's acquisitiveness and greed, and has not felt that its mouth has been stopped, and the purpose of its creation stultified? There is no blessing the Lord, no praise, no "peace" here.

Where do I come into this picture? Here am I, a tiny speck on a world which itself is but a speck in a vast universe. My span of life is short. My contribution to history can be only small. From one point of view, as Isaiah put it, I am "no more than the breath in (my) nostrils" (2:22). And yet, if the thesis I present is true, I am a vice-gerent of the Most High; redeemed in Christ, restored, forgiven; a partaker of the human nature in which Christ was not ashamed to share; for all my transitoriness and sinfulness, of immense value to God, for He gave His Son for my redemption. This being so, *I signify, I matter*; and my life is more than vanity. For it is possible for me, travelling light, to exercise my vice-gerency and, with full heart and mind, to make my assent to the adjuration of the old Psalmist:

"O earth, bless the Lord; sing his praise, and exalt him for ever".

When I do that, eternal life is mine—here and now.

The Ethics of Scientific Farming

MY OXFORD ENGLISH Dictionary gives as one of the meanings of *layman* "an 'outsider' or non-expert (especially in relation to law or medicine)". If you add the words "or science generally", you have the perfect description of the one whom, with great kindness but, I must say, I think with considerable rashness, you have invited to address you. My line—if I can be said to have a "line" at all—has been the study of languages and theology, and perhaps, one could add of people. Of science I know all too little.

I have not found any considerable reference in your symposium to the possible effect of chemicals on fish. This is a matter of considerable moment if, in the coming years, the harvest of the sea is to have an increasingly important part to play in the feeding of the population of the world.

I note that *The Times* of 23rd March, 1964, reported that over five million fish, duck and other birds died in the Mississippi basin as a result of drainage from crops sprayed with insecticide; and it added: "There is some concern because little is yet known about the effect of these ... substances upon humans." I have no doubt that care and thought are being given to this matter, even if it does not occupy a prominent place in this conference.

It is a matter for gratitude that scientists today should have such clarity of vision that, in dealing with a matter which is highly technical and "specialised", they should put first on the agenda of their conference a matter which has to do with the

The Yorkshire Institute of Agriculture, Askham Bryan, 12th April, 1965.

ethics of their theme. Ethics is the science of human duty in its widest extent. We are looking now at the ethics of our particular duty in the field in which you are experts. The title you have given me to speak to implies that you realise that a weight of responsibility rests on us. We have wrested—we are wresting— from nature her secrets. We are increasingly learning how to handle, how to manipulate nature. Though we cannot yet create life, we can lengthen the age-span of the average man. We can ease his pain and obliterate *some* of his diseases. We can at least, to a limited extent, begin to grapple with the problem of the size of his family. (I say "begin", because here I am touching on a problem of vast proportions which we have only started to solve. To this I shall return.)

In the Bible there are laid down certain fundamental principles which, so far from growing out-dated as the centuries pass, stand out as guide-posts for mankind. If they are heeded, men live lives which are happy and fruitful for the good of mankind. If they are neglected, men lose their way and get in a mess. Thus, the truth of the Bible does not depend on the credibility of Genesis or the edibility of Jonah but on the validity of those basic principles which it enunciates. I do not go to the opening chapters of Genesis, for example, for accurate scientific data as to the beginning of things. I have other sources of information for that. But I find in those opening chapters profound insights into the nature of man as an individual, as a member of society, and as a partner in the marriage relationship. So in the Bible once again, I find the general principle of *responsibility*, of *accountability* in regard to nature. In the words of Professor C. F. D. Moule: "Man is responsible for ruling nature . . . He is God's vice-gerent within creation; he is like a provincial ruler in an empire; he is supreme over nature, he is accountable to God alone." It is his duty to use nature, not to abstain from using it; but he must use it as a son of God and in obedience to God's will.

Neglect the principle of responsibility, the "ethics" as you have called it; put the principle of "grab" first in your thinking, and you have the disaster of the dust-bowl, or the wiping out of some precious species of animal life, or the dirtying of the atmosphere. Guard the principle of responsibility, of account-ability, of ethics, and you find man rising to the height of his nature, not giving up the use of nature, but manipulating it

responsibly, maintaining the ecological balance, and thus ministering to the needs of mankind. We do not seek to contract out of
the responsibilities which ensue on the discoveries of the scientists.
We seek to use them to the full but as—in the widest sense of the
term—"pro-creators", like Adam in Paradise cultivating the
earth for the Lord. The biblical principle, in short, is that man is
made to control nature but to do so with an eye to Him who has
given him his powers of mind and hand. "Thou hast given him
dominion over the works of thy hands." Yes. But "Thou hast
given him dominion." With a touch of keen insight the Psalmist
wrote (in Coverdale's rendering): "They had an eye unto Him
and were lightened."

We are not far from that phrase in which Albert Schweitzer
sums up his philosophy—"reverence for life"; even though none
of us would go so far as to follow his example when a friend of his,
about to crush a destructive beetle at Lambarene, found a hand
laid on his shoulder and heard Schweitzer say: "Gently, Noel!
Remember you are a guest in its country"!

I referred earlier to the power man now possesses of limiting
his family by scientific means. If I refer to it again now, it is not
because I have in mind primarily the increasing population of this
country. Rather, I am thinking of that growth in world population
which can only be described as terrifying. I have been thinking
about this in recent years in connection with the problem of
what the millions of newly literate peoples in the emerging nations
will *read*. You, though I hope not forgetful of this vitally
important issue, are primarily concerned with that on which they
will *feed*. The figures are, roughly, that the world's population
increases every year by sixty million; that by the end of this
century, which is only three and a half decades off, it will have
doubled. Some of us hardly dare look beyond the year 2,000!
In view of these figures, it is surely a matter of first importance
that a means of birth-control should be found which can be
understood and operated by people only just emerging from
primitive conditions of life. But even given this, and given it
quickly, the urgency of your task in relation to food production
can hardly be over-estimated.

But here you find yourselves, I imagine, on the horns of a very
difficult dilemma. Just as the long-term effects of "The Pill" on

those who use it cannot be known for a considerable period of years and yet it is imperative that we press on with population control, so it is with the matter of chemicals and the land. It is, I suppose, a fact that there is an element of doubt about the effect of the use of certain chemicals in food production on the health of man in the long run. Yet we dare not wait until we are sure of the effects, for the problem of food production is so immediately urgent as to brook no delay at all. A measure of risk, therefore, must be taken, even if the stakes with which we play are high. When half the world is—not starving but—definitely under-nourished, the call is clear to muster all the forces of scientific research in an international attempt, if not to solve, at least to ease the plight of the non-Western nations. (A somewhat similar problem faces those engaged in forestry. The vast forests, e.g. of North America and Brazil are being devoured faster than we can replace them. The U.S.A., we are told, uses twice as much timber as she grows. Each year we grow one and a half billion cubic metres of timber, and we use two and a half billion. Yet we cannot well cut down on the consumption. This is but another area where we look to science and international co-operation to help us at least to ease the problem).

If then, the first principle in regard to the ethics of scientific farming which we have enunciated is that of *responsibility*, the second and third would appear to be those of *urgency* and of *international co-operation*. Time is against us. The explosion of world population is a fact. This kind of conference, in which Yorkshire is giving the lead today, needs to be repeated and enlarged.

I am told that in 1850, the acreage per head of population was 32·7; in 1925, 18·8; in 1950, 14·3; in 1962, 11·4; and, such is the anticipated rise in population, it is estimated that in 1970, a brief five years hence, it will be 5·7. That is to say, in 120 years, the acreage per head will have dropped to just over one-sixth of what it was in 1850. But as these figures include everything from deserts to cities, and from jungles to swamps, the effective usable land must probably be divided by three. The area is alarmingly small. Your task is correspondingly urgent. Risks must be taken; but risks tempered by a sense of responsibility and of the interdependence of the expert in one field and the expert in another;

of the Russian and the Englishman, of the American and the Continental. Even such a disaster as that which occurred in connection with the thalidomide drug is not allowed to hold up the progress of medical research. Aerial disasters are not permitted to hinder advance in the mastery of space. So in the realm of the use of chemicals in the production of food—the work must go on if the race is to survive. We have to face an ever increasing demand from an ever decreasing acreage.

I touched a little earlier on the problem of the destruction of wild life by means of chemicals used for crop-production. Here we have a matter of considerable delicacy. It is not a question of brute vandalism such as has occurred in parts of Africa where the indiscriminate hunting of certain animals has threatened the virtual elimination of the species and led to desperate efforts in recent years to save them. That is a monstrous abuse of nature for which no good word may be said. Rather, we are thinking here of the loss of certain kinds of wild life by reason of the serious attempt which scientists are making to increase crops desperately needed for the sustenance of men. I do not pretend to know the answer, but I confess, as a lover of nature, to finding the problem a distressing one. If it is a question of the survival of man over against the survival of some forms of animal or bird life, then there is no doubt that man as the highest in the animal series must come first. But is it as simple as that? Do we know what animal life it is vital to maintain? Do we know at what point destruction of animal life may boomerang on us and damage the damager? The balance of nature would seem to be a very delicate thing and will need very reverent handling. A sense of proportion, when scientific issues of a very complicated kind are concerned, is not easy to maintain.

The themes which you will be considering this week are the kind of subjects which tend to generate a good deal of emotional heat. I find in these matters that the greater the emotional heat the less the intellectual light! You will bring to your task the cool balance of the scientist, trained to weigh evidence, trained to follow clues wherever they may seem to be leading, trained to distrust the merely emotional. But with the cool detachment which is called for in the man of scientific research, you will combine a steely determination to do your bit in the vast task of

meeting human need in a world whose imbalance between the
have and the have-not nations cries out for amelioration.

I speak to you as one whose deepest convictions lead him to
cast in his lot with the men called Christians. I hold that all truth,
of whatever kind it be, comes from God. God is not, as we so
often make Him appear to be, only interested in "religion", nor
is He a kind of super-ecclesiastic! Whether it be the theologian
pastor, relating the truth of religion to life with its manifold
needs, or the psychiatrist seeking to "minister to a mind diseased", or the historian seeking to piece together the broken
fragments of history, or the scientist at work in field or laboratory
—in so far as he advances the cause of truth, he is an agent in the
hands of God. He may not realise this—and if he does not, that is
tragic. But it does not alter the fact. If this is true—as I believe
with all my heart it is—then we are committed to press on with
the task before us, and, in our small corner of the advance of
human knowledge, to do our bit with a will!

If I were to sum up what I have tried to say tonight, I would
underline certain words which should, I think, be basic to all our
work. First comes the word *responsibility* or *accountability*, a concept implied in the very idea of the *ethics* of scientific farming.
Then the word *reverence*—reverence for life human and animal, a
reverence which reaches its peak when it springs from a deep
reverence for the Creator-God. Then the word *urgency*, in view
of a population explosion such as man has never known since
first he appeared on earth. To these I would add the idea of
willingness to take risks, and the *duty to co-operate* on as broad a
basis as possible, both on the part of those who are at work in
different but contiguous branches of science in this country, and
on the part of scientists at work in different nations who all too
easily can go on their way ignorant of what others in identical
or contiguous fields of research are doing.

Thy Kingdom Come

St Matthew 6:10
Thy Kingdom come

"THY KINGDOM COME". So Jesus prayed and so He taught His disciples to pray. So they have prayed ever since. So they pray today.

The "Kingdom" means the reign of God, His actual sovereignty, His rule in the affairs of men. The theory behind the prayer is roughly this, that God is King of all the universe and that eventually—no date is given!—His sovereignty will be finally and fully manifested. Meanwhile—and we live in this long "meanwhile"—the full realisation of that sovereignty, the absolute rule of love and goodness and beauty, is challenged, and indeed impeded. "We see not yet all things put under Him." As the second Lesson put it: "The whole created universe groans in all its parts . . ."

There are forces at work which make for hate and wrong and ugliness, forces of great power and mighty malevolence. In fact, a long-drawn-out battle is being waged. World forces are engaged. Every human being is, willy-nilly, in the battle. If one thinks to opt out, one finds oneself on the side of evil, for "he that is not with Me is against Me". But if a man dares to pray with any fullness of meaning the prayer "Thy Kingdom come", he lines himself up with the forces of right and does his tiny part in making the reign of God a reality in the world of space and time.

British Association, 3rd September, 1967.

That is, roughly, the "theory" behind the prayer. Perhaps it is easier for our generation to grasp at least the meaning of the bit about the forces of hate and wrong and ugliness than it was for our fathers, especially if those fathers lived and flourished about the turn of this century. Before the cataclysm of two World Wars, when Western civilisation and domination seemed so secure and the advance of scientific discovery so vastly hopeful, they might be forgiven if they saw the coming of the Kingdom round the corner and the advent of Utopia as being very near. We, however, if we are disillusioned, are at least greatly sobered by the forces that are at work against what we believe to be good and true. Not only have two World Wars pulled up short our optimism, but we find that the fight to maintain international peace is constant and hardly ever wholly successful. And the physical sciences which with lavish hand have enriched us with all kinds of benefits, have put within our grasp knowledge which is appalling in its potentiality for ill; and even its beneficent activities of healing have created enormous problems in world population and in the realm of geriatrics. From another point of view, the battle with disease bids fair to be longer drawn out than we had thought—a cure, for example, for cancer still eludes us, and as soon as one kind of disease looks like being mastered, another rears its ugly head.

What is true in the sphere of physical disease is equally true of mental. To pray "Thy Kingdom come" will likely be to invite wounds which will be bloody, for sin and ignorance and disease, hate and ugliness, are tough foes and the battle shows no signs of lessening.

But *how* is the Kingdom to come and who are to be the agents of its coming? There have been those down the ages—and there are some still today—who answer simply: "The agents of the Kingdom are the members of the Church of Christ." I believe they are right and they are wrong—right in their emphasis; wrong in their implied exclusiveness.

Let us look for a moment at the rightness and the wrongness.

I believe that he alone can *fully* pray this prayer who consciously and of his own free will lives his life, does his work, thinks out his philosophy, in obedience to Jesus Christ, who is Himself the

Word and Revelation of the eternal Father. I believe that the purpose of the Church in the world is to be the worshipping and witnessing spear-head of all that is in accordance with the will of God as it has been revealed in Jesus Christ. To do that and to be that, the Church will have to be infinitely adaptable to new forms and new emphases—far more so than it has often been in the past or often is today—at the same time as it is true to the faith once and for all entrusted to it. Hence there is the need for a constant supply of men and women, clerical and lay, within the Church, who, dedicated to it as the Body of Christ, do not silence their critical faculties when they worship and work within that Body, but, prepared to bear the shame as well as to share in the glory of the Church, are content to live and die within its ranks. In short, I see the Church not as the Kingdom of God itself—along those lines there has been confusion in the past—but as the primary agent of God in making real His Kingdom among men.

So much for the rightness. Now a word about the wrongness, as I see it, of those who say, simply and with no qualification, that the agents of the Kingdom are the members of the Church of Christ. To put the statement thus baldly is to refuse to face facts and to be guilty of an inadequate doctrine of God the Holy Spirit. As I begin to understand His Person and work, the Holy Spirit is the Agent, within God's vast creation, of all that is good and true and beautiful. Wherever truth—in the realms of theology or philosophy, of the arts or of the sciences—invades the territory of darkness, ignorance and error, there the Spirit of Truth is at work. Wherever the forces of disease and death are conquered, there the Spirit of Life is operating. Wherever ugliness is kept at bay, there the Spirit of God who is the God of Beauty is doing His creative and re-creative labour.

God is not some kind of super-ecclesiastic interested only in Churchly things, as many imagine Him to be, but the God behind all discovery and invention and learning, the Source of all truth, the Origin of all beauty. And *therefore*—and this is the point to which I am leading up—whoever he be who is the agent of that work, in laboratory or study or studio or slum, is a servant of the Most High, an agent of the King, even though he be not conscious of that fact in all its glory (and therefore, I think, immeasurably the poorer!).

This, if it be true as I believe it to be, has corollaries of immense importance.

First, it means that Church and science—I use the words in their widest connotation—are colleagues who need never be suspicious of one another, need never stand over against each other, but may—no, *must*—join hands in a joint assault on all that makes this created universe groan and on all that opposes the reign of God. Church and science, of course, overlap and flow into one another, for among the committed members of Christ's Church are great numbers of men of learning in all its branches. But out beyond this, the Church joins hands with those who, as yet unable to yield their obedience to the Church's Lord, seek to oppose His enemies.

Secondly, I hope that, as an outcome of that increasingly close alliance, more frequently and more powerfully, Church and science might speak unitedly to the world on major issues of world concern.

Increasingly the Church is speaking with a united voice, for example through the World Council of Churches. Increasingly the voice of science is making itself heard, for example through the British Association and through its international links with scientists throughout the world. Let these great organisations join their voices, as need arises, to denounce the follies which oppose the coming of God's Kingdom, and to point the way forward to sanity and international well-being. For example, is no word of denunciation called for to rebuke the present madness of importing arms into Nigeria? And if this is called for, who could better give it than World Council and British Association, representative as they are of those who, within the last century, have brought enlightenment to that country? Or again, has the time not come when our united voices might call on Governments, temporarily at least, to slow down the vast expenditure on the "space-race", while we devote the money and expertise thus saved to the betterment of the millions who, physically and mentally, are starving?

The unsuccessful American Survey 4 Moonprobe cost £28½ million—and that was only one little bit of a vast programme. One asks whether this is the best use of resources at this point of human history when ignorance and disease stalk our earth. Could not Church and science become, more in this decade than hitherto they have been, a combined force for sanity in a world groaning as the result of man's madness and inhumanity to man?

I am pleading for two things. *First,* for *a union of knowledge with compassion.* Knowledge, naked and alone, is neutral—capable of being used for weal or woe to mankind. But knowledge combined with compassion at once ceases to be a neutral force and becomes a power for good in the banishing of the enemies of mankind.

Secondly, I plead for *a more concerted approach by the combined forces of religion and science to the power structures of society.* The day is long past when the scientist can be thought of as a man working alone, or with a tiny team, in study or laboratory. He is part of a great international corpus of men and women, often financed by their governments, discovering vast new sources of knowledge which will be used for the curse or the blessing of mankind. The day is equally long past when the man of religion can be thought of as an individual bent on the achievement of his own salvation alone. He is a member of a worldwide Church whose area of concern is as wide as the world for which Christ died. Just because his message transcends the bounds of time and space, he finds himself deeply implicated *in* the affairs of time and space. The love of Christ constrains him. Wisdom, of which our first Lesson spoke so eloquently, moves him to hard thinking. Compassion warms him to translate his wisdom into action.

Knowledge and compassion joined together; science and religion working hand in hand; and both speaking with united voice on behalf of the vast masses of the nations who can hardly make their cries heard in the corridors of world power. It may well be that, along these lines, blows will be struck at the enemies of truth and light and the reign of God advanced among the children of men.

Healing Relationships

St Matthew 8:17
He took away our illnesses and lifted our diseases from us.

YOU CONFER AT a time of perplexity and unrest almost unparalleled in the long history of your profession—but that is true also in the sphere of education and of the Church, to take but two other examples. I could, in selecting my theme, say something about the difficult problem of the relationship of your profession to a Health Service which has but recently come of age, and to touch on the thorny question of the kind of pay which skilled doctors may expect to receive from the government. Or I might take some of the thorny problems which crop up where medicine and ethics interlock—transplants, abortion, the use of foetuses and foetal material for research, the isolation of a group of genes by scientists at the Harvard Medical School which has been described as a first step in human genetic engineering. I do not intend to develop any of these themes this morning, though I am fully aware of their pressing urgency and deeply anxious that increasingly in many areas of our country there should spring up and flourish groups of doctors and "laymen and women" who share a concern for the working out of Christian answers to these problems; or, if that is something too much to expect, groups of men and women who will feel their way towards a vision of the points where Christian insights impinge on medical problems.

What I want to do is take you back to the picture which the

British Medical Association, 28th June, 1970.

Gospels give us of One who spent a great deal of time in doing very much what you are doing day in day out—bringing relief and healing where tension and disease previously obtained. I believe that in thus taking you *back* I may be able to point you the way *forward* in certain areas of great moment. "He took away our illnesses and lifted our diseases from us"; the words of Isaiah came back to people as they watched Jesus at work.

Jesus had no medical training such as you have. He lived in a day of what we can only regard as appalling ignorance as to the cause and the cure of disease. Superstition reigned, and was to reign for many centuries before the winds of scientific knowledge could blow most of its clouds away. But the evidence is strong that Jesus had very definite healing powers and that, as He moved about, touching one here and speaking to another there, He left in His wake a stream of health and sanity which made men wonder and praise God.

Let us watch Jesus at work.

1. I see Him confronted with a man who is crippled (St John 5). The question which He puts to him is deeply significant: "Do you *want* to recover?" It takes more than the doctor to bring healing. There must be co-operation on the part of the patient. Indeed, the task is a joint one, shared by patient and doctor. So Jesus gets alongside the man, in a deep relationship of understanding, and the cure is effected, the paralysis broken. Life begins to surge again in his limbs.

2. I see Jesus faced by a poor tormented wreck of a man (St Mark 5:1 ff.), "not a man but a mob" (as a modern novelist described one of his characters). He was "demon-possessed", as the language of the day had it. Jesus did not immediately launch into an attack on the problem. He first entered into the situation in which the man found himself. "What is your name?" He asked. "My name is Legion, there are so many of us", was the reply. A man with a split personality found himself face to face with One who Himself was a wholly integrated person, whose very presence seemed to bring peace and security. It was not long before something of that peace entered the demon-possessed man and, no doubt to his immense surprise, he found himself sitting quietly at the feet of Jesus, clothed and in his right mind.

There is an interesting epilogue to this story. Naturally enough the man, infinitely grateful for the healing that had come to him, expressed a desire to go with Jesus as He stepped into the boat to leave the district. But Jesus would have none of it. "No," He said; "go home to your own folk and tell them what the Lord in His mercy has done for you."

There are two points of importance here. *First*, the cured man must achieve a healthy state of independence. *Indebted* he will always be, for no man can ever repay in kind one who has brought him sanity and health. But *dependent* to the extent of having his own personality cramped and confined—that he must never be. "Go home," said our Lord. "Work out your salvation. Claim your independence. Grow up."

Secondly: "Tell them what the Lord has done for you." A blessing shared is a blessing doubled. Hug your discovery to yourself and you may well lose it. Share it and you will keep it. It is a principle which holds in all spheres of life—for the individual, for the Church, for the nation.

3. I see our Lord looking at a man let down through the tiled roof on a stretcher and laid at His feet (St Mark 2:1 ff.). Jesus looks into the eyes of the man and says—well, what would you have said? You would presumably have called for a case-history. Or you would have run your hands over the enfeebled body. Or you would have asked the man certain questions about his condition. But Jesus does none of these things. He does not even delay to "get alongside" the patient as in the other cases we have noted this morning. With His keen perception of spiritual realities, He knows that the man has a burden on his conscience, a sense of sin unforgiven, and that *this* is the thing which, as we say, is "tying him up" and crippling his life. "My son," says Jesus, "your sins are forgiven." *This* was the word of release which above all things the man needed. It was like the unlocking of prison doors. The man's shackles fell off. He was free!

We could go on, examining cases in this way. But time makes it impossible. As men watched Jesus at work, so St Matthew hints, they were reminded of a passage in Isaiah which spoke of One who would "not snap off the broken reed nor snuff out the smouldering wick" (12:20). Perhaps the reed which looked so useless might be restored to uprightness, and the wick which only gave out a stench might be persuaded once again to give out light. Here was a relationship of extraordinary tenderness, of compassion and of invincible hope. Here was One who treated persons as of infinite importance—nothing mattered so much as the establishment of a healing *relationship* between the person of doctor and patient.

I do not need, in the presence of an audience such as this, to apply point by point, the lessons which a study of Jesus at work brings home to us. That would be to insult your intelligence. Nor do I need to underline the difficulties inherent in establishing with our patients such relationships as Jesus appears to have had with those who came to Him in distress. We are cumbered about with forms which have to be filled up, generally in triplicate, and are hedged around with restrictions and conditions which make the achievement of personal relationships of any depth very difficult indeed. To a lesser degree, perhaps, this is true in the parson's life as well. But we know that, once we *allow* this to happen, once we cease to fight for person to person relationships with our patients, and that in depth, then the glory is departed from our work. A calling becomes a profession. We become hacks.

In an excellent chapter entitled "The Christian Approach to the Disabled, the Incurable and the Dying" in *Ideals in Medicine* (The Tyndale Press, p. 58), the author writes: "An unashamed but unostentatious Christian conviction, a genuine love finding its outlet in first-class medical care, and a real personal concern for the patient and the patient's family, all these may bear fruit in due course." That is well said. And I myself believe that there is no short cut. When we obey the summons and answer the invitation of Jesus: "Come unto Me . . . take My yoke . . . and learn of Me", then, and only then, do we find that "rest unto our souls" which enables us in some measure to bring a like healing, a similar rest, to others. There is something infectious about the life of a man who daily prays along these lines:

> Grant, O Lord, that this day may be lived in
> the calm of Thy presence,
> the rest of Thy will, and
> the peace of Thy governance.

I leave it with you.

Mind-Hunger

IT IS NOT difficult to bring home to an Englishman or an American the pathos of under-nourishment. We have all felt the pangs of hunger, though most of us have never been without the means of rapidly allaying them. We have all seen pictures of pot-bellied children, with spindly arms and rickety legs. It is much harder for us to conceive what mind-hunger is like. We are the heirs of an elaborate educational system, from which we have all benefited. We take it for granted that the school-leaving age, now fifteen, will soon be sixteen, and that there should be equal opportunity for all to have a university education who can profit by it. We have our own private libraries, big or small. We have access to public libraries. We can buy books when we want them. It takes some imaginative effort to conceive of circumstances in which these conditions do not apply.

As long ago as Shakespeare's day, we were given the picture of "the whining schoolboy . . . creeping unwillingly to school". He suffered from no pangs of mind-hunger! He took education for granted, even if it was limited in its range as compared with its modern counterpart. The description often fits the modern youngster of the West—education and books are his for the asking, even to the point of satiety. He can be—and sometimes is —blasé about them.

But if Shakespeare had written his "Seven Ages of Man" in the twentieth century instead of the sixteenth, and in Africa or Asia instead of in post-Renaissance Europe, he would have had to alter his phraseology radically. Education, in the sense we know it,

The Golden Lecture, 17th March, 1974.

has but recently come to many of these countries, brought frequently by the Christian missionary. Now, increasingly, the governments of newly independent nations are taking over the task of developing what the missionaries began. Sometimes they make but scant acknowledgment of those who first kindled the spark, but that is neither here nor there. The spark is now a flame. Literacy—or at least semi-literacy—and education at various levels are spreading like a forest-fire, and old superstitions, old isolationisms, old cultures are being burned down in its path. The schoolboy is not a "whining" schoolboy. He is a *shining* schoolboy—his face lit up with the prospect of learning. He does not creep unwillingly to school. He *runs*—for will he not find there the key, the golden key, of knowledge?

There is something extraordinarily exhilarating about this passion for literacy and education, be it at the elementary stage of such literacy-campaigns as Dr Laubach's ("each one teach one") or at the advanced stage of Universities like Makerere in Uganda or Legon in Ghana. But there is also something frightening about it. For example, Canon Howard A. Johnson, in that perceptive and thought-provoking book, *Global Odyssey*, has pointed out that if you educate, let us say, African children only up to the age of twelve (as is generally the case), you "spawn a mass of semi-literate people". That sort of education "makes them vulnerable to every sort of demagoguery. Illiteracy is bad, but from a wider point of view it may be even worse when the populace, secure in the knowledge that it can read, has no very mature criteria for judging the reliability of the matter read. People who have newly learned how to decipher a type face are all too prone to take things at face value" (p. 90). Canon Johnson is not suggesting that the education of African children should be stopped. That would be to suggest a Canute-like attitude of great folly! He is simply pointing out one of the perils of literacy, or, rather, of semi-literacy.

My metaphors have been getting mixed. We have watched literacy spreading like a forest-fire, and now we seem to be looking at King Canute! Never mind—fire or flood, it is sweeping over the emerging nations, and nothing will stop it. Indeed, U.N.E.S.C.O. has declared its intention of tackling illiteracy in a way hitherto never dreamed of. Leaving wholly on one side the massive programme of educating children, U.N.E.S.C.O. has taken a steady look at the fact that there are some five hundred million adult illiterates in the world. It proposes, *in this quin-quennium*, to make three hundred and fifty million of them literate! We are getting accustomed to the onslaughts of science on various of mankind's scourges—leprosy, tuberculosis, etc. But here is an onslaught on the scourge of ignorance on a scale never contemplated in the history of mankind.

In bringing this to your attention, I am not asking you to consider some distant problem. I am asking you to open your eyes to a fact that is happening in the world around you, the little world that has shrunk almost unbelievably because of the discoveries of our life-time and which now is on your doorstep; a fact of this decade.

You will have seen what I am leading up to. It is, I think, about the most important question which we in the West can ask today, and we have not got long in which to find the answer. The question is: "What shall these newly literate peoples read? What shall they read as they begin to spell out the letters and frame them into syllables—words—sentences? What shall they read when they leave school at the age of twelve? What shall they read at the universities from which they will emerge to lead their adolescent nations in the heady days of new-found nationalist independence? *What shall they read?*"

We who are committed Christians, or at least are people whose thinking and scale of values have been deeply coloured by the Christian faith and tradition, are not the only ones to be faced by this question. Others have already listened to it and resolved on an answer. There is a flourishing world-trade in pornographic literature and in literature which borders on the pornographic. Here, in the millions newly learning each month to read, is a fertile field in which to sow this deadly seed. Here is money on a scale never envisaged previously. If illiteracy is a vast problem in India and Pakistan, so is literacy.

Mahatma Gandhi once said: "When I look at what is offered on our station bookstalls in India, I am thankful that so many of my fellow-countrymen are illiterate." The literacy rate rises. The standard of books does not.

A little team of men making a film for the British and Foreign Bible Society were preparing their equipment in a remote country area of India, when a crowd of small boys appeared as from nowhere. One lad had in his possession a little book in Tamil. On its cover was a picture of two girls, and the caption in small English print was: "The Story of Christine Keeler". It was all the young lad had. The Bible Society secretary asked if he might have it. The boy said: "Yes, I can easily get another."

There are the forces of Communism whose leaders know that the power of the pen is far greater than that of the bomb. Every year they pour into the emerging nations millions of pounds' worth of Communist literature—specious, attractive, compelling.

There are the forces of materialism, highly attractive to peoples who hitherto have been among the "have-nots" of the world—and still are. The claimants for the attention of the newly literate or semi-literate are many and powerful.

Where do the Christians come in?

They have been working in the field for a long time—and working with great skill and high courage. But if they are left to carry on as they are, the battle for freedom from mind-hunger as Christians understand it may well be lost in the next four or five years, if not sooner. At present, the Christian literacy campaign is the Cinderella of Christian good causes. It must be rescued at once and be seen to be what it is—the most urgent cause to which Christians and men of goodwill can set their hands. The future Christian strategy lies, I believe, not so much in raising new buildings and institutions as in pouring out a flood of attractive and well-directed literature at all levels of intelligence.

Let me mention two spheres of work which call for our immediate attention and on the grand scale.

The first is *the distribution of the Bible*. From earliest days, the Christian Church has gone to the world with a book in its hand. At the start it was what we now know as the Old Testament. The New Testament was soon added. Translations into various languages quickly followed. Since the British and Foreign Bible Society was founded in 1804, the Bible has been translated, in whole or in part, into over twelve hundred different languages, and we have now reached the stage when many of these translations are being revised in the interests of scholarship and accuracy. It is a skilled work of a highly specialist nature—work in which denominational barriers are transcended and in which a combined operation can be undertaken on behalf of the whole Church of Christ.

I am proud to be President of the United Bible Societies, which holds together some two dozen national societies working in over a hundred different countries. I was privileged to launch last Whit Sunday in Tokyo a campaign to treble the world circulation of the Scriptures by the end of 1966—a mammoth task which can only be the beginning of a greater, as world population soars meteorically. In view of this rapid rise both in population and in literacy, I am calling a conference of world Christian leaders to meet next June in Driebergen to plan the strategy of Churches and Bible Societies in this great task. You cannot evangelise without Bibles—but to provide them calls for skills in linguistics, in art, in binding, in trade, and in a host of cousin occupations.

The second sphere of work is as wide as biblical distribution is specialist. We need—in the immediate future—*a flood of literature, at all levels, which incorporates Christian insights and the Christian philosophy of life. At all levels*—this is important. We need books of serious theology and philosophy, written from the angle of the nations who will read them; books on marriage and the family; on the Christian ethic; on Christian biography and history; novels; books and booklets aimed at the instruction of catechumens and Confirmation candidates; books for ordinands; brochures and pamphlets and strip-cartoons for those whose level of literacy is low, and so on without limit.

To sketch this, even as briefly as I have just done, is to envisage an army who have begun to glimpse the fact that to dedicate your life to *this* is to wield about the sharpest weapon for good and for God that any man or woman can handle. I can see them—theologians, philosophers, novelists, journalists, artists, binders, cartoonists, printers, packers, businessmen, distributors, organisers. And behind them a Nuffield—perhaps there is one listening to this lecture—a man of magnanimity of vision and of purse who would invest his wealth in the realm of Christian ideas and of the dissemination of the Christian Good News. And, behind him, a multitude who will spread the message of Christian literacy—by talking about it, by praying about it, by giving to it.

I have already alluded to the world-trade in pornographic or salacious literature. I am one of those who hold the view that the best way to expel evil is to open the flood-gates of good. The best way to deal with bad thinking is to encourage good thinking. The best way to deal with bad literature is to produce, in attractive form and at cheap prices, a mass of positive, clean literature. But, unfortunately, this is not enough. Battle must be done at the point where the evil is most rampant.

Many thinking men are not eager for a repetition of the trials which have comparatively recently taken place over books like *Lady Chatterley's Lover* and *Fanny Hill*. Even if such trials lead to the eventual withdrawal of the book from the bookshops (and there is always a large element of doubt as to which way the judgment will go), the publicity given to such books makes the legal victory a somewhat dubious one. The damnable thing is that, in practically all of our big cities and towns, there are shops where youngsters of any age can obtain books, booklets and papers which can hardly do other than corrupt immature minds, especially the minds of those who are in their years of adolescence.

Two main lines of attack on this evil seem open to us.

The first is to arouse the conscience of local Christians and men and women of goodwill. Here is a sphere of service for the local Council of Churches, and indeed, the help of the local synagogue can be enlisted too. Protests can be made to the proprietors of shops which stock this type of literature. If these protests, made firmly by a large number of men and women who refuse to see their young people subjected to this menace, achieve no results, then those who protest should withdraw their patronage from these shops and transfer their orders elsewhere. Concerted action, quietly and steadily applied, may well force out of business those who poison our young people's mind, or may compel them to destroy the poison.

The second line of attack is to amend the Obscene Publications Act of 1959. *The Guardian* of February 15 this year described this Act as one which "has given pornographers virtual immunity". *The Yorshire Post* remarked that "it is clear that trafficking in filth is a major industry" and supports the London Committee against Obscenity in its efforts to amend the Act. "The law," it says, "ought to make it unprofitable for the purveyors of really damaging, sheer gutter-filth to stay in business, and for shady booksellers to help them to do so."

Pornography is over-produced in certain States of the United

States of America, and rather than "pulp" it, the producers dump the surplus on Britain. This is one of our less desirable imports, and quick action should be taken to stop it. Here is a place where war must be fought and the hitting must be hard, relentless and well-aimed. Let this battle be fought and won here at home; and then the lessons learnt in these islands may be of help to those overseas who, I doubt not, will have a similar war to wage.

This is a destructive work. It could be called negative work, if it were not for the fact that it saves minds and souls and bodies from perdition. I revert, as I close, to that constructive, positive work to which I have specially called your attention here, the provision of sound literature informed by Christian insights, at all levels of literacy and education; written, illustrated, produced, dispersed, sold by an army of intelligent and skilled men and women, and financed magnanimously by those who see that the pen is more powerful than the sword, that a drop of ink may make millions think, that this is *the* issue of our generation. At this point the battle for the soul of the world is joined.

As I walked through the wilderness of this world, I lighted on a certain place where was a den, and laid me down in that place to sleep; and as I slept, I dreamed a dream. I dreamed, and behold, I saw a man clothed with rags standing in a certain place, with his face from his own house, a book in his hand, and a great burden upon his back. I looked, and saw him open the book, and read therein; and as he read, he wept and trembled; and not being able longer to contain, he brake out with a lamentable cry, saying, What shall I do?

The words of the beginning of Bunyan's *Pilgrim's Progress* are familiar to us all. The picture of "a man clothed with rags . . . with his face from his own house . . . and a great burden upon his back" is not a bad picture of modern man for all his affluence. The length of the queue which waits to get the attention of the psychiatrist is evidence of the "great burden" which men have upon their back and from which they know not how to free themselves. For all their television sets and cars and modern luxuries, for all their scientific achievements, their spiritual nakedness is scarce covered by the rags which they themselves supply. They say they are rich and have need of nothing, the while they know not that they are poor and wretched and blind and naked.

Modern man is much like Bunyan's Pilgrim. But, in a sense, he is in worse plight than he was. *He* had a book in his hand. True, he read therein only judgment; but to read judgment is the first step towards finding redemption. Modern man has no book in his hand, and, for lack of it, his plight is made the worse.

This is the task of the Church now—to give to modern man, in the extremity of his need, the book which, by the aid of the Spirit, can convict him of his need and point him to his Saviour. But, such is his ignorance and the ignorance of his parents and grandparents, that he will need other books to make its message plain, to introduce it, to put it in its setting, to expound its relevance.

God has spoken in His Son.
The essence of that revelation is in the Bible.
It is for us to give it to the world.
Only so will its burden fall from its back.

The Abolition of the Death Penalty

My Lords,

The record of the previous debates on the matter before us occupies many pages in Hansard. The arguments for and against retention of the death penalty have been bandied backwards and forwards; the thrust and parry of debate has been keen.

I intervene as one who is unashamedly for the abolition of the death penalty. I do not take this view on sentimental grounds. On the contrary, in casting my vote, as I hope to do today, in favour of abolition, I do so with a sense of deep concern for the furtherance of justice, for the security of the citizens (be they the police officers or prison officers concerned, or the old and defenceless people in our cities), and for the compensation (in so far as any kind of compensation is possible) of those who are related to or dependent on the one who has been murdered.

Your Lordships would not wish me to seek to go over again the arguments drawn from the experience of countries which have, either long ago or more recently, abolished the death penalty. These arguments affect different people in different ways. I am considerably moved by the evidence which seems to indicate that there has been no increase in crimes which hitherto had been regarded as deserving of capital punishment. I note also with deep interest that in such countries as Norway, Sweden and Denmark, where capital punishment does not exist, the police still go unarmed, as I am sure our own police would wish to continue to be. I cannot ignore the statement of such a witness as the noble Lord, Lord Shawcross, that: "I believe that there is not a shred of

House of Lords, 26th October, 1965.

evidence, nothing that any respectable lawyer would dream of adducing in the lowest courts in the land, to support the view that the death penalty in the past had any deterrent effect on the rate of murder in this country" (§511). All these things sway my judgment in favour of the ends which this Bill seeks to bring about.

But on these things I shall not delay this afternoon. Rather, I would beg your Lordships' attention to certain moral issues which, I believe, must be given the most careful consideration.

As I recall the course of previous debates on this subject, I notice that there has been not infrequent allusion to Scripture. This is not to be wondered at, inasmuch as our English law can claim largely to be based on those writings. One of the arguments of many retentionists is that death as a reward for murder is written into the Old Testament, and is therefore a part of the divine intention for the conduct of human affairs so long as time shall last. But it must be pointed out that a good deal of Old Testament legislation no longer is held to be applicable to our society today. I give but one illustration. "If a man be found lying with a woman married to an husband, then they shall both of them die, both the man that lay with the woman, and the woman . . ." The most rigid supporter of a strict code of sexual ethics would hardly wish to see that enforced today! The conscience of mankind has moved on. Indeed, it may be noticed, in passing, that the *lex talionis* ("an eye for an eye and a tooth for a tooth") is not so much a demand for strict vengeance in kind, as a safeguard, a kindly safeguard, that if a man takes your eye, you may not take *both* of his!

I wish to say a word about a phrase—this time from the *New Testament*—which has more than once been quoted in this debate. The noble Lord, Lord Shawcross, in the speech to which I have already referred, said that he would be content to be guided by the advice of St Paul, that vengeance is the Lord's, and that He will repay. The noble Lord added, in parenthesis, "if the Bishops will permit such a curious aberration from modern theology". My Lords, I can only say that if it is an aberration from modern theology to call in evidence this "advice" of St Paul, then I would fain be put down with the *ancient* theologians! For here, surely, is a point of great importance. Men—weak, fallible men like ourselves—have often to be the means of executing judgment. Our

E

officers of law fulfil a function in our national life which is indispensable for its health and well-being. But there comes a point—I believe it is the point whence there is no return, the point of the death sentence—where weak and fallible humans must say; "Hands off. This is the sphere where *we* give place to the divine wrath. Vengeance belongs to God. *He* will repay."

Let me not be misunderstood here. I believe in retribution: I believe not only in reformation but in retribution. Society must say, through its officers of law, that it repudiates certain acts as utterly incompatible with civilised conduct, and that it will exact retribution from those who violate its ordered code. But to adopt that which we condemn and to kill the killer is not, in my view, the best way of exacting retribution. I suspect that to act thus is to take on ourselves a measure of vengeance which is best left to the Deity Himself.

There is about capital punishment a dreadful irrevocability which belongs to no other sphere of justice. It is possible to go over the evidence again, as is now being done in the case of Timothy Evans, but you cannot bring a man back from the dead. As the noble Lord, Lord Morris of Borth-Y-Gest, said in an earlier debate, and said with almost terrible monosyllabic simplicity: "We can put out the light of life: we cannot light it again."

All of us—every one of us—stands under the judgment of God. I do not think that we should ask any of our fellow-citizens—Home Secretary, judge, or hangman—to participate in a function which rightly should not belong to mortal man.

I believe that, if we continue to countenance the infliction of the death penalty, we are placing a burden which should never be borne on the Home Secretary whose unenviable task it is to tender advice to the Crown. I ask: Ought our society to ask any man to shoulder the appalling responsibility of saying Yea or Nay to the question, with all its dreadful imponderables, of a reprieve?

Further, someone has to carry out the order. Or, rather, a number of persons must make themselves responsible for the final act of hanging. It is one thing to debate this issue in the House of Lords. It is another matter to find oneself implicated in the execution of a fellow-member of society, however depraved he may be.

And again, I believe the society which allows this law of hanging to remain on its statute books degrades itself, coarsens itself, cheapens itself.

My Lords, in my opening remarks I referred to my concern for those who were related to or dependent on the one who has been murdered. There is, of course, a sense in which *no* compensation can ever be made to those who by some dreadful act have been deprived of a relative. But there is a sense in which some kind of amends may at least be attempted. In the realm of crime and punishment, I believe that the re-instatement of such ideas as duty and re-payment, of sweat and toil, might be of more avail in many cases than the reference of the criminal to the psychiatrist's consulting-room. I am not one of those who subscribe to what I have called elsewhere "the cult of the easy". A hard way back for the man who has made it hard for others may be the best way for all concerned. Even in the dire case of murder, I believe it should be made possible for the murderer, during the long years of his imprisonment, so to work as to make at least some financial contribution to the remaining members of the family which he has deprived.

In saying this, I have touched on a matter which calls for more attention than it is now receiving. I mean the employment of the prisoner—and I am now thinking especially of the murderer—during his imprisonment. I hold that, wherever possible, he should be given work of such a kind as will be profitable to the community; that it should be paid for; and that a large part of the pay should be used for the compensation of those whom he has injured. Difficult as this is to operate, I am sure that its operation would do something to stop that "rotting" of a man during long imprisonment to which frequent reference has been made in this debate, as well as making some tiny compensation to the bereaved. Compensation and the promotion of self-respect would go hand in hand.

My Lords, I have said enough. With the necessary safeguards now written into this Bill, let us by an overwhelming vote in its favour say to the country: "We will give this a fair trial. If, after a period of years, it can incontestably be proved that there has been a rise in the rate of those crimes which hitherto have involved capital punishment, and if that increase seems to be attributable to the abolition of capital punishment, then we will think again.

But now, in 1965, let us be done with this relic of a bygone age. We in this House invite you to follow our lead. Have done with this thing! In the Name of God, let it go!"

The Ordination of Women

THE REPORT OF the Archbishops' Commission on *Women and Holy Orders* which appeared in 1966 was the outcome of a resolution passed by the Church Assembly in November 1962. It ran: "That the Archbishops be asked to appoint a Committee to make a thorough examination of the various reasons for 'the withholding of the ordained and representative priesthood from women' and to report to the Archbishops." For three years the Commission worked under the chairmanship of the Bishop of Chester, and its 134-page report was thorough and judicious. It was debated at the Spring and Summer Sessions of the Church Assembly in 1967 and was commended by the Assembly "to the consideration of the Church".

Then came the Lambeth Conference of 1968. The committee which had to consider the Ordination of Women to the Priesthood reported: "We find no conclusive theological reasons for withholding ordination to the priesthood from women as such." The conference itself affirmed "its opinion that the theological arguments as at present presented for and against the ordination of women to the priesthood are inconclusive" (Resolution 34), and requested "every national and regional Church or Province to give careful study to the question of the ordination of women to the priesthood and to report its findings to the Anglican Consultative Council ..." (R. 35). That same Lambeth Conference recommended that "canonical provision should be made to enable qualified women to share in the conduct of liturgical worship, to preach, to baptise, to read the epistle and gospel at

In General Synod, 6th July, 1973.

Holy Communion and to help in the distribution of the elements"
—a provision which has been increasingly implemented in the
ensuing five years of the Church's life and work.

When the Anglican Consultative Council met at Limuru in
1971, the issue had been sharpened by the fact that the Bishop of
Hong Kong had asked for advice since his diocesan synod had
approved the ordination of women in principle. By a narrow
majority the Council declared that, if the Bishop decided to
ordain women to the priesthood, his action would be acceptable
to the Council, and the Council would use its good offices to
encourage all Provinces of the Anglican Communion to continue in communion with these dioceses. The Secretary General
was asked to request the Metropolitans and Primates of the
Churches of the Anglican Communion to consult with other
churches in their areas and to report to him in time for the next
meeting of the Anglican Consultative Council.

Our General Synod referred the matter to A.C.C.M. and to the
Council for Women's Ministry in the Church. The latter, having
resolved that "a very large majority of the members of this
Council has come to believe that the Church of England should
now take steps to enable women to be admitted to the Ordination
of Priesthood", joined with A.C.C.M. in inviting Miss Christian
Howard to produce the survey which we now have before us in
G.S. 104 and, in its shortened version, in G.S. 104A. Miss Howard
produced a document both balanced and clear.

The Church of England, unlike some other Provinces in the
Anglican Communion, has been unable to give the Anglican
Consultative Council, due to meet in Dublin soon, a reply to the
question put to it. As the question includes matter of a doctrinal
nature, we are compelled to regard it as Article 7 or Article 8
business and therefore to refer it to the dioceses for discussion
and report. Only then can we return our reply to the Secretary
General of the Anglican Consultative Council.

This, then, is where we now stand. It is important that the
debate in which we shall join today should concentrate on the
issues which matter most and so should give a lead to those
debates in our diocesan synods which will take place in the
coming months. The Convocations of Canterbury and York
debated the matter last May. It might be of help to members of

the Synod to read the record of these debates. The Press tended to highlight some of the less responsible remarks which were made in debates which were, generally speaking, of a very high order.

The path of those who engage in discussion of this subject is perilous. We are *all* prejudiced one way or another. Is there a totally unbiased man or woman? "My mind is made up; don't confuse me with facts"—the Bishop of Liverpool quoted the words during the course of the debate in the Convocation of York! "O Lord, open Thou our" *minds*, might be a good prayer for us all.

Another danger to be avoided is the quotation of texts from Scripture, texts which are sometimes isolated from their contexts and therefore become pretexts. Such a practice fails to differentiate the passing from the permanent in the interpretation of Scripture. The man who engages in such citing of texts often fails to weigh the importance of the movement of history. The circumstances which obtained in the first century and in the Near East are wholly different from those which obtain in the late twentieth century in the West. Before we produce yet again the argument that, because Jesus did not include a woman in the apostolic band, it is therefore impossible to conceive of women priests, ought we not to give consideration to the wholly impossible situation in which the Lord would have found Himself if He had thus flouted the conventions of His day? This consideration may not be thought to decide the issue one way or the other for there are plenty of other factors involved; but at least it should make us cautious in repeating an argument which seems to carry singularly little weight.

Far more fundamental is the question: "What in fact is the basic qualification for ordination?" Is it masculinity *or* is it redeemed humanity? If women are full members of the priestly body, the Church, what precisely is it in them which disqualifies them from ordination to the Church's priesthood? Let me give you an example: Here is a woman hospital chaplain. In her ministrations, say to a woman patient, she can do everything that a priest can do until the moment comes when the patient seeks absolution or the sacrament of Holy Communion. At that point, the woman hospital chaplain must import a priest who is probably unknown to the patient in question. If we can pin-point what precisely it is which forbids that woman chaplain from fulfilling a total priestly ministry, our thinking and our decision will be the clearer. If the ordained ministry is the extended priesthood of Christ Himself, and if He represented and represents the human *race*, does a priesthood restricted to males only lose something of its representative character?

But underlying these basic questions and determinative of our final answers is one question of over-riding importance. It is this: What is our doctrine of the Holy Spirit? And particularly what is it in relation to tradition and the ministry? Was the pattern of the ministry made unalterable and inviolable, at an early date, say around the year A.D. 100? Recent scholarship seems to indicate that no one, fixed, regimented form of ministry is discernible in the documents of the period. There was very considerable variety of local development. Local conditions determined local patterns of ministry. If that is true, might it be argued that change might be conceived not only in regard to patterns of ministry but also as to the sex of the ministers? Indeed, that the metaphors of wind and fire by which the activities of the Spirit are described, might lead us to expect change, even though it be long delayed? Do not these metaphors speak of change of pattern, of diversity of form, of the dynamic rather than the static, of the mobile and adaptable rather than the rigid and unchanging?

As I have thought this matter over, I have been reminded of a change which has taken place within the life-time of us all. If you look up the records of past Lambeth Conferences when the Bishops were debating the delicate issue of birth control, you will see that again and again they declared against it—and sometimes the language was strong. But in 1958 there was a wind of change and the declaration in favour of birth control was in clear and positive terms. Few Anglicans today would question that the Bishops were right and that the change was made in obedience to the guiding of the Spirit. Past utterances were cancelled out and a lead was given to Christendom on an ethical issue of great importance to the Church and to society. I have noted a remarkable change between the debates at the Lambeth Conference of 1958 and that of 1968 on the issue now before us. In the broadest sphere of the liberating of women from the restrictions and inhibitions of a bygone age, who can fail to detect the work of the

Spirit? Must we not ask our diocesan synods to face the question: "Is the Holy Spirit leading us on here too?" Are we, in that area of life which has to do with inter-personal, male-female relationships, at last beginning to move towards a theology of sexuality which does justice to those insights which modern science is giving us and which, in as much as all truth comes from God, must be acknowledged to be the gift of the Spirit?

There are many other questions to which our diocesan synods will need to address themselves. I mention one of them. It is the question whether, if the Anglican Communion gave an affirmative answer to the question before us, action ought to be delayed because it would jeopardise relations especially with the Roman Catholic Church. The issue is a serious one. But this at least should be borne in mind. The thinking of the Roman Catholic Church is far more open today than it was in pre-Vatican II times. Theologians of that Church like Hans Küng have suggested that the issue is sociological rather than theological.[1] It is therefore quite possible that, in the near future, we shall see a change in this area of thought just as, in recent years, we have seen this happen in many other situations. We must recognise that the Anglican Communion, for all its 66 million members, is a small communion compared with that of Rome. Nevertheless, in the history of the Church, minorities have been known to be right and majorities wrong. It has sometimes been the task of a minority, once it is convinced of the rightness of a course of action, to give a lead. Is this such an instance?

The Church of England is but a part of the Anglican Communion. Some Provinces have already indicated their reactions; others are now in process of doing so. "Many of the Churches of the Anglican Communion regard the question as an urgent matter," so the Limuru Resolution (28a) said in 1971. The other Provinces will not be content to await our decision indefinitely. Our Standing Committee, however, realising that some parts of the Church of England having been tardy in studying the matter seriously, also have been slow to see that this *is* an issue on which an answer has to be given. So it is not asking the Synod to commit itself formally at this stage one way or the other. It is asking the Synod to vote that the matter should be referred to the dioceses

[1]See his *Why Priests?* pp. 59–60 (1971, Eng. Trans. 1972, Fontana).

to find out (a) whether they accept the principle of the ordination of women to the priesthood and (b) whether they consider consequent action to be desirable at the present time.

If, as I hope, the Synod gives an affirmative answer to this request, we shall certainly not lay ourselves open to the charge that anybody is being rushed into a decision. We shall however ensure that the matter is taken seriously in the immediate future and, incidentally give some measure of hope to the small group of women, who, in their hearts, realise that God is calling them to the priesthood and who desire the Church to test that call as it tests the vocation of men who are similarly convinced.

I hope the Synod passes this motion this morning. May our debate, and the answer of the dioceses, reflect a maximum of light and a minimum of heat, and so help the Church of England to play a responsible part in a debate which is as wide as the Anglican Communion itself.

The Purpose of Life

I DINED IN London recently. The guests were a mixed group of business men, politicians, and clergy. After dinner there was discussion. In the course of it, a politician who had, at one time, been a distinguished Cabinet Minister, described a conference at which he had been present. Its members consisted of scientists and theologians. My political friend was disappointed in the theologians because, in his opinion, they failed to give any satisfactory answers to such a question as "The Nature of Man". That, he felt, was their job. They had let their colleagues down by failing to give such answers.

I wrote to my friend next morning and received in reply a letter most of which I quote:

> ... I don't think you Rt. Rev. Gents. understand how clearly many of those who run the country in one way or another, and who are not practising Christians, nevertheless have grasped that it is their failure to conceive the nature of man which is behind their failure to manage things better. They think that unless they swallow the doctrines of the Church as enunciated in—say—the Creeds there's nothing in it for them. What they don't want is the clergy to act as though they were better welfare officers than their own trained personnel, or for that matter to try and legislate better than the departments in Whitehall. They want your particular expertise—something they know they haven't got.

Heckmondwike Lecture, 28th May, 1969.

That is a penetrating letter. It is a cry for guidance on such questions as: "What is the purpose of life?" (it was clear to my political friend that the provisions of the Welfare State gave no satisfactory answer to that one); "What is man?"

I want to try and deal with these questions now.

We cannot begin to get a satisfactory answer to the question: "What is the purpose of life?" until we have first tackled the question: "What is man?" If to this latter question we give a purely materialistic answer, we shall approach the former question from an angle quite different from that of the person who thinks of man as a spiritual being.

What is man? A bundle of chemicals worth a few shillings in all? A body made up of a hundred billion or so cells? Will that do for an answer? I think not. "Man is like unto the beasts that perish"—that is a biblical answer, the reply of a Psalmist who was oppressed by the obviously transitory nature of life and whose understanding had not been illuminated by the Christian conception of life after death (Ps. 49:12). That is only one answer—and it is a depressing one—from the pages of the Old Testament, though there are glimpses there, long before the coming of Jesus of Nazareth, of a more satisfying reply.

Another Psalmist poses the question: "What is man?" (Ps. 8:4). He sets it against the awe-inspiring background of a universe which puzzles him by its magnificence: "When I consider Thy heavens . . . the moon and the stars." He knows nothing of the immensities of time and space which we have begun to understand in recent centuries, but he knows enough to make him feel very small. We might imagine that he would reply: "Man is nothing; a puff of wind, a spark soon exterminated." But he gives a wholly different answer. "Thou madest him little lower than the angels," he replies. "Thou hast crowned him with glory and honour. Thou madest him to have dominion over the works of Thy hands, and hast put all things in subjection under his feet, all sheep and oxen, yea and all the beasts of the field . . ." In other words, man, tiny and transitory as he is when compared with the immensities of the universes, is yet God's vice-gerent. He is to have dominion, the while he himself is under the dominion of God.

Now we are at least getting somewhere. If this is true, there inheres in man a certain *responsibility*, an answerability to God, which gives him a dignity unique in creation. The process of the evolution of *homo sapiens* is a mystery, and much of the story is still tentative. Professor L. C. Birch, in his book *Nature and God* (pp. 36–7), has put it this way: "Were it possible, by some act of necromancy, to resurrect our evolutionary forebears, and set them in a long line from earliest to latest, and then to review them as one might review a guard of honour, it is unlikely that we would be able to say: 'Well, here at last is a man; the creature on his left is not'." That is no doubt true. But what is it that constitutes the *humanum*, the distinctive characteristic of man? Is it not his ability to evaluate, to stand over against nature of which he is a part, and to fulfil his function of responsible domination over what has been entrusted to him?

The old creation story of Genesis 2 must not be dismissed as just another of the primitive stories of earth's origins which most primitive peoples have handed down. It has profound insights. When God had made man, He put him in the garden "to dress it and to keep it". So there is *a dignity to labour*. Man is responsible. He is entrusted with soil and plants and trees. Then God formed the beasts and the birds—the language is highly poetic and contrasts strangely with the picture which the scientists present to us. That does not matter. When God has made the animals, He brings them to Adam "to see what he would call them: and whatsoever Adam called every living creature, that was the name thereof" (Genesis 2:19). The point of this strange saying is this. If I know the name of a thing or an animal, still more if I give it its name, that thing or that animal is in my power. I am its master. So we see man as master of the animal world, God's vice-gerent as it were, having dominion over the beasts, but answerable to God for the kind of dominion which he exercises. Man is over nature and under God. (In passing, I draw attention to what happens to our earth when there is no sense of responsibility, of *answerability* to God for being put in trust with nature. Dust-bowls and contamination of the atmosphere by atomic explosions are but two grim illustrations).

The story of the garden and the animals is followed by the story of the making of a companion for Adam. Again, the language is highly poetical. The point of the story is not far to seek. Man, if he is to be truly man, must live in harmony not only with nature, plants and beasts, but in community with others like himself. Indeed, the opening three chapters of Genesis make it abundantly clear that if man is to become fully human, he must learn to live in a right relationship with God, with others, and with Nature. So man can rejoice in God, that is to say, he can live in community; he can develop as a son of the Most High; he can exercise his vice-gerency in humble responsibility.

The old Genesis story is reflected in a powerful sentence in Psalm 100:2: "Be ye sure that the Lord He is God: it is He that hath made us and we are his . . ." This is taken up by the writer of the Epistle to the Ephesians (2:10): "We are God's handi-work . . ." The word is *poiēma*, which has been taken over into English as *poem*. A poem is the noblest expression of the poet's mind, his best expression of himself. That, so St Paul suggests, is what man is intended to be, the finest flowering of God's mind within His creation. The tragedy of life lies in the fact that we, by our folly, spoil the metre and wreck the poem (and, incidentally, in doing so, grieve the Poet, who, if we follow the teaching of Jesus, was not only Artist but Father).

Kierkegaard, the great Danish thinker, says that each man's life is to be a poem, as if we are each to write or compose ourselves. But a Christian allows God to write his life's poem; in so far as that takes place he reaches his full humanity and finds his purpose in living.

We have moved from the question: "What is man?" to our original question: "What is the purpose of life?"

This is a question which presents itself to anyone who is at all serious about the business of being human. It has a way of teasing us, even when we are young. We can seek to stub it out, as a man puts out the fire at the end of his cigarette. We can seek to prevent its recurrence, as something too problematical to worry about. But in doing so, we cannot but feel that we are abandoning ourselves to a method of living which is unworthy of us. The question, even if it cannot be fully answered, must (to use the language of the examination room) be attempted.

Here am I, a mysterious entity of passions and desires, of hopes and fears, of possibilities for good and ill. I came on the scene only very recently, if you compare me with the physical world of which I am a part. I shall disappear from the scene very shortly—

I may live to be ninety or one hundred, but that is a mere second in time if you think in terms of a universe where millions of light years are your standard of measurement. Can you speak of *purpose* for so tiny, so transitory, a thing as that?

I believe you can. I believe you *must* think in terms of purpose, if life is to have a thrust to it which delivers it from being a mere sharing in a succession of random events and then—out into the dark.

There is a wide variety of possibilities open to the man who is prepared to put the question to himself. For example, he may say: I am a bundle of desires which cry out for satisfaction. Hunger, thirst, sex, the whole world of sensation, are there to be fulfilled. The purpose of life, as I see it, is to see that these desires are met as they press their claims on my attention. Most thoughtful people would say that, legitimate as those claims are, important as is the place which man's hungers hold in his make-up, the satisfying of them as a main motive for living is an unworthy one. Even the satisfying of the desire for knowledge, if it be pursued simply for itself and not for the ultimate enrichment of mankind, can be a selfish thing.

What is the purpose of life? We cannot get far with this question without coming up against the profit motive. "I want to make £100,000 before I am thirty-five." That may, or may not, be good. It all depends on the motive behind the desire.

Let me contrast two men of our own time, both of whom became immensely rich. One is King Farouk of Egypt who amassed a huge fortune and lived in fabulous luxury, while the vast majority of his people lived around him in grinding poverty. He died at an early age largely owing to the dissipation of which he had become a victim. The other is William Richard Morris, known to the world as Lord Nuffield. He began work, as everybody knows, in a little bicycle shop in Oxford. He ended life as a millionaire whose wealth has saved thousands of lives through the medical institutions which he founded and the research which he made possible. The profit motive, like ambition in general, is an amoral thing. Everything depends on the forms through which that motive finds expression.

Put our question to many serious-minded men and women

today, and they would reply: "My purpose in living is to leave this world a better place than it was when I entered it." That is good. I shall suggest later that it is not good enough, but, so far as it goes, it is good. It has provided the stimulus for a multitude of noble lives—and anything that does that cannot, must not, be airily dismissed. Life for multitudes of our contemporaries is a grim affair, a pitiless struggle for existence, a battle against elements which bid fair to destroy them. The so-called "third world", the world of dire poverty, of illiteracy, of lack of amenities which we in the West take for granted as minimal necessities is the world in which tens of millions of our fellow-men eke out a short and miserable existence. To strike a blow against *that*, to pit our learning against that ignorance, to bring hope and a fuller life even to a comparative handful of people less fortunate than ourselves—*that* is to give a really meaningful answer to our question. A man who works on these lines may feel, at the end of his life, that that life has not been in vain. It has had purpose.

The Christian gives his whole-hearted assent to this answer to the question. But he goes further. Simply "to leave the world a better place than it was when he entered it", good as that motive is, is not good enough for him. He has a higher point of reference. If he was born north of the border, he is familiar with the answer to the question: "What is the chief end of man?" as it is given in the Shorter Catechism: "The chief end of man is to glorify God and to enjoy Him for ever." We are back with the Poet and the poem. We are back with man's answerability which is the essence of his humanity. The Christian sees his purpose in life in terms of his response to God. His attitude to persons is what it is because of his attitude to God who made them and him. He cannot treat them as things to be manipulated for his pleasure or profit. They are, as he himself is, children of God, designed to be His "poems", capable of almost limitless growth. They must, therefore, be treated with reverence. If Jesus came that men "might have life and have it in all its fullness" (St John 10:10), then it will be the Christian's chief aim to forward that purpose. In that way, he will "glorify God", and prepare for a fuller life when he will "enjoy Him for ever". He will see life, with all its absorbing interest, in its relationship to the Creator, to his fellow-creatures, to nature; and he will see it as a training-ground for life after death.

That is the context of his living.
Everything is *sub specie aeternitatis*.
There is no limit to his horizons.
The prospects are exciting.

With these horizons and prospects, with these terms of reference, and with this overwhelming sense of answerability, the Christian disciple will obviously be prepared for a life of self-discipline and training. The great ecumenical leader, Archbishop Nathan Söderblom, constantly used to avail himself of the metaphor of the race-horse and its rider in this connection. The good horse, he would say, can achieve its highest capacity and its greatest speed only under the sure hand of the rider. Kierkegaard, using the same language of the apostles, said that they were "well broken in". That is true of Christ's disciples at all times. Söderblom said: "Only with God's good hand and strict bridle can the soul be helped to give its best." (Bengt Sundkler: *Nathan Söderblom, His Life and Work*, p. 152). He was right. Or to revert to our earlier metaphors, the vice-gerent exerts his sovereignty rightly only when he himself bows to the sovereignty of God. The poem attains its full power and beauty only when the Poet has a free hand to make of it what He will.

Literature is full of instances of men who have failed to see this, and who, because they have lacked this vision, have perished.

A. J. Cronin, in one of his less known novels, *The Northern Light*, tells the story of the manager of a newspaper who sought to run it on lines which gave its readers the best kind of journalism and avoided the cheap and the salacious. The heart of the story is a take-over bid which Henry Page, the manager, resists. When it is seen that no offer is acceptable, a rival paper is started up in the town with the specific object of ruining *The Northern Light*. It very nearly succeeds—but not quite. The central figure of the opposition is one Leonard Nye. Cronin uses all his skill in describing him. It is not merely his cunning which stands out in the story. It is his closure of his heart to pity, his willingness to use people and to ruin them if by so doing he can achieve his aims, which make Nye so despicable a character. People are pawns in his little game of living. Only one person matters, Leonard Nye, his wealth, his aggrandisement. What matter if he leaves the world a *worse* place than he found it, so long as his own selfish aims are achieved?

Cronin answers our question brilliantly in his character-sketches of Page and Nye. Page lives for the community. Nye has not begun to live in community. God does not exist in his thinking. There is no one to whom he is answerable for the use of his gifts. The centre of Nye's universe is Nye. His horizons are narrow, his prospects beyond this life are nil, his sense of answerability to God, if it ever existed, has died on him. He has lost his soul.

So Cronin has provided us with an illustration of a man who had not a clue as to the real purpose of life. The New Testament will provide us with two instances of those who had.

Saul of Tarsus is a good example of a man who "changed horses in mid-stream". All his considerable energies as a young man were devoted to persecuting the followers of Jesus of Nazareth. Then he met Him and, yielding Him his allegiance, spent the rest of his life in serving His cause and winning men to His service. His letters reflect this dramatic change and give us a vivid picture of a man quite clear as to the purpose of life.

I choose two typical utterances. *First:* "It is God Himself who called you *to share in the life of His Son Jesus Christ our Lord*" (1 Cor. 1:9). Here is human destiny at its highest. The men to whom St Paul wrote knew a good deal about the life of Jesus Christ. Some perhaps had seen Him in the flesh and heard Him. Many had listened to those who had lived with Him in Palestine. All knew of the power and love of that life lived for others, a life which death by crucifixion had been unable to extinguish, a life which was available to them in prayer and sacrament. *Here*, for them, was the purpose of life—"to share in the life of the Son of God".

Secondly: "We make it our ambition to be well-pleasing to Him" (2 Cor. 5:9). The "we" is editorial; this is clearly a statement of personal aim and ambition. We have seen earlier that ambition in itself is an amoral thing—it all depends on that to which you hitch it. Here it is something of immense moral power—every personal desire subjugated to the overmastering ambition of pleasing Christ. This is the one passion of his life. This gives life its purpose and its meaning.

Stephen Neill writes:

Life is filled with meaning as soon as Jesus Christ enters into it.

Man realises himself to be part of a great purpose in which he can participate, and in which all his minor purposes can find place and significance. The knowledge of the ever-present Christ can reach down into the hidden depths and assure lonely modern man that he is not alone. More than that; it can draw him out of his loneliness to the rediscovery of the human race. (*The Church and Christian Union*, p. 279.)

That is not a bad summary, by a modern writer, of St Paul's two statements: "God... called you to share in the life of His Son Jesus Christ", and, "We make it our ambition to be well-pleasing to Him."

If St Paul furnished us with our first instance of a man equipped with a clear purpose for living, a greater than St Paul provides us with the second. I take two sentences from the Fourth Gospel, one of which I have already quoted.

First: "I have come that men may have life, and may have it in all its fullness" (St John 10:10). Here is a life lived with no thought for self but wholly for others. The context shows that such a life involves sacrifice, even to death—"the good shepherd lays down his life for the sheep". And it involves battle; there are forces of evil represented by "the thief" and "the wolf" which must be opposed. The purpose of life depicted here is a stern one.

Secondly: "I have made Thy name known . . ." (St John 17:6 and 26). These words are not purposive in their form, but, taken in their context, they declare the fulfilment of the purpose which Jesus saw as the meaning of life. They are taken from a long chapter which purports to give us the prayer of Jesus at the end of His earthly life, immediately prior to His self-sacrifice on the Cross. He declares that that purpose was to "make known the name of God" to the men whom God had given Him as His immediate followers. It would then be for them, in their turn, to continue to make His name known to others—so the knowledge would spread in ever widening circles.

The "name" represented to a Jew the *personality*. If one made another person's "name" known, one drew aside the veil that hid him. One showed him for what he essentially is. That is precisely what Jesus did. Before His coming, men had a partial or a distorted or a warped view of God. Many were tiring of the crude polytheism of the Hellenistic gods and the emperor-worship of Rome. Many were looking wistfully to the worship of the synagogue and were pondering on the message of the prophets—the rigorous justice of an Amos, the yearning love of a Hosea, the ethical rectitude demanded by the God of Isaiah. Here were glimpses of a religion which could satisfy the deepest longings of men both in their personal religion and in their desires for a satisfying social ethic. And then Christ came and, in coming, drew aside the veil that had partially or almost completely veiled the Face of God, and men saw in Him a King to be obeyed, and a Father to be loved. Here was one worthy of total response. To be the vice-gerent of such a Sovereign was man's highest destiny. To exercise responsibility, answerability, was to live life in all its fullness. To allow such a Poet to create His poem without let or hindrance was to find life that was life indeed.

> To know Him is to live;
> To serve Him is to reign.

I doubt whether we can go further than this, but this is enough to begin to make sense of life and its purpose at least for me. The unsolved mysteries of life are legion. The agnostic element in any thoughtful man's philosophy of life must be great; he must be prepared to say, again and again, "I do not know". "My knowledge now is partial". St Paul said that nineteen centuries ago and, for all the strides which science has made, it is still true, for our horizons are far wider than were his. But we know enough to see that God has a purpose for the lives of His children and that He has made us in such a way that we can enter into that purpose—or spurn it.

I believe that a purpose is found for life when God is seen to be constantly at work within His creation, God who is both sovereign Lord and loving Father. God who has spoken finally in Jesus His Son; God who was in Christ reconciling the world to Himself; God who, by His Spirit, constantly seeks to make us holy, that is to say, to fashion us after the likeness of His Son.

This God treats us as responsible beings, answerable to Him for the response we make to His love shown in Christ, for the way we treat His sons and daughters, for our attitude to nature in its myriad manifestations.

This God never forces our response. As Augustine said, He "asks our leave to bless us". But when that leave is given, He gets on with the making of His poem.

Then, and only then, is the purpose of life achieved.

Uppsala and Lambeth

THE LAST TIME we met, I promised that I would tell you a little about the conferences which I attended this summer at Uppsala and Lambeth.

Come, first to Uppsala in Sweden, to the huge Fyris Hall, normally used as a sports stadium. There, coming from six continents and eighty nations, were some two thousand people, delegates, fraternal delegates, advisers, youth participants, reporters, broadcasters, and so on. The Swedish paper industry gave the World Council of Churches ten tons of paper to use at this mammoth Fourth Assembly—and I doubt whether much of it remained unused at the end! All of us were provided with headphones, so that we could, at the turn of a switch, listen to the speeches in Russian, French, German or English.

I was present at the Third Assembly held in New Delhi in 1961, so the conditions in which we met in this ancient University of Uppsala were different. I found the conference naturally to be full of interest, though it can scarcely be described as a picnic. Tom Driberg, M.P., who was one of our Anglican delegates, described it in an article to *The Times* as a "gruelling business".

The Presidents of the World Council took the chair at the main meetings in turn. In the background hovered the almost legendary figure of Visser t'Hooft who for so many years guided the destinies of the Council, moulded its shape and helped to develop the theology of the World Council of Churches. His influence is still greatly felt.

I mention, but only in passing, the immense difficulties created

York Diocesan Conference, Presidential Address, 12th November, 1968.

by the sheer size of the Fourth Assembly. The biggest Lambeth Conference yet held looked small in comparison with the two thousand churchmen and visitors who gathered at Uppsala. There was a large representation of the Orthodox (first welcomed into membership of the World Council of Churches at the Third Assembly held at New Delhi in 1961). There was a significant number of Roman Catholic observers. Father Roberto Tucci, S. J., of Rome, the first Roman Catholic ever to give a major address at an Assembly, declared in fact that Roman Catholics "no longer regard themselves as outside spectators who are indifferent or merely curious" but as partners engaged in the same quest for unity.

There were 135 youth participants, though my own view is that the participation allowed them was unsatisfactory and called for radical alteration at any future Assembly. They had no voting rights, and sat in a block—so they seemed to be "they" over against "us". I have recommended that at a future Assembly all the major delegations should be *required* to include a certain number of youth delegates, who would have full voting rights and exercise full participation in all the activities of the Assembly.

Against that sketchy background, I want now to concentrate on one point which stood out, perhaps above all others, with a burning clarity. It was the awareness of the delegates and observers and participants at Uppsala of the social miseries and inequalities of our world. True, we met at a time when the Nigeria-Biafra conflict and the Vietnam conflict were at their worst. But these things together with the situation in South Africa, only tended to highlight our awareness of a third world on our doorstep and the fact, as the economist Dr Barbara Ward (Lady Jackson) pointed out, that eighty per cent of the world's wealth is in the hands of twenty per cent of the world's population. Pitilessly the facts were brought home to us—the fact that the world population is likely to double by the year 2,000; the fact that the bulk of this growth will be in the developing lands (more than half the population of country after country in Africa is under twenty years of age); the fact that the incomes of the developed nations, twelve times larger than those of the developing nations today, are likely to be eighteen times larger at the end of this century; the fact that U Thant had said: "There is a clear prospect that racial conflict, if we cannot curb and finally eliminate it, will grow into a destructive monster compared to which the religious and ideological conflicts of the past will seem like family quarrels. Such a conflict will eat away the possibilities for good of all that mankind has hitherto achieved and reduce men to the lowest and most bestial level of intolerance and hatred. This, for the sake of all our children, whatever their race and colour, must not be permitted to happen"; the fact that half the people in the world live near or below the starvation level and 700 million of them are illiterate.

Perhaps in our particular positions of responsibility, we need to stress two developing factors in the face of these appalling problems:—

1. An increasing political awareness on the part of Christians, and so a willingness to press *politically* for reform, e.g. increases in government aid to underdeveloped countries from which we extract great wealth. This is always unpopular, but we must be prepared to face the cost *and to get others to join us*. Alluding to the proposal presented in the section report on economic development, namely, that the affluent northern nations should accept a tax, if only to begin with, of one per cent of Gross National Products, Lady Jackson pointed out that it would merely mean "getting richer slower between Christmas and Easter, and that includes Lent, so it isn't much of a sacrifice. Would we be all that worse off if we paid five cents more for a cup of coffee? Hardly. And yet that might determine the possibility of African and Latin American countries having their development programmes".

2. A realisation of the theological issues lying behind, and indeed giving rise to such political pressure and reform. If all men are in fact sons of God, irrespective of colour or background, then equality of opportunity is theirs by right—opportunity for a life of dignity, education, housing, freedom from the restrictions imposed by dire poverty, illiteracy, etc. Our social concern springs from the theological convictions which sustain it. The theological introductions to conference reports which deal with mundane matters are therefore not pietistic exercises largely irrelevant to these issues. Exactly the reverse is the case, *because* we believe certain things about creation and man's position of dominion within it while he himself is under the domination of God; *because* we believe that man's vice-gerency involves him in a

responsible use of nature and an attitude of reverence to its
resources; *because* we believe certain things about the worth and
destiny of man; *because* we believe in the Incarnation and in the
redemption wrought by Christ. It is because of all this that we
are deeply concerned for man's total welfare in the here and now
as well as in the world to come.

We listened one Sunday afternoon to the negro novelist, James
Baldwin, on "White Racism or World Community", as he gave us
a searing indictment of the white man and his oppression of the
black. It was easy, at the end of his talk, to say that his perspectives
were wrong and that he had been almost totally silent on the
benefits which, for example, the great missionary movements had
brought to Africa and the East. It was easy to say that he had
confused the actions of *so-called* Christian nations with those of
practising Christians. And it was comforting to listen to the
balanced speech of Lord Caradon which followed James Baldwin's. *But* to leave it at that would be wholly irresponsible.
Baldwin represents a seething mass of dark people, millions of
whom are not willing merely to sing the haunting tune which will
for ever be associated with Martin Luther King: "We shall
overcome." The day will come—in Memphis, Tennessee, and
elsewhere it has already come—when marches will give place to
machine guns and songs to even more sinister weapons *unless
the West wakes up.* But—and this is the point we need to emphasise
in our teaching—we who are Christians should take action in
regard to racism *not* because we want to avoid a blood bath in
America or Africa or Birmingham or Bradford, but precisely
because we are Christians who believe that the black man has
rights to certain standards of living by reason of the fact that the
same God made him as made us and our children, and the same
Christ died for him. This is the *theology*, the *religion*, lying behind
the politics and the action. And these are the truths which, week
in week out, year in year out, we must impress upon the minds
and consciences of all Christian people—thoughtfully, steadily,
relentlessly, prayerfully.

I quote a paragraph from the Assembly message which a percipient American theologian has said may be the most important
result of this global meeting of followers of Christ:

"We heard the cry of those who long for peace; of the hungry and exploited who demand bread and justice; of the victims of discrimination who claim human dignity; and of the increasing millions who seek for the meaning of life. God hears these cries and judges us."

I turn now to the Lambeth Conference, held so soon after in Church House, Westminster, because Lambeth Palace was too small for us all. Those present were the bishops of the Anglican Communion in full-time episcopal work (diocesan, suffragan, and assistant), some 462 in all (some, of course, were prevented from attending, for example, some American bishops who felt they ought to remain at their posts in case race riots should take place during the hot summer). In addition to the bishops, there were some seventy-five official Observers representing many Churches, from the Armenian to the Lusitanian, from the Lutheran to the Roman Catholic. And—for the first time—there were twenty-five Consultants, experts who gave their skills for the benefit of the conference.

Lambeth was a big and expensive operation—expensive in man-hours, in energy, and in money. Many have asked: "Was it all worthwhile?" I say "Yes". These conferences have been held roughly once a decade since their inception 101 years ago. No one can say what shape the next one will take, but I hope greatly that there will be another. Some have spoken of Lambeth 1968 as the last; I consider such talk to be ill-conceived and premature. I believe in these conferences, not merely for the statements that come out of them, although these statements often read rather "flatly", for they frequently are the work of more than one mind and bear none of the sparkle of the spoken word. But even these statements are valuable as distillations of hard thinking, and serve as the basis for preaching and discussions in ensuing months and years.

Perhaps the greatest benefits which come out of the Lambeth Conference are the friendships formed and deepened. I mean by this not merely that it can be said at the end of the conference that "a good time was had by all". I mean something much deeper. I mean that men (and women, for some hundreds of wives came to London) get to know one another, to understand the problems of areas which they had never visited, and, out of this deep fellowship in Christ, intelligent and constant prayer is bound to flow. *This* will enrich the life of the Anglican Communion as will nothing else. *This* is our greatest need.

The rape of Czechoslovakia which occurred during the conference only served to deepen that awareness of world tragedy which had so deeply affected the thinking of those of us who had shared in the conference at Uppsala. It was a matter of no small interest that, on the day that the Lambeth Conference opened, the Pope released his Encyclical Letter "On the Regulation of Birth", a document which raises not only questions of grave moral importance in the sphere of sexual ethics, but matters of conscientious freedom which affect all who allow a religious dimension to their life. The Lambeth Conference re-affirmed the findings of the conference of 1958 in which, among other things, it asserted that it believed that "the responsibility for deciding upon the number and frequency of children has been laid by God upon the consciences of parents everywhere; that this planning, in such ways as are mutually acceptable to husband and wife in Christian conscience, is a right and important factor in Christian family life and should be the result of positive choice before God . . . "

What did we all discuss? The theme at Uppsala had been: "All Things New". Ours at Lambeth was similar: "The Renewal of the Church". We divided into three sections, one dealing with *Faith*, another with *Ministry* and a third with *Unity*. I can only here touch on a few of the main subjects which attracted our attention.

I have already mentioned *world need*. *War* as a method of settling international disputes was condemned as being incompatible with the teaching and example of Jesus Christ; and *nuclear and bacteriological weapons* were singled out for special condemnation. Concern was expressed that the Church should uphold and extend *the right of conscientious objection*. *Racism* was described, in the words of the statement of the World Council of Churches at Uppsala, as "a blatant denial of the Christian faith", and the Churches were called upon to give expression to the demands of the Gospel by the inclusiveness of their worship, by the creation of a climate of acceptance in their common life, and by their justice in placing and appointment.

The members of the section which was concerned with the Christian *Faith* realised how difficult it is for many thinkers to express and give meaning to their belief in days when our categories of thought are so different from those of first-century Christians. They sought for an approach which would combine Christian assurance with a bold exploration of theology and society; which would unite Christian confidence and intellectual and social risk. They sought to encourage theologians to continue to explore fresh ways of understanding God's revelation of Himself in Christ, expressed in language that makes sense in our time. That entails respect for tradition on the part of the theologians, and freedom of enquiry on the part of the Church members.

The bishops concerned with *Ministry* were acutely conscious of the fact that every baptised and committed member of Christ's Body is a minister, a servant, a witness of Jesus Christ. Clergy and laity complement each other. The laity, in their daily work, are in immediate contact with more of their fellows and therefore bear the greater responsibility for witnessing to their Lord. Ministry, in a highly diversified society, will take very varied forms. In the *ordained* ministry, there will be full-time and part-time deacons and priests; the diaconate will be sometimes preparatory to the priesthood, sometimes permanent. There is almost infinite room for experimentation.

The position of women ordained to the diaconate was clarified, and their function was clearly seen to be the same as that of male deacons. The conference recommended that "national or regional Churches or provinces should be encouraged to make canonical provision . . . for duly qualified women to share in the conduct of liturgical worship, to preach, to baptise, to read the epistle and gospel at the Holy Communion, and to help in the distribution of the elements".

A further resolution ran: "No major issue in the life of the Church should be decided without the full participation of the laity in discussion and in decision."

As to *Unity*, each bishop was bidden to ask himself how seriously he takes the suggestion of the Lund Conference that we should do together everything which conscience does not compel us to do separately. (For that matter, every parish priest and layman should ask a similar question!) Provision was made for welcoming to the Lord's Table people of other Churches, to meet special pastoral needs or on special occasions when progress towards unity has reached an advanced stage. Special reference was made to the Church of South India (which has led the way in progress toward Church unity), to the Churches of North India and Pakistan, to the Church of Sri Lanka (Ceylon), and to the Anglican-Methodist negotiations in this country. The conference recommended the setting up of a Permanent Joint Commission with the Roman Catholic Church and welcomed the resumption of pan-Orthodox and pan-Anglican discussions.

I have but touched the fringe of the story. Others will fill out that story for you on various occasions in the diocese, for at Uppsala Miss Christian Howard was also present from this diocese, and at Lambeth our three suffragan bishops.

May the inspirations, the insights, and the demands of these two great gatherings "seep through" into our diocesan and parochial life, and, where that seeping comes, may the Holy Spirit grant renewal.

Spirituality

Authority, Religion and the Church

ANYONE WHO ATTEMPTS even to begin a con-
sideration of the subject of authority in religion and in the Church
must start with the Gospels. If he approaches the earliest of the
four, the Gospel according to St Mark, he meets the subject in the
very first chapter. As Jesus taught in the synagogue on the Sabbath,
the thing that astounded His hearers was that, "unlike the doctors
of the law, He taught with a note of *authority*".

This, combined with His healing of the man with convulsions,
made the people exclaim: "What is this? A new kind of teaching!
He speaks with *authority* . . ." (St Mark:1:27). They were accustomed to the teaching which derived its authority from the
number or eminence of those who could be quoted in its favour—
"Rabbi A. in the name of Rabbi B. in the name of Rabbi C. says
. . . ; but Rabbi X. in the name of Rabbi Y. in the name of Rabbi
Z. says . . ." But here was one who quite clearly had an authority
of His own. "You have learned what our forefathers were told.
. . . But what I tell you is this . . ." (St Matthew 5:21 ff.). This
was, indeed, startlingly new, incisive in its demands on conscience,
imperious in its call for obedience.

This question of the authority of Jesus was not something to
be debated as a matter of mere curiosity—as it were at arm's
length. When the chief priests, lawyers and elders, puzzled by
the activities of Jesus, came to Him and said, "By what authority
are you acting like this? Who gave you authority to act in this
way?" (St Mark 11:27 ff.), He gave them no straight answer. He

From Authority in a Changing Society, *edited by* C. O. Rhodes, Constable 1969.

simply asked an embarrassing question of *them*—one they dared
not answer—and sent them away with a blank refusal to debate
at no depth an issue which He could see (though they could not)
impinged on heart and will, on conscience and action.

The question of authority was, for Jesus, not primarily a
subject for intellectual debate. It was a matter which touched
the very roots of His own religious conviction. When He taught
men about the Kingdom of God—and this would seem clearly
to have been the main theme of His teaching—He was not one
lecturing with academic detachment *de Deo*. He was in a very
real sense drawing aside the curtain of His own spiritual experience
and sharing with His hearers the secret of what God's authority
over Him meant. The reign of God, the authority of God, was
a reality with which He had to come to terms every day of His
life—at least from the adolescent realisation that He must be
about His Father's business to the day when, having cried, "Not
My will but Thine be done", He could say, "Father, into Thy
hands I commend my spirit".

The unique authority of Jesus, seen alike in His teaching and
His acts of power, seen, noted and marvelled at by His contemporaries, was His precisely because He Himself was under
authority. He knew, as no one else before or since has known,
what it means to do always those things that pleased the Father.
"I do nothing on My own authority, but in all that I say, I have
been taught by My Father" (St John 8:28). Whether these words
be the *ipsissima verba* of Jesus or, to use William Temple's phrase,
"the interpretative recollection of a memory", they convey the
truth of the point at issue.

It was from this basic position of personal religion that Jesus
proceeded in His teaching work and especially in His training of
the Twelve and other disciples. What He had learned of the
authority of God and what He was continually learning in His
daily religious experience, He *must* seek to impart to them.
It would not be easy. To communicate a system, to teach them
a set of rules, to inculcate a series of directions, would be a simple
matter. But this would not do—not if He were going to produce
men of authority who themselves were under divine authority.
He must treat them as adults, not children. He must, as T. W.
Manson used to say, give them direction rather than directions.
This might often prove tantalising to them, even annoying. He

would often have to refuse to give a straight answer to a straight question, and that is always annoying if you want to be saved the bother of thinking a thing out for yourself. "What do you think?" He would say, and then counter their question with another, or answer their question with a story which made them think much more deeply than they had done when they posed the original question.

"The Spirit of the Lord is upon Me". He had read the words from Isaiah 61 on that first Sabbath of His public ministry in the synagogue at Nazareth (St Luke 4:16 ff.). The Spirit—the wind; who was to say where it would blow? Who could measure its power or predict its direction? Try to contain it, and you may look very silly as you see your puny efforts in ruins at your feet. But put yourself in the way of it, set your sail to catch it, place yourself under its authority, and you may find yourself an instrument of power far greater than yourself. Jesus' ministry was to be a demonstration of precisely that. It was thus that He would be enabled to teach, to preach, to heal, to reach right judgments, to rise to increasing demands, to be stretched and not to break. He would try to train His men along similar lines. He would show them what divine authority really meant.

Such training would call for a radical recasting, on their part, of their value judgments. They had been brought up to think of authority in terms of power. "In the world the recognised rulers lord it over their subjects, and their great men make them feel the weight of authority" (St Mark 10:42). If they wanted evidence of that, they had only to look around them and see it working out in the domination of the whole Roman system. But "that is not the way with you; among you, whoever wants to be great must be your servant, and whoever wants to be first must be the willing slave of all". This was a revolution in the concept of authority! And the revolution was so radical that it would seem that it could not take effect in their thinking until, the passion of Jesus being past and the Holy Spirit having been given, they could work it out in the light of that event and in the power of the Paraclete.

This initial glance at the subject of authority as it presents itself to us in the Gospels—and space does not allow for more than this —suggests some valuable lines of guidance for those whose task it is to exercise authority in the Church of God. "Take thou authority to exercise the office of a deacon in the Church of God . . ." says the bishop to the man kneeling before him. "Take thou authority to preach the Word of God, and to minister the holy Sacraments . . ." says the bishop to the man being ordained priest. And, though the language used in the consecration of a bishop is different, the idea of authority recurs both in the prayers and in the words used by the archbishop when he hands a Bible to the newly consecrated bishop.

The subject of the kind of authority exercised by the clergy is one of great concern to the most sensitive of their number, particularly in a day when there is a general dis-ease about any kind of authority and when, in many circles, the very idea of it is resented. "What right have I," the curate or vicar may ask, "to preach to these people Sunday by Sunday? Many of them are better educated than I am; very many of them far more experienced in life and affairs. Who am I to harangue them?" He does well to ask such questions and to ask them sincerely. Who indeed is he? Who am I? But if he can find no answer to these questions, it will go ill with him and with his ministry. Authority matters.

He must surely begin to find his answer along the lines suggested by our brief study of the Gospels. Our Lord's words and acts derived their authority from the fact that our Lord Himself was under authority. Here is our first and absolutely fundamental principle. He alone can preach who knows himself, in the depths of his spiritual life, to be a man under domination, the reign of God Himself. There is a hand on his shoulder directing him and he is supremely contented to live his life, so far as he knows how, under that direction. In fact, his great ambition is to be able to approximate to his Master in saying, "I do always those things that please Him". The Spirit of the Lord is upon him, and his aim is so to set his sail as to catch the Wind. Unless this is a reality— the great reality of his life—he may read his people an essay Sunday by Sunday, he may give them a few good thoughts drawn from the papers with a dash of scripture added, but he cannot *preach*. For to preach a man must know the authority of being under Authority.

Further, he must know something of the authority which derives from service, from being the "willing slave of all". When a priest seeks to impose his own authority—"I am in control of this parish; what I say goes"—then the real authority goes out of the window. When the week has been spent in lowly service to his people—the service of intercession, of visiting, of the menial job gladly undertaken—then the clergyman need not fear that his Sunday ministrations will lack the stamp of genuine authority. "The Son of man did not come to be served but to serve . . ." (St Matthew 20:28).

In fact and in short, there is an authority attaching to personal holiness which can be found nowhere else. It is the *sine qua non* of any ministry worthy of the name. He alone can exercise an authoritative ministry who often has recourse to the secret place of the Most High, who has learned to listen to the God who speaks, who knows the meaning of obedience, who can say not merely, "I hold this view", but "I am held by this God". There is something self-authenticating about the authority of a man of whom it can be said by the man in the street as it was said of Elisha by the woman of Shunem: "I perceive that this is a holy man of God who is continually passing our way" (2 Kings 4:9).

There is nothing brash or noisy about such authority as we have just sought to describe. This is the very reverse of cock-sureness. When Jesus exercised His authoritative ministry, the people were reminded of the words of Isaiah:

> He will not strive, He will not shout,
> Nor will His voice be heard in the streets.
> He will not snap off the broken reed,
> Nor snuff out the smouldering wick . . .
> (St Matthew 12:19–20)

So sensitive was His dealing with people, so reverent His handling of personality. There was no forcing of His views, no crushing of individuality. The reed whose usefulness seemed to have been finished might perhaps be coaxed back to uprightness; the wick which only gave out an evil smell might be fanned again into a clean, light-giving flame. Who was to know? It was worth trying. Human nature is a tender thing, and it calls for tender and patient handling. And, judging by the Gospels, the greater the sinner, the more tender was the handling given to him by our Lord.

F

This tenderness of approach to the individual, this absence of brashness, betokened no lack of sureness of touch. The surgeon who really knows his job, whose experience has taught him the complexities of diagnosis and of the ills that flesh is heir to, once he has made his decision, will not hesitate to use the knife. St John's story of our Lord's dealing with the woman at the well (chapter 4) shows at once the infinite tenderness of His approach and the rapier-like thrust of His charge—"the man with whom you are now living is not your husband; you told me the truth there" (v.18). Tenderness and authority can go hand in hand. They did in His case. Nor do such insights into the recesses of human character belong only to the learned. Many a university graduate has been humbled by the shrewdness of the "unlearned and ignorant". Such insight is but another illustration of the authority which belongs to holiness.

What has been said above, however, must not lead anyone to retreat behind the cover of a pietistic woolly-mindedness. There is a measure of authority which belongs to the man who is master of his subject. There is an expertise which belongs to the priest's office which has to be worked at and which can only be gained by long and patient study. The preacher, for example, must be an exegete, able by special study and constant application to wrestle with the ancient texts and to indicate their relevance to the people to whom he ministers. Not only is he an exegete; he is a *hermeneut*; and Hermes, be it noted, was the *messenger* of the gods.

The only thing which the bishop hands to the deacon and priest at his ordination, and the archbishop to the bishop at his consecration, is a Bible. Perhaps the lack of authority in the ministry of certain men is due to the fact that they have failed to grasp, or have forgotten over the years, the deep significance of that act, and the significance of the reiterated emphasis of the Thirty-Nine Articles on the authority of Scripture. The authority of the creeds rests in the fact that "they may be proved by most certain warrant of Holy Scripture" (Article 8). The Church has "authority in Controversies of Faith", but is itself under the authority of God's written Word (Article 20). Councils may err— "wherefore things ordained by them as necessary to salvation have neither strength nor authority, unless it may be declared that they be taken out of Holy Scripture" (Article 21).

There is very real authority inherent in the message which we preach. The Christian believes that God has spoken, in a unique way, in the Person of His Son; not only in His teaching and His example, but supremely in His mighty redeeming acts. When St Paul summarised the essential content of the message which he brought to the Corinthians, nervy in himself but confidently assured about what he preached, he put it in credal form: that "Christ died for our sins ... that He was buried ... that He was raised ... that He was seen ..." (1 Cor. 15:3 ff.).

These are the mighty acts of God, to which nothing can be added, acts wrought out once and for all on the stage of human history. This is the *kerygma*, the thing preached; this is the *parathéké*, the sacred treasure committed to us. It can only be expressed in a great series of indicative verbs: God loved; God gave; the Word was made flesh; Christ died for our sins; He was raised by the power of God. These indicatives are the very stuff of which the Gospel is made. There is no good news without them. It is only in the light of them that we can ever face the imperatives of Christianity; but when we have grasped, or been grasped by the indicatives, we find the imperatives to be not only possible but a joy to obey. There is authority inherent in the message itself, for it is the very word of God to *homo viator*.

The expertise of the pulpit—for preaching is, *inter alia*, a craft the practice of which calls for steady and life-long application—can only be learned slowly and, it may well be, with a strange mixture of pain and joy. But the more it is learned, the greater will be the measure of the preacher's authority. This, however, is only one—though it is one of the greatest—of the spheres in which a priest's expertise and his authority will go hand in hand. The skill of the administrator, of the chairman, of the sick-visitor, of the pastor, of the counsellor; these and a dozen others as they are learned will add the sureness of touch which leads the onlooker to say: "This man has the authority of one who knows his job." In an age such as this, the age of the professional, this is not un-important.

I turn for a moment, though with great diffidence (for I have had so far a bare thirteen years in the episcopate) to the particular exercise of authority which attaches to the episcopal office.

There are occasions when a clergyman says to his bishop: "I will go to such and such a benefice if you, as my bishop, order me to do so." I think there are occasions when such an order is called for and must be given. I can only say that in my own experience, I have hardly ever given such an order. I believe that, shall we say in ninety-nine cases out of a hundred, it is vastly preferable to follow that principle which we noticed in our Lord's handling of men, and to give direction rather than directions.

Thus anything approaching domineering authority is avoided, and the man who seeks his bishop's advice is helped to grow towards maturity of judgment. Let the bishop think through the problems with the man concerned. Let him ask questions which will help him to get his thinking straight and which will disentangle the primary issues from the secondary. Let him pray with him, or at least assure him of a place in his prayers, and then leave the decision to him.

Is such a source of action the avoidance of the exercise of authority? I think not. It may well be the exercise of authority at its best and most sensitive. Thus Albert H. van den Heuvel can write: "In order to be able to give authority to any conclusion or event, the recipient must have had some part in its establishment. That is true for parental authority and for intellectual authority, *but also for spiritual authority*." (*The Humiliation of the Church*, p. 82. The italics are mine).

The question of the right size of dioceses is much under discussion at the moment. It is not wholly unrelated to our theme of authority. The matter has been brought to the fore by Leslie Paul in his *The Deployment and Payment of the Clergy* (1964). There he makes much of the loneliness of the clergy and the need for smaller dioceses than those which we have now in England—dioceses in which the bishop can in truth exercise real pastoral *episcope*, knowing his men and being intimately known by them. There is much to be said for this view, though in fairness it should be added that probably hardly ever before has there been such closeness of contact between the bishop and his clergy as now exists. This is partly due to the ease of modern transport and partly to a new, or perhaps one had rather say revived, grasp of the meaning of episcopacy.

Nevertheless, there is a measure of loneliness among some clergy, as one who has charge of a large diocese, predominantly rural in character, can well judge. Nor is this loneliness only due to a refusal on the part of some clergy to share in the fellowship which chapters, ruri-decanal conferences and so on provide, for such men are rare, I am thankful to say. Loneliness is a reality to be reckoned with and its elimination, or at least its amelioration, must be worked at. But is the answer to be found (to put it vulgarly) in the bishop being so close to his clergy that he is constantly breathing down their necks? Is this the best kind of episcopal authority? Is the best pastoral work in the parishes obtained this way? I very much doubt it. Is there not, rather, something to be said for the diocesan bishop at least having a measure of detachment which will enable him to view his intimate diocesan and parochial problems against a wide background and in a broad context? It would be to the loss of the British people if at least some of her diocesan bishops were not national figures.

The best parish priests, I am convinced, do their best parish work if they are given a large measure of responsibility and are left room for the exercise of a large measure of individuality. It is, of course, of first importance that every clergyman in a diocese should know, from the day of his ordination, that he has the right, at any time and on any matter, to go straight to his bishop for consultation and advice. And it should go without saying that the *first* call on a bishop's time and care should be his clergy, their families and their problems. But given these basic facts, and given the constant movement of the bishop up and down his diocese, it may well be that beneficent episcopal authority cannot always be measured in terms of the smallness of the diocese over which he presides. Now that, in view of recent Church legislation, "lawful authority" has been more closely defined, it should be possible to exercise pastoral authority without clipping the wings of local priestly responsibility, initiative and individuality.

It is a fact that many of the main issues exercising the minds of churchmen at the present time have in common problems connected with authority. The revision of Canon Law, which has occupied the Convocations and the House of Laity for many years, is basically concerned with authority in the governing of the Church's life. Now that the work is virtually completed, we may ask ourselves whether we have not at times succumbed to the temptation to legislate in detail and to give directions rather than direction. If, in fact, we have done so, our successors will not bless us. It has been a temptation to others than Christians to lay on men's backs legislative burdens grievous to be borne.

The matter of synodical government, which has perplexed the Church for many years and on which, we may hope, we shall soon see some definitive steps taken in England, has at its heart the problem of authority. Where shall this authority be found, in matters doctrinal as well as practical? Is it to be confined, at least in matters of doctrine, to the bishop sitting in synod with his clergy? Or have the laity the right to share with their brethren of the clergy in discussion of and decisions about matters theological and liturgical? The past few years have seen them doing this by courtesy. I am one of those who hope that the day will very shortly arrive when we shall see them doing so as of right. An authority shared among the whole *laos* of God will lead not to the impoverishment but to the enrichment of the Church of God. I take it that the promise of the gift of the Paraclete, of His leading and of His teaching, was made to the *whole* Church and that the whole Church has the right to go forward leaning on the reliability of that promise.

"By this shall all men know that ye are My disciples, if ye have love one to another" (St John 13:35). It is likely that a future historian of the Church of the first six decades of the twentieth century will have to record that the most remarkable feature of its life has been a growth in love and understanding between different branches of the Church. The century opened with an appalling ignorance existing between the adherents of different traditions. Misunderstanding was rife. Rivalry often took the place of co-operation and asperity the place of a desire to learn and appreciate. But during these decades, and especially since the Edinburgh Conference of 1910, the founding of the World Council of Churches, and the visit of Archbishop Geoffrey Fisher to Pope John, there has grown up a great yearning for actual unity and a measure of loving understanding and of co-operation in evangelism and in Christian philanthropy which could hardly have been dreamed of when the twentieth century dawned. For this we may thank God and take courage as we move steadily forward to further organic union.

Especially may we be thankful that we can detect a growth in the authority with which the Church can speak when the leaders of the main traditions unite to make their voices heard. Disunity results inevitably in lack of authority. How can a world, terribly torn by divisions of race and ideology, be expected to hear the voice of a Church which itself has not found the way to unity? "Physician heal thyself," the world may sadly say, and hardly be blamed for saying it. But with the return of unity— a unity based on the twin foundations of love and truth—will come a return of authority. "By this shall all men know . . ." "May they all be one: as Thou, Father, art in Me, and I in Thee, so also may they be in us, *that the world may believe* that Thou didst send Me" (St John 17:21). The need for an authoritative voice, proclaiming the word of God and declaring the will of God, should act as a constant spur to those whose task it is to promote the unity of the Church; and that does not mean only those who attend the great world conferences dedicated to that end!

We have imagined a future historian writing up the tale of the Church of the first six or seven decades of this century. If he will have to start his story with a substantial section given to the subject of Church unity, it is likely that only second in importance will be the subject of the handing over of authority by the Church of the West to the leaders of the Churches of the emergent nations. No longer does the white missionary go as part of a great and growing Empire structure, the whiteness of his skin suggesting that he may dominate while others serve! Rather, his white skin often constitutes an embarrassment and his national background is a cause of stumbling. He may only remain if he is prepared, in actual fact, to *serve*. So it is that we have watched the handing over by the white races of positions of leadership to men whose faces are dark and, very frequently, whose grand-parents knew nothing of Christianity. Authority has passed from West to East.

A glance at the photograph of the Lambeth Conference of 1968 as compared with that of 1958 or 1948 will illustrate this, as will the fact that during the primacy of Archbishop Fisher four different provinces were inaugurated in Africa: West Africa (1951), Central Africa (1955), East Africa (1960) and Uganda (1961). For all the tremblings and forebodings, is not this cause for unfeigned rejoicing? After all, final authority belongs neither to the Church of the West nor of the East, but to the Lord of the Church. "Full authority in heaven and on earth has been committed to Me. Go forth therefore and make all nations My disciples; baptise ... and teach them ..." (St Matthew 28:18). Such authority as we have is an authority delegated to us by Him and held in trust by us for only as long as He wills.

We began this essay with a reference to the authority which marked the life and teaching of Jesus, and we sought to distinguish between an *authority* in response to which men found— and find—their freedom and life and an *authoritarianism* which cramps and confines. When, on All Saints' Day, 1966, Professor Ian Ramsey was consecrated Bishop of Durham in York Minster, the sermon was preached by the Master of St John's College, Cambridge, Canon J. S. Boys Smith. I quote an extract from that sermon, for, in reverting to that with which I began, it adds point, as I could not, to the principles which I have tried to outline: "He taught them," we are told, "as one having authority, and not as their scribes" (St Matthew 7:29). What kind of authority was this? What sort of following, of obedience, did it, and does it still, demand? Does it demand that the following be absolute, unconditional, that we must (if need arise) leave *all* and follow? To that the answer is Yes. But does that mean that the following of Christ is to be unquestioning, unsearching? Such a following would not be the following of *Christ* at all. It would be to miss the very heart, all the originality and promise of His summons. Had His call been to a blind following, its authority must long since have ceased to carry weight.

"His demand was very different—both higher and harder. He told us that we must have the single eye, that we must *look*, look with direct, unprejudiced sight, look that we may *see*. You cannot tell in advance what it will be that, when you look, you will see; and it is for no man to prescribe it for you. But you can be sure that, unless you look with the eye that is single, it will not be the truth that you will see. And remember that, if no man may prescribe for you what you shall see, still less may you seek to predetermine it yourself. Your duty, and your privilege, is to look that you yourself may see.

"This governs and pervades the teaching of Jesus. It is this, that He Himself had the single eye, single and searching, and that His call to others was to look as He looked that they might see as He saw, and in the end it is only this that gave, and still gives, to His summons and to Himself, an unconditional authority, an authority that derives from insight and rules by conviction."

Faith and Prayer

I BEGIN BY defining our terms. It does not matter if the defining takes up quite a large part of this article, for if we can get our thinking straight about each of these great words, then it should not be too difficult to join them one to the other in a meaningful relationship.

"Faith," so the small boy is reported to have said, "is believing what you know to be untrue." His definition is all too close to what many do in fact think about a word that is at the very heart of New Testament Christianity. Shut your eyes, swallow with determination, take a deep breath, and say the Apostles' creed—*that* is faith! But this is a travesty of the real thing.

"I do not believe in any creed." So William Temple said. If these seem surprising words to come from an Archbishop, remember he went on to say that he used certain creeds to express, conserve and deepen what he believed. But *his faith was not in a formula, however historic. It was a distinctly personal thing and it rested on a person, Christ the Lord.* It could not be expressed in a series of propositions. Though it had an intelligent and an intellectual foundation, it was more than a matter of the intellect. "I believe *that* . . ." will not suffice to express what the Christian wants to say. "I believe *in* one God . . . and *in* one Lord Jesus Christ . . . and *in* the Holy Spirit, the Life-giver." It is not without significance that the Greek preposition is *eis* used with the accusative, that is to say, it expresses motion, transference of trust *from* self *to* God as He has revealed Himself in Christ.

Article in the Methodist Preacher's Handbook, *1972.*

When Jesus, walking by the Lake of Galilee, called two brothers and received from them their response ("they rose and followed Him"), that was the beginning of a faith-relationship. Though it may well be that these young men had known Jesus from boyhood, in fact they knew very little about the real significance of the One who so imperiously and yet so graciously called them. But, that great day, they responded with all that they knew of themselves to all that they then knew of Christ. That is faith. It was tiny as a grain of mustard seed. Thirty years later Peter knew a great deal more about Christ (not to say about himself!) than he did on the day of his call. But that is the way of faith. It begins in a small way. It has such vast potentialities of growth.

Faith begins as an intensely personal response to the outgoing love of God manifested supremely in the Christ of Nazareth, of the Cross and of the empty tomb. But it is soon seen to have an equally important corporate aspect. The "believer", the man of faith, finds himself incorporated into "the blessed company of all faithful people", and it is here, within that company, that he finds his nourishment and the secret of his growth. Here the life of faith is strengthened by the ministry of Word and Sacrament. It is "with all God's people" that he comes to grasp "what is the breadth and length and height and depth of the love of Christ and to know it, though it is beyond knowledge" (Eph. 3:18–19). "The fellowship," as Anderson Scott used to remind us, "is the organ of insight."

So much—or, rather, so little—about *faith*. What about *prayer*?

It would be easy to say that prayer is conversation between God and His children, and there would be this to be said for that definition: it makes clear the two-way nature of the communication. But it would be an inadequate definition. Instead of the word "conversation", let us use the word "intercourse". For intercourse can take place in a wide variety of ways. Indeed, it can be entirely silent.

Here are two old people. They have known one another down the long years. They have lived together in all the intimacies of married life; they have laughed together; they have suffered together, and in so doing, have grown together till in very truth they are one. There are many ways in which they have intercourse together, but not least is the intercourse, entirely silent, of just being together, content with one another. Is not this one aspect and a very important aspect—of prayer?

"I look at Him, and He looks at me; and we are one together." It matters little whether or not words are spoken. The beloved is consciously in the presence of the great Lover. That is enough.

This is surely where faith and prayer meet. It is intensely personal, this meeting of the finite with the infinite. When the man of faith presses his littleness close to God's greatness in prayer, his ignorance close to God's wisdom, his weakness close to God's strength, yes, and (greatly daring) his sinfulness close to God's holy forgiving, it is personal indeed. But faith, as we have seen, is like that—personal contact with God, beginning in so small a way but having within it the potentiality of almost infinite growth.

But to leave it there would be to truncate the true meaning of prayer. For if prayer, like faith, is a deeply personal thing, it is also, again like faith, a fundamentally corporate thing. If, as we have seen, faith functions in the setting of "all God's people", so does prayer.

I believe that it is because we fail to realise this that we become so discouraged in our praying and so despondent about it that we either relapse into mere formality or give it up altogether. God is so great; the universe is so huge and so mysterious; life, suffering, death are so far beyond our comprehension. What is the point of our feeble little attempts at prayer, the broadcasts of tiny individuals in a great echoing vastness?

There are at least three errors in such an argument. The first (on which we need not delay, for the idea of "intercourse" has already answered it) is that prayer is our broadcast to the Almighty. It is not. It is our communion with Him and His with us. It is intercourse.

The second is that it fails to appreciate that, at the centre of the "great echoing vastness", beats the heart of a loving God. Jesus dared to speak of that God in terms of Fatherhood and Kingship, that is to say, of love and authority. Marry those two concepts and you will begin to see what God is like. Was it C. S. Lewis who used to warn us not to think of God as a great managing director who could not be bothered with the newest little office boy? God's fatherly care reaches to the least significant, for "significance" is a human term which has no significance for the heavenly Father!

The third error in the argument is that it over-individualises prayer. It fails to perceive its essentially corporate nature. When I pray, it is not one little piper piping alone. It is certainly one individual, but *joining in an orchestra.*

The whole Church of God makes up that orchestra. It has been playing ever since there was a Church. It began at least as long ago as Abraham. It took on a new dimension when those two pairs of brothers made their response by the Lake of Galilee. It gained a fresh jubilation at Pentecost. Now its members come from all over the world, and the greater part of them have gone on ahead. But it is one orchestra. It is unlimited by space or time—it transcends both. It goes on—and will go on till the Great Day. And then all its disharmonies will fade away. Meanwhile, when I pray—even when I am at my coldest and most formal—I "chip in"; I take my part in the great orchestra; I am one with angels and archangels and all the company of heaven. That helps me to get my perspectives of prayer right.

Prayer is then at once an intensely individual activity and it is a corporate activity. It is the response of the beloved to the great Lover, of the child to the Father. But it is more. It is the response of the subject to the King—for Jesus, when He spoke of God, did so in terms not only of Fatherhood but also of Kingship. The reign of God seems to have been the dominant theme of His teaching. We must pause here.

When I come before God in prayer, I come as a subject who would learn the meaning and the implications of that relationship. Really to pray is to stand to attention in the presence of the King and to be prepared to take orders from Him. It is to concentrate into these few moments what should increasingly be the whole attitude of my life, namely, obedience to the will of God, in things great and small, as He sees fit to make that will known.

When Jesus prayed, "Thy will be done, Thy Kingdom come"; when, near the end of His earthly life, He prayed, "Not my will, but Thine be done", He focussed into those few words a *life-attitude*. It is likely that *He* attained that attitude, and so was able to pray those prayers, not without difficulty. "He *learned* obedience", and learned it "through suffering" (Heb. 5:8).

To "delight to do Thy will" and to do it "with my whole heart" is not likely to come easily to us self-centred sinners, for the sinless Son of Man had His struggles! Hence the need for those oft-repeated moments of will-focusing which, increasingly over the years, will merge into a life-attitude. The saints would appear to tell us that about the *only* prayer that matters is: "Thy will be done." To pray that prayer perfectly, to align my little will with the "good, acceptable and perfect" will of God—that is the end greatly to be desired. That is the goal of discipleship. Then the prayer "Thy will be done" is not uttered in a minor tone as a kind of recognition of the inevitable, but as a triumph-cry—this is the best that can happen to any man living!

St Luke records a remarkable word of Jesus which none of the other Evangelists mentions. The New English Bible renders it: "You are the men who have stood firmly by me in my times of trial" (St Luke 22:28). The setting of the saying is a sombre one. The Eucharist has been instituted. Jesus has told His friends that, in the little group around the table, there is one who will betray Him. Then—of all times and places!—a dispute breaks out as to which of them should rank highest, and Jesus has to give them an object-lesson in the meaning of service. Against that dismal background, He pays His men a glorious tribute: "you are the men who have stood firmly by me in my times of trial." They had been with Him when the crowds in their thousands hung upon His words. That was easy. But, when the crowds disappeared and the numbers who followed Him were small, when the people grew suspicious and their leaders violently opposed Him, still those men stood firmly by Him. That was hard. And it was splendid.

The worst lay ahead, and Jesus was quick to warn them. "Satan has been given leave to sift all of you like wheat." "Hosanna" is to give place to "crucify", and that within hours. "But Simon, Simon, I am concentrating my prayer on *you*" (the plural has given way to the singular) "that your faith may not fail." After all, he was to be the leader. He had singular gifts in that direction—and singular weaknesses too! The great test was round the corner—and with the test, dismal defeat. Talk about unanswered prayer! "I have prayed for you"—and Simon squirmed under the sneer of a servant-girl, and denied his Lord thrice. Unanswered prayer? Yes, and no. Immediately unanswered, yes. In the longer view, wonderfully answered. The prayer was "that your *faith* may not fail". A relationship had been established between Jesus and Simon Peter, a relationship of a most intimate and personal kind. It was to undergo the most fearful stress. From Peter's side it was to be strained to breaking-point, but not from the side of Jesus. Though Peter was unfaithful, Christ was not. After the cross and resurrection came renewal and re-commissioning and, at Pentecost, re-empowering. The faith relationship, established by the Lake of Galilee, strengthened in those "times of trial", did not finally break. On the contrary, over the next thirty years and more, it was to grow infinitely stronger, more resilient, more deep. Like his friend St Paul, Peter was to be "in journeyings oft" and, according to the stories in the Acts, he was to experience the testing fires. If (as there is good evidence to believe) the First Epistle of Peter comes from his hand, it reflects a situation of severe testing, but it reflects also a "faith which has stood the test" and "a joy too great for words" (I Peter 1:7 & 8).

We need not doubt that the exhortation (in 4:7) to a life "given to prayer" sprang out of his own experience of just such a life lived down the long years. The relationship of faith was nourished by the life of prayer, and in the process acquired a depth which Peter could never have imagined back in the Galilean days.

The last quarter of a century, the years since the end of the Second World War, have been "times of trial" for Christ's Church. While the Church has made immense strides in Africa and Latin America, here in Britain and in North America the winds have been blowing fierce and cold. Active, practising Christians have been seen for the minority that they are. Many have lost their faith in any positive proclamation of a Gospel rooted in the historic facts of God's revelation in Christ, and have reached the point where they feel that they can only engage in activities of a social nature as expressing generally accepted Christian principles. They can do little more than ask questions; they cannot "declare". Others have become so absorbed in re-structuring the Church that their vision of what the Church really is has become clouded. Others, again, have so concentrated their energies on such subjects as ecumenism or liturgical revision as to give the impression that these are ends in themselves. The best has been submerged by the good. The fires of a personal devotion to our Lord have burned low. Prayer has become formal—indeed, many have questioned whether prayer, in the sense that the Church has understood it down the long centuries, will avail for "man come of age".

Perhaps two things are called for in these "times of trial". The first is just that endurance for which, so St Luke tells us, Jesus commended His followers. To some, endurance would seem to be a very humdrum virtue. But in the New Testament it is one of the most highly commended. The grace to stick it through when others defect; the power to hold to the essentials when others concentrate on the peripheral; the ability to face, undiscouraged, the implications of belonging to a minority movement, in fact to endure—and endure joyfully—the shame of the Cross; all this, in part, is the meaning of Christian endurance.

This is a very unspectacular virtue, but it is one of fundamental importance. It is commended of our Lord to be honourable among His men. I can conceive of no higher honour than that, at the end of the journey, He should say of me and my fellow Christians: "You are the men who have stood firmly by me in my times of trial." The relationship of faith, at once so intimately personal and so powerfully corporate, has been deepened by the life of prayer—and it has stood the test.

The second thing that is called for in these "times of trial" is a new grasp of the meaning of *hope*. After all, hope is faith-looking-forward. Hope is confidence in the God who is not only the God of Abraham, Isaac and Jacob, but the God "who *will become* what He will become", the God not only of the historic past, but of the future.

The man of faith, who is necessarily also the man of hope, knows that God has not abdicated. He is the God of surprises. "The best is yet to be" precisely because "best of all, God is with us."

In an article in *The Critic* (November-December, 1971), entitled "Why are you a man of hope even in these days?", Cardinal Suenens wrote powerfully about hope:

I am hopeful, not for human reasons or because I am optimistic

by nature, but because I believe in the Holy Spirit present in
His Church and in the world—even if people don't know His
name. I am hopeful because I believe that the Holy Spirit is
still the creating Spirit, and that He will give us every morning
fresh freedom, joy and a new provision of hope, if we open
our soul to Him.

The story of the Church is a long story, filled with the wonders
of the Holy Spirit: we must remember the saints and the
prophets bringing, in hopeless times, a gulfstream of graces and
new lights to continue on the road.

I believe in the surprises of the Holy Spirit. The Council was
such a surprise, and Pope John was another. They took us
aback. Why should we think that God's imagination and love
might be exhausted?

On similar lines, Bishop F. R. Barry in his autobiography,
Period of my Life, wrote:

There are certainly strong reasons for fear. But there are
stronger reasons for hope. I have hope for the future in which
our grandchildren will grow up because I believe in God and
the providential government of history. I believe that God
raised Jesus from the dead and committed Himself to the cause
of Christ as His own cause. Good, yet undreamt of, is
within man's reach if we have the faith and courage to take it.
Have we?

And again:

I believe in God through the Man. Therefore I am able to
believe in man, and, under God, in a future for man, and the
victory of good over evil. And though the Church may seem
now to be in decline—*all* institutions seem now to be in decline
—yet, because I am able to hold to the Easter faith, I believe it
will rise again in power and glory.

All this has an immediate bearing on prayer. The Christian, in
entering into a faith-relationship with God in Christ, has by the
same token entered into a hope-relationship with that God. It
follows, then, that when, in prayer, he approaches God, he does

so in a "waiting attitude of expectation", in a stance of questioning. Study the Psalms, that prayer-book of the ancient Jewish Church, and you will see how many of the prayers are in the form of questions put by the petitioner to God. This is not quite the same as the point made earlier, that prayer is standing to attention in the presence of God and awaiting His orders. This, rather, is coming into the presence of God, with the question posed: "What surprises have You got today, Lord? For You are the God of the new, the hitherto unrevealed, the unexpected."

So it is that an article entitled "Prayer and Faith" might equally well be entitled "Prayer and Hope", for, as we have said, hope is faith-looking-forward, and ours is the God of hope (Rom. 15:13). But it might also equally well be entitled "Prayer and Love", for living prayer issues from a relationship with the God of love who Himself makes the first move towards us, and by His Spirit of love, is at work within us when we pray.

After all, outside the room where a man is praying, the appropriate notice is not so much: "Quiet! Man at prayer", as "Look out! *God* at work!"

Spirit of Flame

FOR THE LAST half century or more—and this is a point I am constantly making—in the sphere of Christian doctrine, our attention has been focused on the doctrine of the Church more than on any other subject. Since the great conference held at Edinburgh in 1910, we have been busy pondering on, writing on, conferring on the Church—its nature, its unity and disunity, its glory and its shame, its function in society as the Body of Christ, and so on. This has been good. It has led, among other beneficial results, to a concern for re-union which has led us a long way and has already resulted in much joint worship and activity. Indeed, some of the younger Churches are striding on ahead of us. Nigeria, for example, is about to consummate a union of the Anglican, the Methodist and the Presbyterian Churches, and it looks as if Ghana will not be long in following Nigeria's example. But in many other parts, Great Britain included, the march towards union is very slow. There is something of a log-jam, to use a phrase familiar to Canadians. Why is this? I do not know, but I ask this question: Have we been so occupied with the doctrine of the Church that we have given little thought to the Person and work of the Spirit? Have we concentrated on the Body and neglected the Breath? Have we studied the limbs and neglected the Life? Have we been absorbed in the theology of the Church and almost by-passed Him through whom the Church came into being, the Lord, the Life-giver?

If the answer to these questions be "Yes", we may excuse ourselves by recalling that there is a certain "self-effacingness"

C. J. Cadoux Memorial Lecture, 24th February, 1965.

about the Holy Spirit. It is of the essence of His work to take of
the things of *Christ* and show them to us. "He shall not speak
of Himself." And we remember that in the early centuries of the
Church's history, attention fastened on the Person and work of
the Holy Spirit only after the Church had dealt with the doctrine
of the Person of Christ. All that is true. But it is no excuse for
twentieth-century Christians having a feeble and anaemic doctrine of the Third Person of the Blessed Trinity.

Frederick Denison Maurice, writing as long ago as 1849,
referred to "the reformation in our day, which I expect is to be
more deep and searching than that of the sixteenth century". He
prophesied that it would "turn upon the Spirit's presence and
life, as that did upon justification by the Son". Four years earlier,
he had written of the "one thing needful to speak of—the prophecy
of a breath which could come into (a dead, divided Church) and
make the dry bones unite and live". It looks as if Maurice, in this
as in so many other matters, was a prophet speaking before his
time. The twentieth-century Reformation has not come. Does its
coming hinge both upon our attention to the doctrine of the
Spirit and upon our obedience to Him who is Wind and Fire?

I turn to another aspect of the life of the Church to which we
must give heed today. I by-pass any reference to certain local
manifestations of Pentecostalism which have largely appeared
within the historic denominations in England, and ask my questions against the larger background of ecumenical life and thought.

We have been accustomed to think, in discussions about unity,
of the two elements which can generally be characterised as
Catholic and Protestant. But there is a third element which we
can neglect only by shutting our ears to facts which are shouting
at us. I refer to what can roughly be called the Pentecostal element.
Its roots are in the New Testament, even if some of its fruits are,
to our thinking, not always in strict accord with New Testament
teaching. If we do not see a great deal of it in this country, remember that in Latin America four out of five non-Roman
Christians are Pentecostals. We may complain that they are
deficient in many of the things we hold dear. We may complain
that their worship is at times noisy (a complaint that cannot be
levelled at least at most *Anglican* congregations!). But to pass
by on the other side and neglect what is one of the most extra-

ordinary features of religious life in the twentieth century is to show a lack of responsibility or an unreadiness to face evidence.

Why is it that these sects are growing at such a phenomenal rate? Is it possible that they have gifts of the Spirit which we have not? Do we need to heed the reminder of Bishop Stephen Neill that "not infrequently true religious life is to be found in the sects when it has died down in the orthodox; the nonconformists have been from time to time the salvation of the Church"? And if this offends you, as well it may, remember that one of the effects of the Holy Spirit on the members of the early Church was that they were so joyful that people thought they were drunk. And— if I may be allowed to press a point—may I ask when that accusation, *for identical reasons*, was levelled (a) against you as an individual, (b) against the church where you worship, and (c) against the Church of which the church where you worship is an integral part?

So far, I have touched on what I believe to be a weakness in the present ecumenical situation, due to a neglect of the doctrine of the Holy Spirit, His Person and work.

But I suspect that there is a weakness, in this same matter, to be seen in the field of pure theology. I suspect that, if you were to do a tour of theological libraries, you would find precisely what is to be found by an inspection of hymnals, namely, a good, vigorous section on the Church and a feeble, anaemic section on the Spirit! One could list some good books since H. B. Swete enriched the doctrine of the Spirit by his books in the first decade of this century, but how short and poor is that list compared with the flow of books on the Church in an identical period.

I will give only one example of the danger of soft-pedalling the doctrine of the Spirit, and I will give it to you through the comments of a percipient theologian.

Some of you will recall reading with great pleasure last year, as I did myself, Bishop Stephen Neill's book *The Interpretation of the New Testament, 1861–1961* (OUP). It is full of good things, as are all his books. Chapter 6 is entitled "Re-enter Theology". It consists of an appraisal of the work of four great theologians— Albert Schweitzer (b.1875), Karl Barth (b.1886), Edwyn Clement Hoskyns (b.1884) and Rudolf Bultmann (b.1884). Against the background of wide reading, Neill appraises their work with a critical but sympathetic eye. In the closing pages of the section on Bultmann, Neill fastens on this as the essential problem with which Bultmann is grappling, namely "that Jesus of Nazareth remains obstinately and irrevocably in the past; nineteen hundred years have sped away since He lived among men. How then are we to make Him present? How is the challenge implicit in the *Kerygma* to become a living and existential challenge to me?" The Bishop comments: "The whole work of Bultmann can be summed up as a gallant attempt to solve the problem, to make the challenge existential—without belief in the resurrection of Jesus Christ as something that actually happened, and without a doctrine of the Holy Spirit".

With regard to the resurrection, Neill says: "Can anything become historically significant, if it did not first actually happen? If words mean anything, the answer must be "no". Can Christ effect in me life through death, victory and deliverance from transitoriness, if He was not Himself first raised from the dead, literally and in the completeness of His manhood, by the glory of the Father? . . . . This is the burning question which will not stay for an answer." There is no doubt what the Bishop's answer would be, but this is not the point with which at the moment we are concerned. It is his second criticism which concerns us—the absence of a doctrine of the Holy Spirit, or, as he puts it, the "lack of a theology of the Holy Spirit, as the One through whom time and distance are annihilated, and through whom the Word of Jesus becomes the living and contemporary word, whether preached by the eloquent orator in the great cathdreal or read by the simple fishwife by the light of a guttering candle in her lonely room".

Then, just when we are sitting back, self-righteous in the belief that we have put our finger on the main weakness of Bultmann's theology, Neill stabs us with a home-thrust: "But who shall cast a stone? Polite references to the Holy Spirit at suitable intervals are to be heard in the preaching and worship of all the denominations. But who has developed a theology of the Holy Spirit that really does justice to the part that He plays in the whole New Testament revelation?" (pp. 233-5).

We shall do well to give heed to Stephen Neill's warning.

I believe that we need to pose quite a lot of questions. If they are old, then let us not be ashamed to ask them again, in the light of new knowledge and of the changed contemporary situation in the Church and in the world. For example, what is the significance of the biblical metaphor of wind and of fire in relation to the Spirit, in such passages as St John 3, Acts 2, and 1 Thessalonians 5:19 ("quench not the Spirit" or "do not stifle inspiration", NEB)? Certainly there is *power* in wind and fire. Wind breaks down barriers and blows away cobwebs, as well as renewing, reviving and freshening. Fire burns dross and brings about union by heat (as when, in welding, two hitherto separate pieces of metal are made one), as well as warming and comforting. I notice there is an element of chaos about wind and fire—a tornado is only wind in action. Have we not all seen a stately building after fire has ravaged it? Is there a hint here that God, though He is the God of order, is not always greatly impressed with our tidy schemes and that we may have to be prepared to see them blown to bits and burnt to cinders if the doing of His will is not to be inhibited?

Wind and fire are never *safe* elements. They are full of risk and danger. But, then, was not Abraham rash when he took the leap of faith and left the security of Ur for an unknown destination, with no finalised blue-print nor map in his hand? Was there not in his very faith that which is the human correlative to what in Deity is the unpredictability of wind and fire?

Or again, I would ask this question: Have we not often been guilty in our thinking of restricting the activity of the Holy Spirit to spheres which we label "sacred"? Have we not tended to shut up the Spirit within ecclesiastical barriers? To confine His working within the bounds of the Church, and to ignore, or at least to minimise His activity through those who are not Churchmen?

Last year I found myself writing as follows in regard to the prayer of our Lord "Thy Kingdom come":

To pray this prayer is to ask for something wider than the extension of the Church. It is a mistake to think of Church and Kingdom as synonymous. They are not. It is truer to think of the Church as the agent of the Kingdom. The sovereignty of God may be advanced, the Kingdom may "come", through those who are unconscious of being its agents. The *scientist* who, while acknowledging no allegiance to God, makes inroads against the forces of disease, is, unwittingly, advancing the Kingdom. The *politician* who lays the foundations of a peaceful society is advancing the Kingdom, inasmuch as God is a God of order and of peace, rather than of confusion and war. We may regret it—we do regret it—if that politician is not a committed Christian. We may hold—we do hold—that if he were to lay his foundations securely on Christian principles, his building would be the surer. But in so far as the forces of peace and truth are strengthened by his endeavours, so far is the Kingdom advanced. The *writer* who though not a Christian, writes beautiful and clean prose or poetry, advances the Kingdom. Wherever the bounds of beauty, truth and goodness are advanced there the Kingdom comes. Wherever the forces of darkness, disease and hate are driven back, there the Kingdom comes, and God enters in more fully to the sovereignty of His world.

I hope I carry you with me in this. But if those sentences be true, then we must gladly grant that, in every activity that makes for the health of the children of men, the operation of the Holy Spirit is to be seen. It was only after I had written those words, that his son, David Blunt, gave me a copy of the late Bishop Alfred Blunt's *Visitation Charge to the Clergy of the Diocese of Bradford*, given in 1947 and entitled "The Spirit of Life". In this excellent booklet, the Bishop works out in considerable detail the theme that—and I put it in the words of Milner-White (*Essays Catholic and Critical* p. 336)—"the paths of the Spirit do not move merely in the province of what we call so narrowly the 'religious' or still less 'ecclesiastical'." Blunt breaks a lance with the writer of the hymn "Our blest Redeemer, ere He breathed . . .", for there, he complains, "the Spirit's operation . . . reaches no wider than to inspirations towards religious or moral progress" (p. 7). He rejects the idea of "God as a Being of strictly limited interests, concerned only with piety and morality, i.e. with that which is the subject-matter of ecclesiastical people and ecclesiastical organisations" (p. 11). God the Holy Spirit "is 'the Life-giver', as our Creed calls Him. He is the Spirit of all life; and all life is therefore sacramental in its character, for within all life, God is at work. Nothing therefore is merely secular, in the sense that it may not be a vehicle of the Spirit and therefore 'spiritual' " (p. 15).

If this thesis be right, then our attitude to men of science and of industry will be one, not of suspicion but of co-operation. We shall view them as colleagues in so far as, in selfless research and toil, they are seeking the health of the peoples of the world.

Similarly, in our approach to men of other faiths, we should be more ready than were our forefathers to see the activity of the Holy Spirit in all seekers after truth. If we dare to follow Max Warren in holding that, *in some measure*, every nation is a chosen people, that is not to deny the uniqueness of Israel's call nor of the Judaeo-Christian revelation. It is only to insist that the Holy Spirit has not ceased to be at work, however much man has marred and dimmed the truth. In some sense, He has, through the Word, been lighting every man coming into the world (I am not ignorant of the fact that there is an alternate rendering of that mysterious phrase in St John 1:9). It is to assert that "of all that is good and true in any religion, He is the teacher; in any man's groping after God, however blindly done, the Spirit is the mover" (Blunt, *op. cit.*, p. 26). Milner-White, in the essay from which I have already quoted (an essay written in 1926 and now very dated but containing some valuable material) puts the point well: "Holy Spirit came by a people. This is not to say, that the Spirit of God worked only in Israel. He worked and works throughout His own poem of creation. But in Israel His life was concentrated, confined, guarded, fostered in an institution dominated by that vocation only" (p. 328).

In speaking in an ecumenical context, I have referred to the Spirit as the Spirit of unity. In speaking in a theological context, I have referred to the Spirit as the Spirit of Truth, the One who, according to the divine promise, is to lead His Church into all truth. But, above all else, the Spirit is the Spirit of *holiness*, and it is to this aspect of His Person and work that I must now briefly turn.

The sign of true sonship of God, says St Paul in a searching passage, is that we are, in fact, driven by the Spirit of God (Romans 8:14). The verb is identical with that used by St Luke (4:2) of the Son of God Himself in the wilderness. It was "a strong *driving* wind" which came upon the disciples at Pentecost (Acts 2:2). That is to say, it was a power *which got things done* in the realm of creative thinking (George Adam Smith's note that the marks of the Spirit outlined in Isaiah 11 are primarily intellectual is worth remembering). It got things done in the creation of Christlike character, so that cowards became martyrs, sinners became saints, the ugly became lovely, yet all the time their own individuality was retained, even heightened. To put it simply if profoundly—the likeness of Jesus was focussed in His followers by the operation of the Spirit of Jesus. That Spirit made Jesus so real to them that they saw Him as their great Contemporary. They lived with Him, even when His physical presence was withdrawn. They spoke with Him, even when they could no longer hear His voice. Their sonship of God was becoming an increasing reality as they companied with the Son of God, driven, led, activated by the Spirit of Jesus.

If this process of growth in holiness is to go on unimpeded, it will involve us in two things which, though apparently contradictory, are in fact complementary.

(1) *It will involve us in lonely encounter with God.* There is a loneliness about Christian experience. Just as I am born alone (though into a family), I am born again alone. I die alone. I face God alone. *In a sense,* I grow alone; for there are spiritual battles which, for all the goodwill in the world, no one else can fight for me, battles which have to do with pride, and purity, and service and holiness. What it will mean for me when the Wind and the Fire of the Holy Spirit come upon my sinfulness and selfishness, only I can find out in personal encounter with the living God.

(2) *It will involve us in close contact with the community of the Holy Spirit, the Church.* The Spirit is the Spirit of the *Body.* It is in the companionship of the Body that each limb grows to its fullness. It is "with all the saints" that we come to know the unknowable love of Christ, not sitting by ourselves in the pious detachment of an "I am better than thou" superiority.

The Church is the Body of Christ, through which He deigns to feed His people in the ministry of Word and Sacrament; through which He moves out to His world in the ministry of love and compassion.

The Church is the fellowship of the Holy Spirit, in which man's great barriers of sex and race and class are transcended in a unity of love and holiness.

I close with a prayer:

> Spirit of flame, whose living glow
> Was known to prophet, saint and seer,
> Where faith is cold Thy fire bestow,
> Where love is distant draw Thou near!
> Our fathers ventured in Thy power,
> So fill us in this present hour.

The Spirituality of the Gospels

"THE SPIRITUALITY OF the Gospels"—the phrase comes from a letter to me from Bishop Wheeler. This letter was the outcome of a talk which we had together in April 1968 when we discussed the subjects with which we might deal at this Conference, itself the brain-child of the Bishop. I suggested "Prayer". In a more recent letter the Bishop wrote: "I am sure we shall only maintain the right balance in the life of the Church by an increased stress on the priority of purely spiritual values."

This subject is one which concerns us very deeply as leaders in the Church, pastors of the flock in our capacities as bishops, theologians, retreat conductors, etc. *We* know how arid, how shallow our work becomes if our prayer life grows thin. As one who knows himself to be very much a beginner in the school of prayer, I should not have the impertinence to talk to you about how we should conduct ourselves in the life of prayer. But I should like to seek your help in answering this question: How can we help our clergy and our serious laity in the life of prayer? They look to us for guidance and leadership; how best can we give it to them? I mention three matters.

1. In the Anglican Communion, there are those who are abandoning what the Church down the ages has understood as the ordinary methods of prayer (though, of course, they maintain a certain round of public liturgical services). They pray at their work, or perhaps they regard their work as their prayer. Perhaps

Wood Hall Ecumenical Centre, 4th June, 1969.

as they walk the streets of their parishes and think of their people, they do so God-wards, and that is their prayer.

There is much that is valid in this. "Making mention of you in my prayers" is a common Pauline phrase of great insight (e.g. Eph. 1:16, Phil. 1:3, 1 Thess. 1:2, 2 Tim. 1:3, Philem. 4). So John Baillie can write in his *A Diary of Private Prayer*: "Prayer is, after all, but thinking towards God." And George MacDonald wrote to a friend: "I will not say that I will pray for you. But I shall think of God and you together." *But* may not this all be too easy a way out? Will it do to sit loose to regular periods of prayer and to almost regimented discipline? And to dismiss it with *laborare est orare*? It sounds good; but will it do? Of course we must learn to pray walking along the road. We must learn to shoot up a prayer before knocking on a door or answering a letter or beginning an interview. And the visit or the letter or the interview carried out in the name and for the sake of Christ is in a sense a prayer offered to God. But I do not believe that this is enough, if we are to grow, with roots healthily downwards and fruit abundantly upward. This *by itself* lays us open to all the perils of activism, which one of my clergy recently described as one of the main diseases in the Church today. By activism I mean the refusal to stop, to think, to read, to listen, to resolve; the confusion of the perspiration of activity with the inspiration of God.

I came across the following in a book of Fr C. S. Dessain entitled *Why Pray?* sent to me at the instigation of the Bishop of Leeds:

Why is it that prayer requires to be justified? By all accounts a number of Christians are questioning its value, undermining it and giving it up. They maintain that activity in helping our neighbour, concern for him, takes the place of prayer, or rather is prayer – in loving our neighbour we find God. There is a truth, or rather, a half-truth here, to which we must return, but half-truths can often do more harm than genuine error, which is more easily detected. The ordinary earthly man, the average man finds it so difficult to pray, clutches so readily at an excuse for not praying, that those Christians who encourage him and provide him with an excuse, bear a serious responsibility. The writing by Christians about adapting ourselves to the secular age in which we live, about our duty of serving the community will have much to answer for, if they disparage prayer or omit it from their scheme of things. In Germany the teaching of some modern Christians is summed up in the phrase "God is only a code-word for human togetherness". Instead of a living religion which puts men in immediate relationship with a personal God, we are in danger of having an ethical system linked with a vague and pantheistic sentiment about the world.

Much is heard today of "religionless Christianity". To many who use it somewhat cavalierly, it means the throwing over not only of set forms of service but of those disciplines of the spiritual life which, in one form or another, have marked the Church all down the ages. But let us be careful here. Eberhard Bethge, who was Dietrich Bonhoeffer's closest friend and who has become his definitive biographer, has said: "The isolated use and handing down of the famous term 'religionless Christianity' has made Bonhoeffer the champion of an undialectical, shallow modernism which obscures all that he wanted to tell us about the living God" (quoted in Mary Bosanquet: *The Life and Death of Dietrich Bonhoeffer*, p. 279). To quote Bethge again: "Secret discipline without worldliness becomes pure ghetto; worldliness without secret discipline pure boulevard." Now Bonhoeffer escapes the perils both of ghetto and of boulevard, of withdrawal from the world into an "other-worldliness" which is un-Christlike, and of involvement in the world ("boulevard-ism") which neglects withdrawal for thought, communion with God, prayer.

Let us never talk about "religionless Christianity" with a kind of nod of acknowledgment to Bonhoeffer until we have read his life. If ever there was a man who learnt and practised the discipline of daily withdrawal, who worked at his prayer life, it was Bonhoeffer. Listen to this: "Our relationship with God must be practised, otherwise we shall not find the right note, the right word, the right language when He comes upon us unawares. We have to learn the language of God, learn it with effort. We must work at it, if we too would learn to converse with Him; prayer too must be practised as part of our work" (*op. cit.*, p. 70).

An indispensable part of this daily withdrawal was, for Bonhoeffer, the slow reading of the Bible. In a letter to a friend he wrote: "I read (the Bible) in the morning and the evening, often during the day, as well, and every day I consider a text which I have chosen for the whole week, and try to sink deeply into it, so as really to hear what it is saying. I know that without this I could not live properly any longer. And I certainly could not believe ..." (*op. cit.*, p. 110). "This steady attempt to follow Jesus," says Mary Bosanquet of Bonhoeffer, "was supported by the inspiration of the daily reading and prayer which was now a discipline never omitted, and whose power was penetrating ever deeper into the hidden roots of his life, to issue more and more frequently as the years went by in the direct and powerful insights which so often set him apart from those who were not capable of this kind of perception" (*op. cit.*, p. 148).

In *L'Osservatore Romano* (24th April, 1969), there was an interesting report of an address given by the Pope in reply to an address given by Mgr Willebrands, who was accompanied by Fr Abbott at an international Biblical Conference held in Rome. In that address, His Holiness said: "In the course of each day there are many things to which We must give Our attention for the good of the Church and for the good of souls everywhere, but an occasion like this meeting with you today gives Us the welcome opportunity to stress the fundamental importance of God's revealed Word in all that We do and say. 'The word of God should be available at all times', declared the Second Vatican Council. Yes, always, and easily, and ever more widely. It is not only priests, religious brothers and sisters who should have the Scriptures, read them, meditate on them, and meet Christ our Lord daily in this way. As the Second Vatican Council said, 'all the faithful' should have easy access to the Scriptures, in the liturgy, through the Scripture readings and the homily, and also in daily private life. All are called to this meeting with Christ our Lord."

This was a fine follow-up to the statements of Vatican II, particularly in that section entitled *Sacred Scripture in the Life of the Church: Documents of Vatican II*, p. 125-128. I quote but one sentence: "Just as the life of the Church grows through persistent participation in the Eucharistic ministry, so we may hope for a new surge of spiritual vitality from intensified veneration for God's Word which 'lasts for ever' ".

I now want to mention a subject closely related to this. I believe that we need help—and that we need to give help—in the matter of the Offices. I am aware of a restlessness about the regular use of the Offices on the part of some of the clergy, perhaps particularly of the younger ones. I understand this, for I am one who only came to appreciate their value after some years in the ministry. A group of liturgiologists from the Anglican and Free Churches, with an observer from the Church of Rome, produced *The Daily Office* (SPCK and Epworth Press, 1969) which puts forward suggestions for a daily Office which is shorter and more varied than our present one and which, while embodying traditional elements familiar to Anglicans, seeks to meet a need felt by a significant number of Free Churchmen. I believe that there is room for experiment and enrichment in this field. The laity as well as the clergy need a simple structure of daily devotion, and I am glad to see that some work has been done on this in a booklet by John Wilkinson entitled *Family and Evangelistic Services* (CIO).

2. We need help—and we need to give help also—in attaining and maintaining a right balance in worship and prayer between awe and intimacy.

Awe is the antiseptic element in religion. The suppliant addresses God as Father, but he immediately remembers that the Father is "in heaven". "God is in heaven and thou upon earth . . ." This element of awe is reflected in our traditional prayers. It is resented by some moderns who maintain that we are morbidly obsessed with our sinfulness and insignificance. They would say that we tend to grovel in the presence of God: "We are not worthy so much as to gather up the crumbs . . ." Is such resentment right? Or are we in the Church infected by the egalitarianism of an age whose children call their fathers "Pop" and whose junior clergy talk to their bishops with their hands in their pockets? How far is it right to let the current rebellion against ideas of empire invade our religion? Certainly the idea of God as the great King is a strongly biblical one, and one of the two great concepts of Jesus was that of the Kingdom with its implied concept of God as Monarch. By all means let us stand or sit to pray. By all means let us call God "You". But let us beware lest the antiseptic element of awe fold up its tent and silently steal away.

In tension with this we hold to the other great concept of God as Father, with the implied concept of the Church as a family. Joachim Jeremias has brought this home in his study of the word "*abba*". He wrote:

With the help of my assistants I have examined the prayer literature of ancient Judaism—a large, rich literature, all too little explored. The result of this examination was that in no place in this immense literature is this invocation of God as *abba* to be found ... *Abba* was an everyday word, a homely, family word. No Jew would have dared to address God in this manner. Jesus did it always, in all His prayers which are handed down to us, with one single exception, the cry from the cross: "My God, My God, why hast Thou forsaken Me?"

Jeremias then draws the implications of this for our own prayers: "In the Lord's Prayer Jesus authorises His disciples to repeat the word *abba* after Him. He gives them a share in His sonship and empowers them, as His disciples, to speak with their heavenly Father in just such a familiar, trusting way."

Similarly, C. K. Barrett can write: "Jesus was aware in a peculiarly intense and intimate way that God was His Father." St Paul took the matter up in Romans 8:16 and Galatians 4:6. How seriously has recent spirituality taken the idea of "boldness" (see especially Hebrews 4:16 and 10:19, 1 John 3:21, 5:14, etc.)? Gordon S. Wakefield in a valuable booklet *The Life of the Spirit Today* (Epworth Press, 1968), writing of New Testament prayer says: "There is more of joy, expectancy, and triumph in it than of grief and penitence, though it is always mindful of Christ's passion as well as His victory." Perhaps it is because so many of us fail to have an adequate grasp of the significance of God's acts in Christ that our prayer fails to echo those notes. "The solid fact of what God has done is always the 'perch' (so to speak) from which Christian prayer takes its flight and to which it returns" (C. F. D. Moule, *Colossians*, p. 48).

The prayer *Veni, Creator Spiritus*, scarcely reflects New Testament pneumatology. J. E. L. Oulton points out that Christians of the early centuries would never have thought of praying such a prayer, for the knowledge that God had already given them His Holy Spirit was clear in their minds. (*Holy Communion and Holy Spirit* pp. 130–135). And H. B. Swete says: "The attitude of the primitive Church towards the Spirit was rather one of joyful welcome than of invocation; the cry *Veni, Creator Spiritus* belongs to a later age when the Spirit was sought and perhaps expected,

G

but not regarded as a guest who had already come, and come to abide" (*The Holy Spirit in the New Testament*, p. 96). That is well said.

Here—in awe and boldness—there is a tension which I do not attempt to resolve. Perhaps it is *in* this very tension that the virility of prayer is to be found. I do not think it will be found in the lessening of either element in our personal and corporate dealings with God.

3. Do we need to look again—and to help our people to look again—at the idea of the *interceding* Christ? The idea is certainly rooted in St Luke 22:32. J. B. Lightfoot in his *Ordination Addresses*, p. 135, writes: " 'I have prayed for thee.' What else shall we need if only we realise this! Christ interceding for me, Christ concentrating His prayer on me, Christ individualising His merits for me, Christ pleading for me His atoning blood before the Eternal Throne!"

The idea is developed in Romans 8:34 and Hebrews 7:25, two different but converging strands of New Testament evidence. I believe that H. B. Swete's work on this idea is still valuable, not least his *The Ascended Christ*. ". . . the intercession of the Ascended Christ is not a prayer, but a life. The New Testament does not represent Him as an *orante*, standing ever before the Father, with outstretched arms, like the figures in the mosaics of the catacombs, and with strong crying and tears pleading our cause in the presence of a reluctant God; but as a throned Priest-King, asking what He will from a Father who always hears and grants His request. Our Lord's life in heaven is His prayer."

St Paul speaks of another intercessor in Romans 8:26 ff., the Holy Spirit who interprets our groanings which can find no words, into the ears of the Father, *coming to our aid* in His gracious activity (the verb is the same as that in St Luke 10:40 where Martha asks our Lord to bid Mary "come to her aid" in the kitchen).

These ideas, infinitely precious to us who have had the opportunity of pondering upon them, need re-stating, if this aspect of prayer is to become real to a modern generation.

Christ and Our Crises

I. *Death*

The last day of Holy Week is a strange day. It is a day with some kind of a hush about it. We look back to Good Friday with horror—to think that we could do *that* to the Son of God; yet we look back with deep thankfulness—to think that He could do *that* for us! And we look forward to Easter Day, with hope and joy.

So between Good Friday and Easter Day we can pause and think.

The crisis that came to Jesus on the first Good Friday was the crisis of death. He tasted it for every man. He went through it— in its most terrible form.

Sooner or later, death comes to us all. Many people try to run away from it, for they dare not face it.

The wise man stops and thinks about it.

Has Christianity anything worthwhile to say about death? It has! Man's mortality has always puzzled him. Life is so brief. There is so much to do, and so little time in which to do it. There is much to experience, but there are so few years to enjoy it all! We feel sympathy with the old pagan British chief who said that human life was like the passage of a bird coming out of the dark night, flying swiftly through the brightly lit hall, and then out into the dark again.

We can understand his perplexity. Out of the darkness—into the dark! But that *is* a pagan, an un-Christian view of things.

BBC Broadcasts, April 1973, elaborated in a book published by Word Books in America, 1975.

For the Christian does *not* believe that he goes from this life out into the dark. He believes, he *knows*, that he is in touch with One Who Himself went down into death, grappled with it, and won the victory over it.

In doing so—as the Bible says—"He has broken its power and brought life and immortality to light through the Gospel".

I like the way the *Te Deum* puts it: "When thou hadst overcome the sharpness of death, thou didst open the Kingdom of heaven to all believers". That is realistic. Death is sharp in its sting. But the sting has been drawn, overcome, by the victory of Jesus. This means, then, that death, when it comes to the Christian, can be welcomed as a friend, not dreaded as an enemy. The crisis of the sloughing off of our present body will lead to an even more glorious experience of closer union with Christ, the vision of God Himself.

Two Nazi warders came to the cell of the young German Christian martyr, Dietrich Bonhoeffer. "Prisoner," they said, "take your things and come with us." Bonhoeffer sent a last message to his English friend, Bishop George Bell. "Tell him," he said, "that for me this is the end, but also the beginning." Next morning, he was executed.

In the midst of death, he was in life.

Good Friday, Easter Eve, and Easter Day hold the answer to the crisis of death.

Thanks be to God!

A Prayer:

> O Lord Jesus Christ, Son of the Living God,
> who as on this day didst rest in the sepulchre,
> and didst thereby sanctify the grave to be a
> bed of hope to Thy people; make us so to abound in
> sorrow for our sins which were the cause of Thy
> passion, that when our bodies lie in the dust our
> souls may live with Thee; who livest and reignest
> with the Father and the Holy Ghost, world without
> end. Amen.

2. *Fear*

The Gospels indicate that Jesus went about His work telling people not to be frightened. "Fear not!", He would say, again and again.

There was every reason for Him to speak in this way, for He came to a people ridden by fear—fear of their Roman invaders, fear of disease in a community that had no hospitals, fear of death, fear of so many other things.

On the first Easter morning it is recorded that Jesus appeared to His friends when they were gathered behind locked doors "for fear of the Jews". We cannot blame them for being frightened. If men had crucified their Master last Friday, who was to say whether those men might not do the same to *them* today or tomorrow?

Fear of the unknown future. They had failed their Master just at the point of His greatest need, so they feared that that would mean the end of their wonderful contact with Him. And so fear of this mysterious Figure who presented Himself before them—so unlike the Jesus they had known, and yet so strangely like Him, the Figure with the wounded hands and the pierced side.

"*Peace* be with you", He said. That was precisely what they needed, the peace that would cast out their fear.

He brought them release from their fears. He brought them the peace of forgiveness. He re-commissioned them in His service: "as my Father sent me, so send I you".

How marvellous it must have been to be re-instated, to be re-commissioned! What a transformation that Easter evening encounter with Jesus made!

For all the sophistication of our "brave new world", for all our scientific advance, fear still abounds in our world and still invades our lives. It is a bogey to many, as we wrestle with fear of the unknown future, the fear of our own inadequacy, the fear of the consequences of our failure in discipleship.

This, surely, is the point where the message of Easter Day comes in—with power to release us from the bondage of fear. Christ is not dead. He is alive, even standing beside you. "Peace be with you," He says.

If that seems to you to be too good to be true, remember the wounded hands and the pierced side of Jesus which He showed to His friends. That was to them the measure of His *love*—and is, to us.

Remember too, the empty tomb which He left behind when He rose triumphant from the dead. That was—and is—the measure of His *power*.

In face of that powerful love and that loving power, there need be no fear for the Christian disciple, no fear for *you*.

Let us turn all this into a prayer:

> May the God of peace who, as on this Easter Day,
> brought up from the dead our Lord Jesus, that
> great Shepherd of the sheep, free you from your
> fears, fill you with His peace and joy, and by His
> power make of you what He would have you be; and
> may the blessing of God Almighty, the Father, the
> Son and the Holy Spirit, be among you and remain
> with you, always. Amen.

3. *Success*

We are thinking together about Christ and the crises of our lives—things like death and fear. I speak now about the crisis of *success*.

Does that seem almost a contradiction in terms? Is not success always to be welcomed as obviously right and good?

It often is just that; and the man who achieves it can thank God for it.

But when you have got both feet firmly on the ladder and you are mounting the rungs, it is just worth asking: "What price am I paying for this success?" Don't we all know cases where success has been bought, say by a business man, at the price of his family life? His wife has been practically deserted, and his children have grown up without the real chance of getting to know their father who is little more than a lodger in the house, at home for bed and breakfast but little else. That is a heavy price to pay for a fat salary and a bigger car.

Don't we know too of cases where the rat-race has made the man or woman engaged in it brittle of temper or as hard as nails? Up goes the wage-packet, but down goes the character!

That is a crisis of major proportions. But where does Christ come into this picture?

He comes striding in, asking this pointed question: "What does a man gain by winning the whole world at the cost of his true self? What can he give to buy that self back?" He forces us to do our sums, to tot up our profits and losses. The stakes are very high —cash or position over against character and eternal life. Which is it to be?

It is an uncomfortable bit of reckoning. But how good of God not to let us get away with madness—at least without being confronted by the price we pay for losing our eternal welfare!

Christ forces us to do our sums, I have just said. That is not strictly true. He puts the sums, the credit and debit account, fairly and squarely before us, and urges us to face the issues involved. But He never forces us into action. He asks our leave to bless us; and if we refuse that leave, if we refuse to do our sums, that is our infinite loss.

We have been given the power of choice. We are not mechanical robots; and Christ always respects our freedom of will. The responsibility is squarely on us.

So success can present a man with a crisis. Jesus says: "Anyone who wishes to be a follower of mine must leave self behind; he must take up his cross, and come with me ..." For, after all, "what *does* a man gain by winning the whole world at the cost of his true self?"

The man who drew up our Litany had a pretty shrewd insight into life. He included this clause: "In all time of our tribulation; in all time of our *wealth*; in the hour of death, and in the day of judgment. Good Lord, deliver us". By "wealth", he meant not just financial success. He meant success of any kind.

It is the time when things are going right and all seems well that can be crisis time, just as surely as is the "time of our tribulation". This is the time to look to Christ and His deliverance, lest we lose our soul, our true self.

At this Easter Season then, we pray sincerely:

By Thy cross and passion; by Thy precious death
and burial; by Thy glorious resurrection and
ascension, in all time of our *wealth*, good Lord,
deliver us. Amen.

4. Despair

St Luke is brilliant in the way that he paints pictures in words. His Gospel is full of them.

One of the most vivid pictures is his story about two people walking the seven or eight miles that stretched between Jerusalem and their own village. It wasn't a bad walk, usually; a bit hot and dusty, perhaps, but they would normally take it in their stride.

Today was *not* usual, or normal. You could tell that by taking a glance at them. Their steps dragged heavily; their faces were full of gloom. They were in despair.

It was indeed crisis day for this couple.

The crisis of their despair lay just here. They thought Jesus was dead. They *knew* He had died—had they not been in Jerusalem that ghastly Friday when it all happened? Wasn't the Cross a fact—and the nails—and the spear—and the stone rolled against the tomb? No one could deny these facts. He was dead. That was that.

But was it? Who was this young man who fell into step with them and strode alongside of them, somehow making the miles shorter, and lifting their sights as they walked? Who was this man who opened up their Bible to them and made sense of it in a way nobody else had ever done? They were strangely drawn to Him, though they did not recognise Him. There was something about Him which made them press Him to enter their home and share their evening meal with them.

He accepted the invitation. Somehow it seemed natural that the guest should act as host, say the grace and break the bread and give it to them. As He did that, there was some characteristic turn to the action which made them recall previous meals which (now they remembered!) they had shared with Him. It was Jesus, gloriously alive. Death was behind him. He was victor over His foes and theirs!

It was a revelation. Their eyes were opened and they recognised him. Jesus their friend and their Lord, was with them.

So despair gave way to joy. Things began to piece together, and life started to make sense. If this were true, life could not be an idiot's tale, full of sound and fury, signifying nothing. On the contrary, it took on new meaning and purpose.

They set out on a return journey, back to Jerusalem where they had so recently come from. They found the disciples, and breathlessly and joyfully blurted out: "It is true; the Lord has risen; He has *appeared* . . . !" Simply they told the story of how He had walked and talked with them.

Despair was defeated!

At one time or another, despair knocks at most people's doors, not least at thinking people's doors. Sometimes, naturally, the reason for our despair is largely physical. We are just tired and worn out; so sleep or a holiday or a tonic from the doctor may be the answer. But often the reason is deeper. What is life all about? What is at the heart of the universe? Was there no sequel to Good Friday? Is truth always on the scaffold? Is goodness always defeated?

The answer to despair like this is to be found in the young man who joined the two on their tramp from Jerusalem to Emmaus; in Him and in no one else. He says to us: "Why are you so perturbed? Why do questionings arise in your minds? Look at my hands and feet. It is I myself."

> Lord Jesus Christ, crucified and risen again,
> draw near to us when we are near to despair.
> Shew us Thyself; drive away our fear; and whisper
> to our hearts and consciences, "It is I myself". Amen.

5. Doubt

Every age, I suppose, has been an age of doubt; but our own age is more an age of doubt than any that has preceded it. After all, we are the children of a scientific upbringing. We believe in laboratories and test tubes and experiments, the results of which can be seen and handled.

Where does faith come into all this? What are we to do when doubt comes gnawing at our vitals and bids fair to leave us with nothing to hold on to, no under-girding for life and death, no answers to the problems which the science lab can raise but never solve?

The question is made the more painful because doubt is often accompanied by a sense of guilt, as if it were *wrong* to ask questions. Then doubt assumes the proportions of a crisis which can, at the worst, turn to cynicism or even to despair.

Let us lay it down as a basic axiom that questioning is never to be condemned, if that questioning takes place against the background of a desire for a living faith. "Lord, I believe; help thou mine unbelief."

Suppression of doubt does nobody any good. Rather let it come out into the open where it can be faced. Truth is big enough and strong enough to stand the consequences.

Perhaps it is time we stopped condemning Thomas so self-righteously! "Doubting Thomas" we call him, disapprovingly, as if we never had doubts ourselves! "Honest Thomas" might have been a better way of describing him. He had enormous, menacing doubts. But he blurted them out and was ready, if the evidence allowed him to do so, to banish them and to build up a faith of his own.

Read his story, told so vividly by St John in the twentieth chapter of his Gospel. The Lord was dead. There was no question about it. "Unless I see—unless I put my finger in—and my hand—I won't believe." Christ met him where he was, at the point of his questioning and of his unbelief.

Thomas was no died-in-the-wool atheist. Far from it. He longed for a living faith. "Reach your finger here," says Jesus; "see my hands; reach your hand here and put it into my side; and don't become an unbeliever but a believer."

So far from becoming an unbeliever, Thomas became the great apostle to India, if ancient tradition is to be believed. "My Lord and my God," he said.

No such evidence as Thomas had is given to the would-be believer today. We have no chance to see and touch and handle. But other evidence there is in plenty, evidence which becomes weightier with every year that passes and the numbers increase of those who, in their own experience, find that the crucified Christ is their living Lord and God.

Let us pray:

> Come to us, Lord, when the clouds of
> doubt are dark and menacing, and say
> to us, as You said to Thomas: "Happy
> are they who never saw me and yet have
> found faith". So may we look up—and
> trust—and say from our heart: "My Lord
> and my God".

6. *Disillusionment with Self*

"I can never forgive myself. I've done it and there's no going back on it. But I made a colossal mistake. I've damaged the people I love. I can never forgive myself".

Haven't you heard some such confession as that? Haven't *you* made such a confession?

How bitter it can be! A cutting word spoken which can never be recalled, or a rotten deed done which can never be undone. "I'll never forgive myself". He *thought* he was such a fine type, and to think he could sink to *that*! The bubble of his pride has been pricked. He has been humiliated by his own act. He is utterly disillusioned—not with others but—with *himself*. He has let himself down. The rest of life is lived under an enormous burden of guilt.

Here indeed is a crisis! If nothing can be done about it, he will go through life warped and twisted and embittered. There is only One who can handle that crisis creatively, and that is Christ.

Let me tell you what I mean.

This crisis of disillusionment with self can be a disaster. But it can equally be the beginning of new life. For look at what has happened. Someone has seen that he is not quite so good a fellow as he previously imagined. On the contrary, there is a weakness, a core of rottenness, which has led to disaster. We are sinners, we need God's forgiveness and re-instatement. We need to be made new creatures. *But is that possible?*

The answer is in a true story.

Simon Peter had reason to believe that he was a bit of a lad. At least so he thought. Was he not the leader of the band of apostles? Had not he had that wonderful flash of inspiration which enabled him to confess Jesus as the Christ of God? Had he not sworn that, though all others might forsake Jesus and flee, he never would? Didn't he mean every word of that? Of course he did. Then that wretched servant girl who curled her lip at him and laughed at him for being a follower of Jesus caused all the trouble. Talk about a pricked balloon! He had collapsed. He had denied his Lord, with cursings and swearings.

What a fool he had been! What a sinner to let his Lord down! "I'll never forgive myself," he muttered. "I'm utterly disillusioned with myself. How *can* I forgive myself after what I've done?"

It was not long after that the risen Jesus met him and took him on one side. "Now it's coming," Peter must have thought. "He'll dismiss me, and that will be the end. After all, that's all I can expect."

The reverse happened. "Do you love me, Peter?" "Of course I do, Lord." "Then there's work for you to do. You are a forgiven man. Go—and feed my sheep. Go—and tend my lambs."

If Jesus could forgive like that, how could Peter continue unforgiving to himself? There was no need for disillusionment any longer. He was now a man re-made, re-commissioned.

It is at that point that life begins.

The re-making began with the breaking.

When Jesus turned and looked on Peter, he went outside and wept.

"Lord Jesus, look on me."

7. *Disillusionment with the World*

We have been thinking together about the way Christ has of meeting us at the point of such crises as death and fear and success and despair and doubt and disillusionment with ourselves. There is another crisis I want to discuss and it has to do with the crisis that comes to many people when they consider the mess the world is in. This feels to some so overwhelming that they get disillusioned with life as a whole. So life goes sour on them, and they go sour on life. And that is very sad.

Our world has two very different sides to it. Part of it is so beautiful that it takes our breath away, and the Christian finds himself saying: "If that is but the outskirts of God's ways, how wonderful God Himself must be!" But there is another side to life. It has its ugly, terrifying facet. Wars and disasters and man's inhumanity to man, disease and suffering are terrible realities.

What are we to say in face of them?

First, in the light of Christ's coming, of His life and death among us, we can never think of God as far removed from our agonies. Jesus wrestled and fought with mankind's great enemies of sin and ignorance and disease and death—and won through. He has made a bridge-head into enemy territory, and this gives us the assurance that victory lies ahead. So, while we do not yet see all things brought under His kingly rule, we know that the day must come when just that will happen. The victory won by Christ on the first Good Friday and Easter Day will reach a triumphal conclusion.

Secondly, our God is the God of history. The Jews believed that God did not set the world going (as a watch-maker might wind up a clock) and then leave it to lurch on to its fate. Through the twisted processes of history, He is working His purposes out as year succeeds to year.

Sometimes it is hard for us, with our near sight and short vision, to detect the pattern of His working. We find it hard to answer our own agonised questions as to why the world is made the way it is, why people get hurt the way they do; why, in fact, we make such a mess of so beautiful a world. We can begin to see that part of the answer is that God made men able to exercise their free-will and not to be mere machines. Our own sin and selfishness are responsible for a great deal of what we and our fellows suffer.

So we get back to the question of what actually is such a mixture of the god-like and the beast-like, and so desperately in need of re-making, which only God in Christ can do for us. When that begins to happen, we catch a glimpse of a glorious fact. It is this; that the man who puts his life into the hands of Christ lines up his tiny forces with those of the God of history in working His purposes out. He becomes a fellow-worker with God in the defeating of evil and in the establishing of God's reign.

The man who sees *that* begins to see the meaning of the universe and of his part in its onward march.

O Lord, Who hast set before us the great hope that Thy Kingdom shall come on earth, and hast taught us to pray for its coming; Give us grace to discern the signs of its dawning, and to work for the perfect day when Thy will shall be done on earth as it is in heaven; through Jesus Christ our Lord.

Music in Church

I STAND BEFORE you as an amateur in the field of music. Almost exactly forty years ago, my father came to me and said: "I'm going to give you a present." I wondered what was coming. There was nothing visible, nothing tangible in his hands. He went on: "I've paid for you to have sixty organ lessons."

It was one of the loveliest presents I have ever had. Over two years, strenuous years when I was preparing to go up to Cambridge, these lessons provided me with an outlet which I sorely needed. They opened up a new world. Though I had played the piano for years, the organ demanded a new technique and introduced me to a new galaxy of music writers. They taught me the joy of accompanying church services. I can still recall the terror of looking in the glass in front of me and seeing the white-robed choir enter, and realising that, for better, for worse, I, in that little box of an organ-chamber, was responsible for the accompaniment of the music, pointed Psalms and all! They also taught me the necessity for what I would call unobtrusive control —to the adjective I shall revert a little later. As to the noun, I would only add that in those years in the twenties, I came to realise that, once an organist was "bossed" by his congregation in the singing of Psalms and hymns, he might as well retire! He must be *in charge*—which is quite a different matter from being overwhelmingly dominating!

The busy-ness of the ensuing years has meant that what very little skill I once had has been largely lost, though I still occasionally know the joy of swinging my legs over an organ-stool

Westminster Choir College, Princeton, New Jersey, 25th May 1966

and trying out some mighty instrument. And, when I was principal of a theological college, I used to enjoy myself hugely in accompanying services and even taking choir practices—the "choir" being the whole college. In those days the instrument was in fact a piano. What instrument is better suited to "lift" the weight of the voices of a solidly male congregation?

I am grateful to my father. Music is one of God's best gifts. No wonder that the writer of the Book of the Revelation, when he was straining himself to find language suitable to depict the joys of heaven, had a good deal to say about singing songs and playing harps!

Have you ever allowed the thought to suggest itself to you that you would have been saved a great deal of suffering if you had not had a note of music in you? If one tune was the same as another to you? If you had not the faintest idea of what was going on around you—musically? If in the sphere of music, you were a complete boor?

Let me illustrate this terrible and utterly unorthodox suggestion.

I have a friend, an Englishman, who is bishop of a diocese in Africa which could scarcely be called advanced in learning and culture according to Western ideas. When he was enthroned in his little cathedral in Africa, the powers-that-be thought that there ought to be trumpets on so great an occasion. So far, so good. But the idea got around that, *whenever* the bishop appeared, trumpets were more or less *de rigueur*.

It happened that one Sunday, he went to confirm and to celebrate the Holy Communion at a tiny church in the veriest backwoods of his diocese. Trumpets—or was it a single bugle?— greeted him as he advanced towards the church. The service was long and the weather hot. By the time all was through, he had forgotten about trumpets. But not so the trumpeters (or was it the bugler?). As he came out into the mid-day sun, tired and not a little famished, sharp and raucous rang out the trumpet. And the tune? "Come to the cook-house door, boys!"

Now my friend knew enough music to recognise the tune. Had he been wholly unversed in the art to which you are giving your lives, he might have thought it was "God save the Queen" or some equally appropriate piece. Alas for him! He knew too much.

That is my point! During the course of a year, I visit a very large number of churches and—let me confess it—I suffer a good deal! I suffer when the organist loses control, and every verse of the hymn gets slower than the preceding one. (Low be it said, but I have been known to stop such a performance, and occasionally—*very* occasionally—to conduct from the pulpit!). I suffer when the clergyman decides—for reasons best known to himself—to intone the prayers, but does not realise that he drops about half a tone each time. I suffer when the organist over-sentimentalises a canticle by liberal use of *tremolo*, and converts the *Magnificat* (which is the nearest thing in the New Testament to the "Red Flag") into slop! I suffer—and here the totally unmusical join the musical—when people will sing nonsense, for example, lusty confirmation candidates being forced to describe themselves as "frail and trembling sheep", and thoughtful congregations being made to sing Coverdale's version of Psalm 22:29: "all such as be fat upon earth have eaten and worshipped". What on earth does that mean?

So much of this is, of course, wholly unnecessary. May I say what I have said on other occasions. If the clergy would not insist, in small parish churches, on apeing cathedrals, but would make worship the beautifully simple thing which it is meant to be, we should be saved much agony (and I suspect would have many more level-headed laity within our doors). There are multitudes of first-rate hymns, at once biblical and closely related to life as it is, set to first-rate tunes, if only we could learn them and use them and steadily refuse to sink to the level of the sentimentally sloppy. And what about the Psalms? Of course, there are parts which no wise man would ever use in public worship. But many of them are superb. And there are versions and settings which make sense and are not difficult to use.

I had the privilege of presiding for four years over a commission charged with the revision of the Psalter. Its members included T. S. Eliot, and C. S. Lewis and Dr Gerald Knight who is one of your honorary graduates. We were glad to avail ourselves of the skill of experts in English, in Hebrew and in music. The result is an edition of the Psalms which makes sense, retains Coverdale's lovely rhythm, and is easy to sing.

Music, especially the kind of music to which you are giving

yourselves, is a *ministry*. The musician is a *minister*. And a minister simply means a servant.

"Servant" is an unpopular word today. But it is a glorious word. It is the word which above all others described the ministry of Jesus. He was the Servant of the Lord. And His followers are servants of Him and of His Word. It becomes a servant to be (and here I come back to the word) *unobtrusive*. All great artists have an element of the unobtrusive about them. *Ars est celare artem*. The supreme art is to conceal art. The *real* preacher, when he descends from the pulpit, does not want to hear people say: "Wasn't he wonderful!" He wants to hear them say: "Isn't his Master wonderful!" The reward of Myra Hess, when she had finished playing Beethoven, was to hear her audience whisper: "Wasn't that Beethoven superb!"

Try to be unobtrusive. Try to get out of the way. Be a minister. Be a servant, using the art with which you have been entrusted to make much of the One who entrusted you with it. That will call for a wide discipline of study, embracing many subjects and reaching out into wide areas only distantly connected with your immediate sphere of music. But remember—

> Who keeps one end in view
> Makes all things serve.

Let your music be the medium through which you serve the Lord Christ.

Unobtrusive in his manner, broad in his culture, dedicated to his Master, the servant of his Master's world. This is the man needed at this hour.

The Bible

The Bible in the Modern World

TAKING THINGS FOR granted is a curse. It shuts
our eyes to wonder, and wonder is a faculty much to be prized.
In one of his poems called "An Expostulation", C. S. Lewis
brackets it with Beauty:

> Beauty that stabs with tingling spear,
> Or Wonder, laying on one's heart
> That fingertip at which we start
> As if some thought too swift and shy
> For reason's grasp had just gone by.

We are inclined to take the Bible for granted. Our grandparents used to read it at family prayers or, if they were not all
that devout, would prop up the aspidistra with it and enter the
family names in it. Our parents saw to it that there was a copy
in our trunk when they packed us off to school or, later, to sea,
or to take a minor share in the dismemberment of the British
Empire. We ourselves must have a copy to go alongside Shakespeare or Dickens on our shelves, for it looks well. Who knows
whether we may not need it for a crossword clue?

The Bible is part of the English way of life. We take it for
granted, like the English parish church, or our digestive system,
or the *Radio Times*.

That there is an epic story behind it we rarely stop to ponder.
But I take the opportunity to do precisely this now. How to
cover 2,000 years, in such a short space, is an impossible journey

Guildford Cathedral, 1965.

to tackle. Still, "to travel hopefully is better than to arrive, and the true success is to labour". Robert Louis Stevenson was right. In that spirit, we set off on our travels.

Perhaps a series of sketches, or brief outline drawings of our theme at different stages of its development, may be the best way of attempting our task.

1. We begin with a synagogue in Nazareth, c.AD 26. The young Preacher had a Bible from which to choose His text. It corresponded to what we now call our Old Testament, the Law, Prophets, and writings. On it He fed His soul. From it He preached. The Church which He founded went out to its task with that book in its hand. "This is that," they constantly claimed, as they saw happening within them and around them what they believed was foreshadowed in their Scriptures.

It was not long before there was added to those Scriptures, first, a collection of letters and then some books called Gospels. Of the majority of those books there was no doubt, though the complete twenty-seven did not finally "congeal" as the canon of the New Testament for a couple of centuries or so. But, right from the start, the Church was "the people of the Book". The Scriptures were the Church's indispensable handmaid in the task of evangelisation.

2. Our second sketch could take us equally well to Edessa or to North Africa. Edessa (the modern Urfa) was from a very early date the centre of Syriac-speaking Christianity. Greek was, of course, the *lingua franca* of the world of Jesus and St Paul. "The Babel of tongues was hushed in the wonderful language of Greece"; and this lovely tongue, almost universally understood, paved the way for the spread of the Gospel. But there were corners of the Roman Empire where other languages persisted. Edessa was one. North Africa was another. It was necessary that the Scriptures of the Christian Church should be translated into the languages most readily understood by the natives. So it was that the great Versions of the Bible came into being—the Syriac versions in and around Edessa; the Latin versions in North Africa.

Because of their very early date, the Syriac versions are of great value to the textual scholar, preserving a text which enables him to trace the original with a good measure of certainty. Of

the Latin versions, the best known is the Vulgate, the work of
that rugged ascetic St Jerome. He found the study of Hebrew a
good answer to the lusts of the flesh! He translated from the
original tongues into Latin, and his Bible has been that of the
Roman Church from earliest days until now. Even Ronald Knox
in the 1940s translated from the Vulgate, with constant reference
to the Hebrew.

There were other translations into other languages, but the
mention of these two important ones serves to illustrate how the
Scriptures began to spread in languages other than those in which
they were originally written.

3. My third sketch takes us to the diocese of York I know so
well, and to the town of Whitby. There, thirteen centuries ago,
that remarkable woman St Hilda, of royal lineage and abbess of
a monastery for both men and women, "reigned"—is there any
other word for it? And is she not a standing rebuke to those
timid souls who would hold back women from positions of
leadership in the Church? There, so tradition has it, Caedmon,
simple herdsman that he was, sang his songs "to praise the Maker
of the heavenly Kingdom, the power of the Creator and his
counsel, the deeds of the Father of glory". He "versified" on the
great themes of the Biblical revelation, thus popularising Christian
doctrine for a largely illiterate people. No wonder that he came
to be known as the father of English poetry.

4. For my fourth sketch, we travel north from the diocese of
York to that of Durham, from Whitby to Jarrow where, in the
monastery Caedmon's biographer, Bede, spent all his life. Well
has he been called "the Venerable" down the centuries. A student
of Latin, Greek and Hebrew, he was, as he himself tells us, "ever
intent upon the study of the Scriptures. In the intervals between
the duties enjoined by the disciplinary rule and the daily care of
chanting in the church, I took sweet pleasure in always learning,
teaching or writing." Precisely how much of the Scriptures he
translated into the vernacular, it is impossible to say, but that he
pioneered in this field is clear.

The well-known picture of his death in 735 is known both in
art and from the account of his disciple Cuthbert. The old man
was busy on St John's Gospel:

Ascension-day drew near. His illness increased, but he only laboured the more diligently. On the Wednesday, his scribe told him that one chapter alone remained, but feared that it might be painful for him to dictate. "It is easy," Bede replied. "Take your pen and write quickly." The work was continued for some time. Then Bede directed Cuthbert to fetch his little treasures, pepper, scarves and incense, so that he might distribute them among his friends. So he passed the rest of the day to the evening in holy and cheerful conversation. His boy-scribe at last found an opportunity to remind him, with pious importunity, of his unfinished task: "One sentence, dear master, still remains unwritten." "Write quickly," he answered. The boy said, "It is completed now." "Well," Bede replied, "thou hast said the truth: all is ended. Take my head in thy hands, I would sit in the holy place in which I was wont to pray, that so sitting I may call upon my Father." Thereupon, resting on the floor of his cell, he chanted the *Gloria*, and his soul immediately passed away while the name of the Holy Spirit was on his lips.

5. Six hundred and fifty years slip by between the death of Bede and that of Wyclif, whose great aim it was to restore the Scriptures to their position as the unique and sole authority for life and doctrine in the Church. Though it is very doubtful that Wyclif translated the whole of the Bible himself, yet two years before his death the whole work appeared, a work (in the words of G. M. Trevelyan) which was "a great event in the history of the English language as well as religion". In a day when many of the clergy could not construe or expound the Lord's Prayer, the creed or the ten commandments, such a translation was desperately needed. What must the plight of the laity have been like! Unattractive as Wyclif would appear to have been as a man, his life-work was of immense significance.

Thomas Fuller, the historian, in a quaint and delightful passage, saw something symbolic in what happened to the remains of Wyclif some forty-four years after his death. "The Pope ordered the Bishop of Lincoln 'to proceed in person to the place where John Wyclif was buried, cause his body and bones to be exhumed, cast far from ecclesiastical burial and publicly burnt, and his ashes to be so disposed of that no trace of him shall be seen again." "Thus," commented Fuller, "this brook (the River Swift) hath conveyed his ashes into Avon; Avon into Severn; Severn into the narrow seas; they into the main ocean. And thus the ashes of Wyclif are the emblem of his doctrine, which now is dispersed all the world over."

The claim would seem to be little more than sober fact.

6. My sixth sketch is set between Westminster Abbey and the Embankment. Pause at the former, not to admire that wonderful church but to ponder on the fact that, in 1477, under its shadow Caxton set up his printing press. (It was only twenty-one years earlier that Gutenberg had issued the first printed book in Europe, a Latin Bible).

The invention of the printing press launched a revolution. No longer need every book be copied out by hand, at the expense of immense labour and inevitable error. Now the liberating news of Holy Scripture could be disseminated by a turn of the printing press.

Nor could this invention have happened at a more opportune time. John Colet at Oxford and Erasmus at Cambridge, against the background of the Renaissance, were helping men to see that the great doctrines of the New Testament were not the preserve of dry as dust scholastics, but that they held within them the secret of new life in Christ for the man in the street. Tyndale and Erasmus were at one in their desire that the truths of the Bible should be available to all. You remember the lovely words of Erasmus: "I wish that even the weakest woman should read the Gospel—should read the Epistles of Paul. And I wish these were translated into all languages, so that they might be read and understood, not only by Scots and Irishmen, but also by Turks and Saracens . . . I long that the husbandman should sing portions of them to himself as he follows the plough, that the weaver should hum them to the tune of his shuttle, that the traveller should beguile with their stories the tedium of his journey."

Turning your back on Westminster, and taking your stand in the gardens on the Embankment, take a steady look at the statue of William Tyndale. Our debt to him and to his translation is incalculable. Ninety per cent of it stands unaltered in our Authorised Version. Professor Greenslade has justly called him "the man who more than Shakespeare or Bunyan has moulded and enriched our language". He was a master of monosyllabic simplicity, and in that simplicity was the secret of majesty. Listen to him: "in Him we live and move and have our being", or "until the day dawn and the day-star arise in our hearts"; or, "for here we have no continuing city, but we seek one to come".

It is hard, if one has a scrap of imagination in one, not to grow a little lyrical about Tyndale. Driven out of London, forced to do his work on the Continent, martyred by strangulation and burning at Vilvorde in 1536, he writes to the Governor of the Castle from his damp prison.

> If I am to remain here during the winter, you will request the Procureur to be kind enough to send me from my goods which he has in his possession a warmer cap, for I suffer extremely from cold in the head, being afflicted with a perpetual catarrh which is considerably increased in this cell. A warmer coat also, for that which I have is very thin: also a piece of cloth to patch my leggings: my overcoat is worn out. He has a woollen shirt of mine, if he will be kind enough to send it. I have also with him leggings of thicker cloth for putting on above; he also has warmer caps for wearing at night. I wish also his permission to have a lamp in the evening, for it is wearisome to sit alone in the dark. But above all, I entreat and beseech your clemency to be urgent with the Procureur that he may kindly permit me to have my Hebrew Bible, my Hebrew Grammar and Hebrew Dictionary, that I may spend my time with that study.

"Lord"—such was the martyr's dying prayer—"Lord, open the King of England's eyes." That prayer was to be answered in the very next year by the royal recognition of the Coverdale Bible, which itself was vastly indebted to Tyndale's.

7. It is cruel that the tyranny of time forces me to pass by Coverdale with only a glance. Do not blame *him* when you sing his version of the Psalms in church if sometimes they do not make sense—the study of Hebrew has advanced since the sixteenth century. Rather can you be thankful for his sensitiveness for beauty of rhythm. "He sings his way through the Psalter like a choir-boy enjoying his anthem."

We pass by various editions of the Bible such as the Geneva Bible, known as the Breeches Bible (Adam and Eve sewed fig leaves together and made themselves "breeches", Genesis 3:7); the Bishops' Bible of 1568, and so on, and come for our eighth sketch to:

8. *The Authorised Version* of 1611. It is fashionable to make rude remarks about committees, but the Authorised Version did come out of one, or rather six committees. They were at work behind the main committee, two at Westminster, two at Oxford and two at Cambridge. Culture, learning, humility and piety were the ingredients which produced this wonderful version.

It is easy to look back from the vantage point of the passage of 350 years and to detect errors in scholarship that the researches of later years have brought to light. We know much more today about the Hebrew language and about Greek manuscripts than did Lancelot Andrewes and his colleagues. But I think Macaulay was right when he described the 1611 version as "a book which, if everything else in our language should perish, would alone suffice to show the whole extent of its beauty and power".

It was a matter of extreme good fortune that the King James version came into being just when it did, for this was the period when our language reached what G. M. Trevelyan has called "its brief perfection". It was the age of Shakespeare and Marlowe, of Spenser, Hooker and Bacon. There is a kind of monosyllabic simplicity and yet majesty about much of the language. Consider this: "Thus will I bless Thee while I live: I will lift up my hands in Thy name." Or: "The Son of Man is come to seek and to save that which was lost." Or again: "The flowers appear on the earth; the time of the singing of birds is come, and the voice of the turtle is heard in our land." For sheer beauty, it would be hard to improve on sentences such as these. It was this kind of English that fixed the standard for centuries to come.

9. We may pass by the translations of the seventeenth and eighteenth centuries which followed in the wake of the Authorised Version, some of them as banal in their effect as they were well-intentioned in design. We come directly to that great period of translation which began with the Revised Version and which is not finished yet.

The Revised Version came out in three parts—the New Testament in 1881, the Old Testament in 1885, and the Apocrypha in 1895. It was a useful if not epoch-making piece of work, and in accuracy a great improvement on the Authorised Version. If its appearance was wrongly timed, its producers were hardly to blame for that. They were not to know that, just about the time that their work was nearing completion, the dry sands of Egypt were to throw up material which would cast a flood of light especially on the New Testament documents. I am referring to the ostraca and papyri, preserved during long centuries in the dry sands of Egypt—the *ostraca* being old broken bits of pottery which housewives would use for making lists and others for odd notes and jottings (the days of paper were far future); and *papyri* being the reeds which grew in the Nile valley which, pressed together and smoothed with pumice, made excellent writing material for letters and so on. These ostraca and papyri, gathered in their thousands and pored over by the scholars, proved that the New Testament was not written in some special "language of the Holy Ghost" (as had been the view of scholars hitherto) but in the ordinary language of home and market-place. True, the subject-matter with which the New Testament dealt raised the language to a new nobility, but just as Jesus took on Himself the ordinary flesh and blood of us mortals, so the language in which His revelation was expressed was the ordinary language of every day. Had the Revised Version appeared early in the twentieth century rather than late in the nineteenth, it could have availed itself of these rich discoveries. In spite, however, of that not being possible, a version was produced which was an improvement on what had gone before and a stepping stone towards what lay ahead. That is hardly to be wondered at, when two of those who took a big share in the work were the great Cambridge scholars, Westcott and Hort.

Since the appearance of the Revised Version, there has been a spate of new translations. I can only mention a few. Perhaps pride of place must be given to Dr Moffatt's production—New Testament 1913, Old Testament 1924, the whole Bible finally revised 1935. If some of his rearrangements in the order of the text prove annoying to the ordinary reader and seem dubious to the modern scholar; if the version often does not "read" well in public and sometimes sinks to the comic (Job, lamenting over the day of his birth, is made to say "Perish ... the night that said 'It's a boy.' " !), it remains true that this was indeed a valiant and scholarly attempt to break away from old styles of translation and to give the Bible to the people in the idiom of modern English. It brought the Bible alive to those who were in danger of being lulled to sleep by the lovely cadences of the Authorised Version of 1611. A great Scotsman had done a great service to readers of the Bible.

In 1946, thirty-two American scholars put out the Revised Standard Version of the New Testament. The whole Bible appeared in 1952. Many of you possess it. Many others hear it read in your churches, and only rarely pucker a puzzled brow at a passing Americanism. Others of you enjoy dipping into Ronald Knox's monumental achievement. It is astonishing that one solitary man produced in 1949 his translation of the whole Bible including the Apocrypha and, just for good value, gave us two translations of the Psalms! As we have seen, it was a translation from the Vulgate (as became a Roman Catholic) but with a careful eye to the originals (as became a good scholar).

For sheer punching power—and the New Testament is powerful and is meant to punch—it would be hard to beat the version of J. B. Phillips, a contemporary of ours who has tried his hand, not without some success, also at four of the Old Testament prophets. It was fortunate for Phillips that C. S. Lewis wrote a preface to the first volume, *Letters to Young Churches*, and so gave this vigorous translation a flying start. It has deserved the success which it has achieved on both sides of the Atlantic.

Of the *New English Bible: New Testament*, I need say little. I would hope that everyone in this audience has a copy and uses it frequently. Within a year of publication, over four million copies were sold. Work is presently going ahead on the Old Testament and on the Apocrypha, and publication is now not too far away. I share with C. H. Dodd, the master-mind behind this production, the view that the New Testament will need but little revision when the whole work is put out—a few unfortunate phrases like "loose livers" must go, but I think most of it may stand unashamed in the face of its critics.

So much—or rather, so little, for we have only touched on

some of the great features of the story—for the epic of translation. What of the epic of distribution?

Here we must be even more sketchy in our approach to the subject. Right from the start, the Church has gone on its task (if I may repeat a phrase I have used at other times) "with a book in its hand". That this is still so is symbolised by the fact (and it is a fact worth repeating) that the only thing which the Bishop hands to a priest at his ordination—or the Archbishop to the Bishop at his consecration—is a Bible. Here is at once the source of his doctrine and the rule of his conduct.

It stands to reason, therefore, that, as I say often, the work done by the Bible Societies of the world is the indispensable work of the Church. To produce the Bible in the languages of the peoples of the world is one of the basic tasks of the world Church. It is one of your inescapable duties, if you are committed to the advancement of Christ's Kingdom. It cannot be regarded as the concern of a few people who "have a thing" about Bible distribution. The Bible Societies are an arm of the Church, doing a highly skilled work of scholarship, conducting a vast business organisation, on behalf of the rest of us who provide the wherewithal for a job we are not ourselves qualified to accomplish.

When in 1963 I presided in Tokyo over a conference of some two dozen national Bible Societies of the world, we determined to treble by the end of 1966 the output of Bibles and Testaments and portions. We did this in view of the meteoric rise both of world population and of literacy-rate among the emerging nations.

Of the first, the rise of world population, I need only repeat that it is expected that our present population will be doubled by the end of the century. Of the second, the rise of literacy-rate, I would remind you that nations like Venezuela and Iran, where hitherto literacy-rate has been depressingly low, are bending every energy to alter the situation. In Venezuela, for example, illiteracy has dropped from forty-seven per cent to thirteen per cent in six years! In Iran, the Shah has made an impassioned plea for the diversion of some money from armaments to literacy work. The world spends thirteen million dollars per hour on arms: could it not give a few "hours-worth" to promote literacy?

The great campaign *To Feed the Minds of Millions* has as one of its two aims the provision of literature which will show the relevance of Christianity to life in all its facets—home, sex, education, farming, etc. The other aim is that concerned with the translation and distribution of those Holy Scriptures which have brought light and the message of life to our own people and have been the basis of all that is best in our civilisation.

There are plenty of other competitors in the world for the minds and souls of the fast multiplying millions of men, women and children. A battle of vast dimensions is joined. Which way it will be decided will be determined in the near future, for events are moving fast and time is not on our side. In one sense, it will be decided by those who pour their skills into writing, translating, illustrating, disseminating, selling, giving—the front line troops. But the real decision rests with the folk at home, the back-room boys (if I may change my metaphor), the ordinary people like you and me, who cannot leave our homes for Mbonga Mbonga, but who provide the wherewithal of prayer and interest and good hard cash.

It is a privilege and a joy to be part of an epic such as this.

The Relevance of the Bible
for Today

WHAT DO WE mean by relevance? My *Oxford English Dictionary* says *"relevance.* 1733 ... relevancy". That does not help very much. *"Relevancy.* 1561 ... the quality or fact of being relevant". That is little better. *"Relevant.* 1560. Bearing upon, connected with, pertinent to the matter in hand". That is better still. "The matter in hand" is, presumably, life in the twentieth century and how to live it—modern man, his life, his thought, his conduct. The question then reduces itself to this: What bearing, if any, has the Bible on such a man? What connection? What pertinence to his life, his thought, his conduct?

The question can be put another way. In arranging your library, on what shelf should you put the Bible? Alongside the classics of Greece and Rome? In the comparative religions section, so that Jesus may be compared with Socrates or the Buddha or Zoroaster? In the history section, so that we may read the story of an extraordinary race, its fortunes, and especially its misfortunes? Or should it be placed not on a wall-shelf at all, but in that little rack which you keep actually on your desk for constant reference, in the company, perhaps, of a dictionary and an address book and a telephone directory? Is this book ancient or modern? Which? Or is it both? That is the question. It is not an unimportant one.

On the face of it one would scarcely expect to find the Bible relevant, for consider the world from which it comes and contrast the world in which we moderns live. It comes straight out from the ancient world. True, it is not very ancient. *Six Thousand*

The University of Western Australia, 15th March, 1967.

Years of The Bible is the name of a book by G. S. Wegener. But what is six thousand years in the evolution of man, or in the emergence of our tiny planet in the vast universe of which it is an infinitesimally small part? In that perspective, Abraham was alive last night and Moses was at work this morning. It is nevertheless an ancient book, even though we now know that many of the stories and the thought-forms of the people who gave us the Bible were dependent on those of peoples more ancient than themselves. And what an extraordinary mixture the Bible is—a mixture of "old unhappy far off things, and battles long ago" and love stories, of myth and ritual, of poetry and prose, of letters and theological theses, of history and apocalyptic. Here cries for vengeance—"happy shall he be, that taketh and dasheth thy little ones against the stones" (Ps. 137:9)—mix with passages of infinite tenderness—"can a woman forget her sucking child, that she should not have compassion on the son of her womb? Yea, they may forget, yet will I not forget thee" (Isa. 49:15). Here great passages of mighty doctrine, which have affected the history of human thought and indeed of national government, mix with intimate requests from a man in prison for a cloak and for "all my note-books" (2 Tim. 4:13), or for a room ready for him when he arrives (Philem. 22). Here parables of Jesus—Who "spoke of lilies, vines and corn, the sparrow and the raven"—jostle dark and threatening outpourings of apocalyptic vision, in which distress of nations is depicted under the imagery of natural and supernatural upheavals. Here the contributions of the nations converge—the rivers of Hebrew, Egyptian, Babylonian, Persian, Greek thinking flow together. Who can read Proverbs—still more Ecclesiasticus—without seeing a combination of Greek and Hebrew minds, each enriched by the other? Here is an extraordinary amalgam. In face of this, ought one to speak of the Bible in the singular at all? True, we get the world *Bible* from the Latin *biblia* which is a feminine singular, but that feminine singular is the Latinising of a Greek neuter plural—$\tau\acute{a}$ $\beta\iota\beta\lambda\acute{\iota}a$. Were the Romans right in making a singular out of a plural? Or, to put the question more theologically and less philologically, is there a unity within these sixty-six books which justifies us in speaking of the Bible, an overmastering theme which allows us to speak of this conglomeration of writings in the singular?

To this we must return a little later.

I said that we could scarcely expect to find the Bible relevant, considering the ancient world from which it comes and the modern world in which we live. Ours is an age of technology. We find ourselves more at home with pipettes than with psalms, with atoms than with Adam, with spaceflights than with journeys by donkey. "Genesis" to us is a biological term and "Revelation" the name of a suitcase. Our world differs, *toto caelo*, from the world of the Bible. It was easier for our grandparents, even for our parents, to feel at home in the atmosphere of the Bible than it is for us, for we belong to those who take for granted the conquest of space, the manufacture of jet-engines, the invasion of the home by radio and television, the use of the pill, and so forth. God—so awful a reality to Moses when he met Him at the bush, to Abraham when he heard His call, to Jesus when He prayed to Him on the mountain or in the Garden—God has been pushed out to the periphery of things in the thinking of the modern man who likes to say that he has "come of age". Would it not be easier to sign on the dotted line with Bertrand Russell, dismiss God altogether, admit that "when I die I rot" and relegate the Bible to the limbo of things now out of date and totally irrelevant to the "matter in hand"?

Yes, of course it would be easier. But the university man or woman, if he has glimpsed the purpose of university education at all, is not concerned with ease. He is concerned with *truth*, the discovery of it and the relevance of it to the society of which he is a part and to himself in all the complexities of his personality. Heaven knows that is difficult enough, for the field of knowledge is immense; specialisation necessarily becomes more and more intense; and the specialists in different departments of human knowledge increasingly find themselves less and less able to understand one another. Nevertheless the student, be he scientist or arts man, cannot afford to leave out of consideration that vast area of human experience which has been radically and fundamentally influenced by biblical ideas and by the biblical writings. In the field of music and of art and of literature, this is obvious enough—here, the Judæo-Christian influence is stupendous (I need only mention at random two great names in each of those three spheres to hint at the scale of the thing—music, Bach and Handel; art, Botticelli and Leonardo da Vinci; literature, Milton and Bunyan). Any man who aspires to be a man of culture must learn about these things and take cognisance of them as he works out his philosophy of life. Else he will run the risk of deserving the epithet of tyro.

I revert to the questions with which I began. Is this strange library of books, this collection which reflects the interaction of so many nations down so many centuries, simply a collection of ancient writings, to be put with the Vedas and the Upanishads or alongside of Plato and Ovid? Or can it also be called a modern book because of its relevance to modern man in his living, his thinking, his conduct of himself and of his affairs? Is there a master-theme which ties the sixty-six books together and makes the contributions of the nations captive to it? Has it a word of eternal significance to man, whether that man be the sophisticated creature of a highly developed scientific culture, or whether he belong to a pattern of society which has as yet hardly felt the impact of Western civilisation?

I believe it can be called a modern book, more relevant to twentieth century man than today's newspaper. I believe there is a master-theme running through it. I believe it has a word of immense importance to say to present-day man in the differing stages of his social evolution. If I did not believe this, I should not have spent many years lecturing on and trying to expound the message of this book, nor should I bother to be President of the United Bible Societies (to which it is a privilege to refer so often) which hold together thirty-five national Bible Societies whose one task is to provide the Bible, in whole or in part, in the languages of the nations of the world. I would add this: I would say that I believe it to be of the utmost importance that the word that this book has to say should be listened to intently and intelligently, should be digested and lived by, should in fact become a guide to modern man in the complexities of his development. I would go further: I would hold that any university which by-passes the word which the Bible has to say is not only impoverishing, but is actually endangering the life and development of its undergraduates.

Sir Walter Moberley, in his book *The Crisis in the University*, points out that the work of a university is not finished when it has taught the student how to make a bomb or a cathedral or a healthy body. It must go on to ask such questions as whether or why you want such things at all. That brings you to the heart of such questions as the nature of man, the idea of God, the meaning of life here and hereafter. To by-pass such issues is to do the student great harm. As Moberley says: "It is a fallacy to suppose that by omitting a subject, you teach nothing about it. On the contrary, you teach that it is to be omitted, and that it is therefore a matter of secondary importance . . . If in your organisations, your curriculum, and your communal customs and ways of life you leave God out, you teach with tremendous force that for most people and at most times, He does not count . . ."

I can only indicate here three areas in which I see the message of the Bible to be of vast importance and of intimate relevance. They are the subjects of man, of God and of life.

1. *Man*

It is, I think, the down-to-earth *realism* of the Bible on this subject which most impresses me. Shakespeare makes Hamlet say: "What a piece of work is a man! how noble in reason! how infinite in faculty! in form and moving how express and admirable! in action how like an angel! in apprehension how like a god! the beauty of the world! the paragon of animals!" (*Hamlet* II. ii. 315-20). There is that in the Bible to which Shakespeare might have appealed for corroboration when he wrote this. In one of the creation stories of Genesis, when God had made man, with his procreative powers and his authority over nature, He saw what He had made "and behold, it was very good" (1:31). The Psalmist, even with his tiny view of what constitutes the universe, sees how small is man in comparison. "Yet," he goes on (Ps. 8:5 ff.), "yet thou hast made him little less than God, and dost crown him with glory and honour. Thou hast given him dominion over the works of thy hands; thou hast put all things under his feet." He elaborates "all things" in terms of man's mastery over cattle, birds and fish. Had the Psalmist been living in the twentieth century AD instead of several centuries BC, he would no doubt have spoken of man's mastery over bacteria and the problems of space flight and so forth.

"What a piece of work is a man!" But the Bible, while granting this, never sentimentalises over it. It accepts, with a stern realism, that there is in man an element which, if unmastered, can make

H

him sink lower than the beasts. It was perhaps alien to the
Hebrew way of looking at life to linger long over the question
which perplexed the Greeks and drew from them such a wealth
of literature—"where does evil come from?" True, the Hebrews
had in their primitive creation stories the picture-story of the
man, the woman, the serpent and the fruit. But even this story
is more concerned with the nature of man's rebellion and its dire
consequence in the breaking of fellowship between man and God
than with the origin of evil. If the typical Greek question is
"Where does evil come from?" the typical Hebrew question is
"How can evil be conquered?" It is to this that writer after
writer addresses himself, and does so with a seriousness which
shows that he has faced the strange paradox of man's nature—a
nobility which makes him akin to the angels, and a sinfulness
which can make him create a Belsen or kill his wife by nagging
even while he is a churchwarden or mayor of the local muni-
cipality.

Looking back over the history of the last century one can but
wish that the realism of the anthropology of the Bible had been
taken more seriously. Had that been the case, we should have
heard less of that philosophy of life which seemed to hold that,
given a little more knowledge, Utopia was round the corner.
We *were* given a little more knowledge—indeed, a great deal.
But World War I and World War II were round the corner,
with all the horrors of atom-bombing and concentration camps.
"What a piece of work is a man!"—much depends on what tone
of voice you quote your Shakespeare in!

The Hebrew realism in regard to the nature of man needs to
be taken seriously. It calls upon us to put a question-mark
against the gnostic view of life that the answer to man's wrongness is more knowledge—by itself. Did not T. R. Glover say
somewhere that the Greeks thought that man had only to follow
his nose and he would arrive at blessedness? But the Greeks had
forgotten that man had a broken nose. The Hebrews never forgot
it. Hence the sternness of their writings. Hence the insistence on
the need of divine succour, of redemption, of a Hand stretched
out to rescue us. Hence the conviction which sounds again and
again, in history, in poetry, in prophecy, in apocalyptic, that
there is a moral core to the universe, a principle of judgment to
be reckoned with. God may be regarded as the Father of His

people—that is propounded in both Testaments. But He is also Judge. Divine love is not sentimentalism. Man, if he is to rise to the heights for which he was intended, must come to terms with this. He must exercise his moral responsibility, if he is to *live*—and life, as we shall see later, is for a Hebrew much more than physical existence.

2. God

If we go to the Bible expecting to find there a closely enunciated argument for the existence of God, we shall be disappointed. His existence is taken for granted much as the air we breathe is taken for granted. If there were no air, we should not be here. We may comment on the kind of air it is—warm, cold, blowing fiercely, breathing gently and so on. But we don't often argue about its existence! It was something like that when the Hebrews came to think and speak—and eventually to write—about God. "It is He that hath made us and we are His" (Ps. 100:3, Revised Psalter). We should not exist if He were not. But what He is *like* —that is another matter. That He cannot be depicted in stone or in art became early in Hebrew history a fundamental tenet of their faith. Hence the contribution of Hebrew religion to the idea of monotheism; and hence, incidentally, the poverty of the Hebrew contribution to art. "Thou shalt not make unto thee any graven image, or any *likeness* of any thing ..." (Exod. 20:4). Hence the surprise of Titus when, during the sack of Jerusalem in AD 70, on entering the Holy of Holies in the Temple he found— *nothing!* "No man has seen God at any time" (St John 1:18). He may not be depicted or His image be formed. But He may be *known.*

This is the great fundamental conviction of the Hebrew prophets. If the Greeks preached self-knowledge (γνῶσθι σεάντον), the Hebrews preached that knowledge of God was everything, and man could only truly know himself when he was at least beginning to know God. "My people are gone into captivity for lack of knowledge", laments the prophet Isaiah (5:13). When he speaks of knowledge, he does not mean merely the acquisition of intellectual facts or the equipment of mental furniture. He means that knowledge of God which is at once the worship of the creature directed to the Creator and the acknowledgment of a relationship of the most intimate kind. Indeed the verb to *know* used with reference to God is the identical word which is used of physical *knowledge*, intercourse of man and woman. This theme is worked out in great detail by a series of Old Testament writers, who depict Israel as the Bride of Yahweh and speak of her defection from Him as adultery. The nuptial element in Hebrew religion is strong precisely because anything less would fail to express the intimacy with which this God may be known.

The element of the numinous is strong. The links with nature are close. God appears to Abraham as he gazes at the stars; to Jacob in the open during a dream; to Moses in the flaming bush. Sometimes man's reaction is sheer terror; sometimes a trembling hope; sometimes a steady confidence. Slowly but surely, as we read the ancient documents in roughly chronological order, we see the emergence of a people from crude and inadequate ideas of God to a vision of Him which almost blinds us with its majesty. Slowly the magical gives way to the ethical—the idea of naked power to the concept of the demands of divine justice, mercy, and love—till at last, with the eighth century prophets, we see the kingly majesty of Isaiah's God (depicted in chapter six against the background of the failure of the prophet's hero-king); the stern justice of Amos' God, dispensing judgment to Israel's heartless neighbours and—on the principle of "the greater the light the greater the judgment"—sterner judgment on privileged Israel herself; the infinite tenderness of Hosea's God; till at last we see a God whose rule is not confined to His chosen people but is as wide as the bounds of His world. Israel is given as a light to lighten the Gentiles. There is no limit to the vision of Deutero-Isaiah's God. He is the God of all the earth to whose worship, in the fullness of time, all men shall come. Even Cyrus is regarded as an agent in His hands, His anointed, His "Messiah" whom He uses in the fulfilment of His purposes.

Such, in briefest outline, was the backcloth against which Jesus painted His picture of God. The metaphor of backcloth and picture, however, is wholly inadequate to convey the manner of His teaching and the content of His lessons. For He taught as much by His example and life as by His verbal formulations. As His disciples watched Him at prayer, they said "Lord, teach us to pray." They saw One who, to use the Old Testament language, knew God in a manner at once intimate and reverent. The contact between the One who prayed and the God to whom He prayed was patently close and real and alive. Seeing that, and listening to Him as He prayed, they could not argue the existence of God, as it were, at arm's length. They were in the company of One who was in the company of God. Here was the knowledge of God indeed! His teaching in a sense was extraordinarily simple —a child could begin to understand it. He said that *only* a child— or the childlike—could understand it. All of them knew what fatherhood meant—loving, personal, constant care. And all of them knew what kingship meant—authority and demand. Combine the two, fatherhood and kingship. Combine the two— care and authority. And you will begin to see what God is like, and the nature of the human response for which He looks.

A father seeks the response of love, a king the response of obedience. That is the essence of the religious life—loving obedience. That is the road to the knowledge of God. That is the path to the *summum bonum*.

When the early Christians looked back on the life and death of Jesus of Nazareth, and especially on the events connected with His passion, crucifixion and the immediately ensuing days, they found it hard to give expression to what they considered as having happened in what we might call the Christ-event. Some put it one way, some another. But however they put it, they were at one in the conviction that in the Person of Jesus of Nazareth there had been an irruption of goodness and power, of grace, of the mind and activity of God for which the events of the Old Testament Scriptures were indeed a preparation but to which they could provide no adequate parallel. Here was something unique. The reign of God had broken in; the Finger of God had been at work (the phrase is used in the Old Testament only of God at work in creation, in the giving of the Law, and in the redemption of His people from slavery); the Son of God had come; the Word of God had been made flesh.

Perhaps the last phrase is the most expressive of all. We owe it to the writer of the Fourth Gospel (though the thought behind the phrase had been expressed, but not in identical language, by St Paul and by the writer of the Epistle to the Hebrews). In using the word λόγος, St John availed himself of a term well known to Hellenic and Hebraic thinkers and writers. In this

term, the two great streams of thought flowed together, though
I myself have little doubt that the Hebraic stream was the
stronger of the two. St John was not content to think of Jesus
as one more, or even as the greatest, of the prophets. *Their*
task was to be the bearers of the word of God to man. Indeed,
they spoke of the word as a burden which they had to carry and
deliver. But Jesus *was* the Word. He, in human flesh, *was* what
God had to say to men. In His Person, the mind and heart and
will of God were uniquely disclosed. Hence the voice at the
baptism and again at the transfiguration—"hear *Him*!" Hence the
extraordinary religious phenomenon that Jews, monotheists
born and bred, found themselves praying to Jesus only a very
short time after the withdrawal of His body from the earthly
scene. Hence the incipient trinitarianism of such a passage as this:
"Through Him [i.e. Jesus] we both have access by one Spirit to
the Father" (Eph. 2:18). Hence the daring phrase of the writer
of the Book of the Revelation when he refers to the shared "throne
of God and of the Lamb" (Rev. 22:1). These are facts of a phenomenon which cannot be explained in any other way than by the
conviction that in Jesus Christ, in His life and supremely in His
death and resurrection, God had broken into this world-order in
rescuing activity never so seen before.

This irruption, this invasion of grace, did not cease when Jesus
was seen no more. Many thought it would. In fact, it did not.
On the contrary, what was a localised movement soon showed
itself to be possessed of extraordinary powers of expansion. The
doctrine of the Holy Spirit grew out of—what? The Old Testament teaching? Yes, in part. But far more out of the experience
of a group of ordinary men and women who saw the life of Jesus
continuing at work within them and who were conscious of
the outworking of His love and power in their lives.

Christian pneumatology, which occupies a much larger place
in the New Testament than many theological books deign to
accord it, was no arid doctrine neatly thought up by a synod of
theologians, but was an attempt to express, albeit in faltering
language, the inexpressible power of God at work.

3. *Life*

What the Bible has to say about human life emerges from the
fundamental conviction of its writers that the only worthwhile

life is the holy life, that is to say, life lived according to the mind and will of the holy God who is Himself the origin of life. If there are passages of Scripture which depict God mostly in terms of crude power—"how *awesome* is this place; this is none other than the house of God . . ."—the concept of power soon gives place to the overmastering concept of the holy, thought of in terms of the *ethical*. The later prophets inveigh in terrible language against any concept of ritual, of the cult, divorced from the ethical (Isa. 1:10ff. is a case in point). Our Lord's condemnation of the worst characteristics of the Pharisees springs from a similar background of thought. St Paul insists far more on the harvest of the Spirit—love, joy, peace, self-control and so on—than on the more showy gifts of glossolalia and the like. "As He which hath called you is holy, so be ye holy" (I Peter 1:15). Only so can man live the life for which he was destined as a son of God.

"As a son of God". It is this concept which makes it impossible for the New Testament writers to believe that the dissolution of the physical body can be the end of *life*. Life as a biblical concept is more than the continuation of a heart-beat. It is the continuation of a relationship entered into in the here and now and reaching its fulfilment when physical life as we know it is transcended. St Paul struggles to express it in terms of a "spiritual body". St John, in a passage marked by a delightfully frank agnosticism—"we know not what we shall be"—pin-points the essence of the thing when he says "we shall be like Him, for we shall see Him as He is" (1 John 3:2). That is to say, physical dissolution cannot destroy a union of love entered into here. Perhaps it is unfortunate that we have to use such words as "endless" or "everlasting" which to our English ears have a temporal connotation which misses the qualitative meaning of the New Testament concept.

This is something more than what the Greek meant by the immortality of the soul. This is the fulfilment and the consummation of a relationship between Redeemer and redeemed.

That the life of the redeemed in the hereafter is depicted in *corporate* imagery is not to be wondered at, for the Christian life on earth is always described in corporate terms. Those who enter into life eternal are depicted as members of a worshipping community (though there is no need of a Temple wherein to worship), as citizens of a heavenly city whose King is the Lord God. This is but the consummation of the life of the Christian here on earth. In the here and now he is a member of the *family* of God; he has come within the sphere of the *Kingdom* of God; he is a member of the *people* of God. Christian experience, while allowing full range for the exercise of individual choice and individual development, is always *corporate* experience. The doctrine of the Church is not an addendum to the main corpus of Christian doctrine, an after-thought added on to the original Gospel. It is part and parcel of the Gospel. Incorporation into Christ means incorporation into the Body of Christ, where alone is to be found the nourishment of Word and Sacrament.

The Church is a venerable institution. If you ask me when it began I would reply, "Not at Pentecost". It is older than that. Pentecost saw the renewal and the empowering of the Church. The *Christian* Church began when Jesus, walking by the Sea of Galilee, saw two pairs of brothers and called them and they followed Him. But, of course, long before that there was a Church. It can be traced back to the days of Abraham, that man of faith who, at the call of God, went out though not knowing whither he went, and became the father of the faithful. Of that Church the believing and baptised Christian is a member, and if at times he is tempted to be scandalised by its failure, he checks himself by reminding himself that it is made up of sinners like himself, *simul justi et peccatores*. There is no other Body of Christ. Here the holy life of the sons of God is nourished, and given for the life of the world.

It is themes such as these, which all too briefly and inadequately I have sketched, which bind together the strange conglomeration of books which we call the Bible. It is such themes which give to it its unity and which constitute its relevance. For man, whether he lives two thousand years before Christ or two thousand years after Him, needs to know about himself and his nature, about God and the revelation of Himself which He has given to man, and about the meaning of life here and hereafter.

Central to all its affirmations is the announcement of the Word made flesh. Before the imperatives of its ethics come the indicatives of God's grace. Luther was not far wrong when he called the Bible the cradle which bears to us Christ. We do not worship the cradle. We can see the variety of workmanship which has gone to the making of it. But we venerate it for the holy Burden which it bears and we approach it with the humility it deserves.

Unity and Scripture

As I LOOK at the matter of Christian unity, I am at once encouraged and disheartened. I am encouraged, because I am old enough to appreciate how great have been the advances made in the last half-century, even in the last few years. The contrast between, say, 1920 and 1970 is very notable. In social work, in joint scholarship, in understanding and in worship, we have been drawn together by the Lord, the Spirit. This does not mean that we blind ourselves to the reality of our differences. It does mean that we face them in love. We talk together. We pray together. We work together. I am encouraged.

But, I confess, I am also sometimes disheartened. Some of our schemes of union are very slow in coming to fruition—I think particularly of our hopes for Anglican-Methodist union in England. I feel rebuked by the progress made by some of the younger Churches—I think again of India and Pakistan. I long for visible unity in truth and love; because I believe it to be the will of God; because any barrier, especially at the sacrament of union, is an offence; because the enemy is at the gates, and we need the strength of unity to do battle with him.

Against that background I try to peer into the future. I ask myself in what main direction or directions we may look for advance in unity. I suggest that it will be in prayerful study of Scripture; in the united declaration of the truths of Scripture; and in the joint dissemination of Scripture.

The Catholic University of Louvain, during a visit to Cardinal Suenens, Archbishop of Malines-Brussels, May 1971.

1. *Prayer and Bible Study*

I put first and foremost the way of *prayer and biblical study*. This is not the expression of a pious sentiment uttered because an Archbishop is expected to say it *qua* Archbishop! It is, rather, the expression of a conviction born of observation. It was not many years ago that Roman Catholics and non-Roman Catholics could not pray together in public. Sometimes they were allowed to join together in the Lord's Prayer—sometimes not even that. Thank God, those days are past, never to return. We are learning to pray together, to worship together. Those who engage in that activity at any depth cannot long remain apart.

The Holy Spirit is spoken of in Scripture in terms of fire. One of the functions of fire is (as I have said in other contexts) to join together, to solder, pieces of metal which otherwise cannot be joined. This, I believe, the Spirit of God is doing by means of prayer undertaken by two Churches, or by two bodies of Christians, hitherto divided. What God is joining together, let no man put asunder!

We are moving towards unity in prayer through an increasing agreement as to "prayers we have in common". Those last five words constitute the title of a booklet published in 1970 which gives a series of agreed liturgical texts proposed by the International Consultation on English Texts. This Consultation, which is international and ecumenical, has agreed on, and presented to the Churches for experimental use, a text of the Lord's Prayer, the Apostles' Creed, the Nicene Creed, *Gloria in excelsis*, *Sanctus* and *Benedictus*, *Gloria Patri*. The Consultation is still working on *Sursum Corda*, *Agnus Dei* and *Te Deum*.

This is all to the good and we can confidently expect progress here. It is frustrating and annoying if, when we meet for joint worship, we find ourselves using different "versions" of liturgical texts.

The weeks of prayer for Christian unity have achieved much in the field of unity among Christians. We think with deep gratitude of men like Abbé Paul Couturier (1881–1953), with whom the concept began. I think I am right, however, in detecting a measure of disenchantment—is "disillusionment" too strong a word?—in regard to these weeks recently in England. True, the people still come, often in large numbers. But I think I should not be far wrong in saying that some of the most thoughtful of those

who attend such gatherings are beginning to say: "Where is all
this leading? We meet. We sing. We listen to speeches in which
our disunity is lamented. We shake hands. We part. Next year,
we meet again, and repeat the exercise. But little advance seems
to be achieved."

There is some justification for such an attitude. If I try to analyse
it, I think the reason may lie here: too often, weeks of *prayer* for
Christian unity have become weeks of *speeches* for Christian unity;
and in the realm of spiritual warfare, speeches do not effect what
prayer effects. I believe that more might be achieved, and greater
advance made, if there were fewer great gatherings to hear people
talk (however eminent those people might be), and more groups,
little groups maybe, intent to hear "what the Spirit is saying to the
Churches". I envisage these groups meeting, as often as not, in
livingrooms and kitchens, by no means always in churches. I
envisage an atmosphere of waiting on God, of silence, of expectation, of informality. Such groups would experience the truth of
the saying of Christ: "Where two or three are gathered together
in my name, there am I in the midst." They would soon find that
once a year was not enough for their meeting. The ear has to be
trained to listen. Friendships formed in prayer have to be culti-
vated. Prayer often issues most fruitfully from biblical study
engaged in together. In short, I see the way forward through a
proliferation of groups of ordinary men and women, studying,
praying, waiting on God together, discovering together an
already-existing unity in Christ which only calls for deepening
and expressing.

You will note my reference to biblical study in connection with
joint prayer. I must elaborate this a little. The great new biblical
movement which is stirring in the Roman Catholic Church is one
of the most significant movements of the Spirit in many centuries.
Non-Roman Catholics are deeply grateful for the Jerusalem Bible
—the Convocations of the Church of England have given
authority for it to be used, *inter alia*, in the liturgical lections of
our services. Roman Catholics use extensively the Revised
Standard Version and the New English Bible, while the New
Testament in Today's English Version has received a Roman
Catholic *imprimatur*. Here in the Bible we have a focal point of
unity. Vatican II was explicit in what it said about the importance

of the Bible in the life of the laity. I quote from chapter VI (22):
"Easy access to sacred Scripture should be provided for all the
Christian faithful"—to which the editorial note is added: "This
is perhaps the most novel section of the Constitution. Not since
the early centuries of the Church has an official document urged
the availability of the Scriptures for all." And again (26): "Just
as the life of the Church grows through persistent participation
in the eucharistic mystery, so we may hope for a new surge of
spiritual vitality from intensified veneration for God's word,
which 'lasts forever'." Who can tell what will be the outcome
of these words from "the fathers of the Council to all men"?

Bishop Stephen Neill, that prolific and illuminating writer and
student of ecumenism whom I quote frequently, towards the end
of his Peter Ainslie Memorial Lecture entitled "Rome and the
Ecumenical Movement" (delivered in 1967 at Rhodes University,
Grahamstown), writing of the many commissions which have
been appointed by various denominations to discuss with Roman
Catholic brethren, asks what they should do when they meet.
He answers his question thus:

> I do not believe that anything at all is to be gained at the
> present stage by talk about such marginal subjects as the
> Infallibility of the Pope or the Immaculate Conception of the
> Virgin Mary. We have to get down to the basic question of
> the way in which we read and understand the Scriptures
> themselves. So, when the Anglican Commission meets with its
> Roman Catholic opposite number, I would like to shut up all
> these learned gentlemen, as the Cardinals are shut up when
> they meet for a Conclave, under not too comfortable condi-
> tions, and tell them to read and study together the Epistle to
> the Romans, verse by verse, phrase by phrase and word by
> word. They would not be let out until they had satisfactorily
> completed their task. This might take a month or more—the
> important thing is that they should not be in a hurry—rations
> would continue to be supplied for as long as was needed. We
> all profess faith in the same Scriptures; we all take them as the
> basis of faith and practice, though with differing views as to the
> place of tradition in the life of the Church. But we do not
> agree in our understanding of Scripture. Why? We all accept
> today the same principles of scholarly interpretation. Is the

source of difference to be found in presuppositions, largely un-
expressed and uncriticised, with which we come to the sacred
text, and, if so, is not our joint task the elucidation and criticism
of these presuppositions? Without such common work, it is
unlikely that we shall advance much further in the direction of
fellowship and the elimination of those things that still divide us.

On the highest level, this is obviously a task for scholars and
specialists, but I ask myself whether the principle is not suscep-
tible of much wider application. I detect throughout the
Christian world a certain weariness in the matter of ecumenical
meetings and discussions. When we have met a number of
times and enjoyed the experience of fellowship, do we really
get any further? Do we not go round the same rather weary
circle of affirmations and negations? Is there any way out of the
cyclical into the linear?

I believe that the field of Bible study provides the answer.
If groups of lay people, and ordained ministers, of the various
confessions could meet not once or twice, but for fairly long
periods, to wrestle together with the words of Scripture, as
found in a Gospel or Epistle, not evading any difficulty, not
attempting to reach premature agreement where difference
really exists, using the best helps available from all sources, it
might be possible to build up over the years a solid body of
common opinion throughout the Churches, and so to create
a climate favourable to the further advances, the new experiments, for which we wait at times impatiently.

Here then, I believe, is the most effective way of advance—the
formation of countless little groups for prayer and biblical study.
They might well prove to be like a thousand rivulets which,
individually weak, would, coalescing, form a river whose progress would prove irresistible.

In the facilitating of such study, many things are already
working together for good. In Holland, for example, those who
produce, on a biblically conservative basis, the Scripture Union
Bible reading notes are co-operating with Roman Catholics in
their production. And the more liberal Bible Reading Fellowship,
of which I have the honour to be President and which has a big
world-wide circulation, now numbers among the authors of its
notes writers from the Roman Catholic Church as well as from

the Anglican, Orthodox and Reformed traditions. The latest venture of the Fellowship is the production of a series of ecumenical Bible Readings entitled *Word for the World* which is commended by Dr Visser 't Hooft, Cardinal Heenan and Dr Ernest Payne. The Bible is proving to be a powerful agent in the cause of unity.

2. *Joint Evangelistic Endeavour*

I now come to the second way forward. I have called it "the united declaration of the truths of Scripture". I might equally well call it the way of *joint evangelistic endeavour*. Dr John Mackay, Presbyterian missionary and theologian, used to speak of truth being found "on the road". He contrasted this with what he called "the balcony approach" to reality. He propounded the thesis that progress in the discovery of truth is more often made in the sweat and dust of the road than on the cool and shady balcony, where those concerned for truth engage in leisurely discussion. The thesis could, I think, be verified from the experience of men engaged in many spheres of search for truth.

Now I believe that what is true of the search for truth is true also of the search for unity. I am not suggesting that we should abandon the theological dialogue into which we have entered particularly in recent years. Dialogue at *greater* depth and of *greater* intensity is called for in the years ahead. The work, e.g. of the Anglican/Roman Catholic International Commission must be continued and extended. Our theological understanding must be deepened. But I am saying that the Church of Christ—using that term in its broadest sense—is faced by a world unbelieving, or at best wistful, in its attitude to Christian belief and conduct, and I ask if we must wait until organic re-union has taken place before we can present a sufficiently united front to state our case and commend our Saviour? Have we not enough which we hold in common to enable us to face the world unashamedly and, on the basis of that common belief, to present Christ to the world?

Professor Karl Rahner has recently been making the point that Christians already hold the fundamentals of their faith in common, though they are sometimes divided more by misunderstandings and misinterpretations of their own position and that of Christians in other Churches than by real disagreements.

Let me illustrate the kind of thing that I have in mind. The

Province of York consists of fourteen dioceses in the North of England stretching up to the Scottish border. Within that area, which includes some of the most beautiful of the English countryside and some of the most densely populated industrial areas, are many millions of people, the majority of whom have either no connection or only a very formal connection with the Christian Church in any of its branches. But in that area there is also a very considerable number of committed, practising Christians, owning allegiance to a wide variety of denominations. Often the witness of these Christians is pathetically weak because of their divisions—a small village may have a considerable number of different "church" buildings. The sceptic has some justification in taunting the Christian: "You talk about reconciliation. You do very little to manifest it." What can we say in reply? Must we wait till the consultations of the theologians issue in schemes of organic reunion? Or can we, on the basis of our baptismal unity and of a very great measure of doctrinal agreement, say unitedly to a sceptical world: "Divided we may be in organisation and in certain matters of belief. But in the great basic doctrines of our faith we are one. We know the love of God—it has invaded us. We know the grace of our Lord Jesus Christ—it has come to us through the Scriptures; it comes to us through the Sacrament of his Body and Blood. We know the fellowship of the Holy Spirit—not fully, God forgive us, but in very truth we are finding out more of it every year. This tri-une God has laid hold of us. Him we adore. Him we commend to you."

With this as a background to my thinking, and with an almost desperate longing that the Churches should be able to say something unitedly to the North of England, I called a meeting of leaders of all branches of the Christian Church in May 1969 at Bishopthorpe, which has been the home of the Archbishop of York since the early thirteenth century. The response could hardly have been better or more representative. We faced the realities—grim realities—of the situation in the North of England. Many of us felt that there was a divine compulsion behind our meeting. The leaders went back to discuss the matter with their people. They met again in May 1970 and went a step further. We are meeting again almost at once. We hope then to decide to launch, in Holy Week 1972, a plan for a year of preparation and study, so that, in Holy Week 1973, we shall be able, unitedly, to say to all who have ears to hear: "Christ crucified is risen. We commend Him to you."

This will have to be spelt out in a wide variety of ways. We are aware that the Christian vocabulary is not understood by the "man in the street". We are aware that we are addressing men of a technological age, whose thought-forms differ vastly from those of the New Testament era. We do not intend to have any one stereotyped form of presentation. The "Call to the North", as it is coming to be known, will be made—here by the organisation of a study group, there by the presentation of drama or music; here by the witness of changed lives, there in a meeting on a scale which will demonstrate the strength of the Christian forces in a given locality. If it is true that in times past God spoke "in divers manners", it will certainly be true in Holy Week 1973 in the North of England! But that is all to the good, providing there can be a demonstration of our unity in Christ and in our belief in the essentials of Christian faith and conduct.

I turn for a brief moment from this particular piece of joint evangelistic endeavour to another sphere where I believe increasingly co-operation will be possible and fruitful, and which indirectly will lead to a more effective presentation of the Gospel of Christ to the people.

In 1960 the College of Preachers was born in England. Drawing some of its inspiration from the long-established and well-endowed College of Preachers in Washington, D.C., it is an Anglican foundation which during the past eleven years has conducted intensive refresher courses for small groups of priests most of whom have been ordained for ten years or more. Some 1,200 clergy have taken the course, which deals not only with the techniques of preaching but also with the content and theology of preaching. In the March 1968 number of *Concilium*, which was devoted to the theme of *Preaching the Word of God*, reference was made to the work of the College. The last sentence of the article in which this reference occurs ended with the words: "The Preachers' College is not yet an ecumenical effort" (vol. 3, no. 4, p. 73). This is becoming less and less true. Free Churchmen are now members of the Council of the College, though the majority of its members are still Anglicans; and the Church of Rome is beginning to show a keen interest in its activities. Thus in 1968, a Roman Catholic priest, a member of the Order of Preachers, attended a day conference organised by the College. In 1969 and 1970, members of the Order attended training weeks as "students". Last year, when the College celebrated its tenth birthday by a great Festival of Preaching held at the University of York and attended by some 400 clergy, Fr Agnellus Andrew, Director of the Catholic Radio and Television Centre, was one of the preachers, and the Roman Catholic Bishops of Middlesbrough and Leeds sent representatives. The Director of the College, Canon Cleverley Ford, willingly accepted an invitation by Fr Lemass, Director of the Communications Centre in Dublin, to lecture there.

These are not easy days for the preacher. There are even those who say that the day of preaching is over. I believe they are grossly mistaken. Nevertheless, the common denigration of preaching has been such as to make the atmosphere exceedingly difficult for the preacher and sometimes his worst enemies "are they of his own household". I hold that so long as there is a God of love and judgment on the one hand, and man in his sin and need on the other, there is a place, a vital place, for the preacher, even though the form and manner of his preaching may be, must be, very different from those of an earlier generation. But the fact that our Lord has committed to His Church the ministry of the Word as well as of the Sacraments, and that, as is undoubtedly the case, he uses that Word to the salvation of men and women, must surely be a powerful reason for His servants joining hands in this ministry.

We have much to give each other. In face of the divine commission and in face of the desperate need of the world, we dare not stand apart in the equipping of ourselves and in the refreshing of ourselves in this basic ministry.

3. *The Dissemination of the Scriptures*

Let me pass now to one area of endeavour which I believe is of immense importance in world evangelisation, and in the joint pursuit of which we may discover our unity. I refer once again to a theme dear to my heart, the translation and dissemination of Scripture, and of course I speak in my capacity as President of the United Bible Societies.

Launched in 1946, the United Bible Societies (if I may repeat the basic perhaps well-known facts) hold together some fifty national Bible Societies, ensuring a wise economy of man-power and finance throughout the world, a high standard of scholarship, and a world-view, as distinct from a partial appreciation, of needs and opportunities. It recognises that, from the beginning, the Church has always gone to the world with a book in its hand as the indispensable tool of its evangelistic work—at the beginning that book was the Old Testament; from the second century onwards it has been the complete Bible. It seeks to ensure that every Church, in every nation, shall have the Bible—at first, it may be, in part, but eventually in whole—in its own tongue, in an accurate translation and at a cost within the means of the people concerned.

From its inception, the United Bible Societies have worked on the principle, which was the principle of its constituent national societies, of *inter-denominational co-operation*. Indeed, this co-operation played no small part in making possible the ecumenical movement. But up to the time of the Vatican Council the Church of Rome, while casting, at least in recent years, a kindly eye on this work, stood aloof from any active share in it. Then things began to happen. Men of great vision like the late Cardinal Bea and Cardinal Willebrands saw, especially in the light of the statements of Vatican II to which I referred earlier, that here was a field in which Roman Catholic and non-Roman Catholic might, or rather, must, work together, not waiting for further advance in schemes of union but tackling together, and at once, a task of great urgency and of vast proportions.

At the very start of the Bible Society movement, early in the nineteenth century, the British and Foreign Bible Society was in frequent communication with Roman Catholic leaders and at a very early stage sanctioned and circulated as many as eight Roman Catholic translations of the Scriptures in the principal languages of Europe. A few years later, Roman Catholic churchmen were invited to share in the formation of the American Bible Society. Then followed a long period of mutual misunderstanding and mistrust, and Roman Catholics and non-Roman Catholics went their several ways.

In 1964 at a world gathering of Church leaders, at which I had the privilege of presiding, called together by the United Bible Societies and meeting in Driebergen (Holland), a call was made for the full co-operation of biblical scholars, regardless of confessions, in the preparation of agreed texts of the Hebrew Old Testament. On January 5th 1967:

> Informal conversations took place between Bible Society experts and staff members of the Secretariat for Promoting Christian Unity and Roman Catholic scholars. Consideration was given to the implications in the field of translation, production and distribution of the Scriptures according to the recommendations of the Second Vatican Council on the use of the Bible. The meeting took place on the occasion of a session of the UBS Translations Committee and a visit to Rome of Bible Society leaders, connected with the development of Bible Society work in Italy. Common recommendations were made for the consideration of Roman Catholic authorities and Bible Society constituencies as to the patterns to be applied and the procedures to be followed in undertaking joint projects wherever local churches ask for them. Consideration was also given to the basic requirements of Bible translation work. Reports on experiments made in various countries, particularly in French-speaking Europe where new inter-confessional translations are in process, were received with considerable interest. It was agreed that the Secretariat for Promoting Christian Unity and the United Bible Societies should keep each other informed of developments in their own spheres of activity.

At that meeting in January 1967, Cardinal Bea said:

> As you know, Pope Paul VI has authorised this Secretariat to study the possibility of co-operation with the Bible Societies in translating and distributing the Sacred Scriptures. Our meeting today is an important part of that study.
>
> How far we have come! It is the remarkable growth of objective scholarship on both sides that has brought us where we are today—yes, objective scholarship and the grace of God. The Holy Spirit is surely at work drawing us together through the Bible: through the effort to translate the Sacred Scriptures together and through the work of distributing the Sacred Scriptures together. As the conciliar Decree on Ecumenism

puts it: "In the dialogue itself, the Sacred Word is a precious instrument in the mighty hand of God for attaining to that unity which the Saviour holds out to all men."

Through the studies and discussions over the past two years we have learned much about each other. Misconceptions have given way to facts; prejudices have given way to mutual esteem. For many years, of course, we had esteemed the Würtemburg Bible Society for its critical editions of the Hebrew Old Testament by Kittel, the Septuagint by Rahlfs, and the Greek New Testament of Nestle. I think it is safe to say that the Bible Societies have long esteemed the work of such Catholic institutions as the Pontifical Biblical Institute.

It is necessary that we persevere firmly in this effort to know each other: who and where the experts are, what the resources are and how they can be deployed. For all this we need on-going dialogue, sharing of information, co-ordination of studies and activities. We need experts on each side who are also friends, who can give guidance and encouragement and direction to their confreres, who can frankly recognise problems and difficulties—not being deterred by them but being determined to overcome them.

It does not seem to be an exaggeration to say that the possibility of our co-operation is one of the most important developments in contemporary Christian history. It challenges decades, even generations of suspicion and, in some cases, hostility. It draws us into deeper probing and more honest appraisal of our different attitudes.

We stand on the threshold of a great enterprise. Taking stock before we enter upon it, we know in our hearts that the Christian virtues of faith, hope, and love already bind us together. We shall invoke these virtues and proceed with trust in each other in the name of the Lord Jesus.

Much has happened since 1967. Co-operation has grown steadily closer, and the appointment, in a full-time capacity, of the Rev. Walter M. Abbott, s.j., as executive Secretary of the Office for Common Bible Work in Vatican City, has done much to facilitate and further this collaboration. To this collaboration the Pope bore witness when on his visit last November to the Philippines. He referred to the "wonderful work" which the Bible Societies are doing for the Christian Church and the world, and again to "that world-wide organisation, the United Bible Societies, with which the Catholic Church now shares many fruitful co-operative programmes."

The United Bible Societies organisation seeks to be the servant of the Roman Catholic Church as it is the servant of all the Churches. It is beginning to receive from Roman Catholics financial support of a very considerable order as is evidenced by the gift of the Vatican of £25,000 for interconfessional scholarly work on the original texts of the Bible. And there are now Roman Catholics on the governing bodies of Bible Societies in many countries and on well over one hundred translation projects throughout the world.

The present healthy relationship can be summarised in the words of the Executive Committee of the World Catholic Federation for the Biblical Apostolate which met in September 1969: "that the Federation co-operate wherever possible with the United Bible Societies to secure ever wider circulation of the Scriptures, especially among non-Christians, and that, to show their concern for this basic work of Christianity in accordance with the documents of Vatican II . . . Roman Catholics should be encouraged to work with and for the Bible Societies."

At the conclusion of the meetings of the Anglican/Roman Catholic International Commission held in Venice in 1970, the three main documents were published as working-papers in the February 1971 issue of *Theology* and in the *Clergy Review*. In the paper on *Church and Authority* come these sentences: "It will be seen that within the disagreements and agreements many lines of convergence have already appeared. The theology of both Churches today recognises the primacy of Scripture. This point is no longer an obstacle to unity. The practice of both Churches also acknowledges the freedom of scholarly enquiry."

It is the thesis of this lecture that we may confidently hope for advance in unity precisely on the basis of that agreement; that, as we prayerfully study Scripture, with all possible aids of scholarship, as we unitedly proclaim the truths of Scripture, and as we collaborate in the world-wide dissemination of Scripture, we shall find truth "on the road" and unity "on the road".

There are at least good biblical grounds for that hope, for it was as the Risen Lord expounded the Scriptures to the two disciples on the road to Emmaus that minds were opened and hearts set ablaze (Luke 24:25 ff.).

The Bible as a Means of Grace

THE BIBLE IS a dated book; or more accurately, as I have often described it, a little library of dated books. How could it be otherwise? The most recent of the books was written nearly 1,900 years ago; the most ancient, many centuries earlier than that. It tells, in picture language, of the beginning of things, of primitive times and ancient love stories, of battles long ago. It is a strange mixture of poetry and prose, of parables and letters, of prophecy and history.

How, then, can the Bible be included in a series about growing to maturity? Can the Bible still be a way in which God comes through to us in power and love? The Eucharist? Yes. Prayer? Yes. But the Bible?

The fact is that it has proved just that—a means of grace—to men and women of all kinds down the long centuries and still is just that to millions today. This is in spite of modern man having "come of age", as that much-quoted phrase goes; in spite of his being a highly sophisticated, scientifically orientated creature, so very different in many ways from those who wrote the Bible and from those for whom it was originally intended.

What is the explanation of this undoubted fact?

It lies, I think, partly in this—that the Bible is very largely a book of biography. It consists of life-stories of men and women looked at as individuals and as members of communities.

While it is true that we humans change from century to century in many respects—men who lived before the discovery of the wheel were very different from those, like ourselves, who live

BBC broadcasts, March 1974.

in the space age—yet, beneath these surface differences lie certain characteristics which do not change from millennium to millennium—our need for love, for forgiveness, for happy community relations, for light on the basic problems of human existence and on life after death, and so on.

Another reason why this ancient book, dated as it undoubtedly is, seems to transcend the centuries and becomes a means of grace to modern man is this. It talks about GOD. Indeed this is the main burden of its message. From one point of view, it is the story of man's search for God—and there are parts of that search-story which, in the full light of the Christian revelation, do not prove very edifying or enlightening. But, from a much more important angle the Bible can be viewed as the age-long story of God's search for man: "Adam, where art thou?" *Here* lies the permanent value of the Bible, for Christians believe that God is still on the search for man, and that His great heart of love is not satisfied till man comes to himself and comes to his Father, and so finds his rest in God.

That much must be said by way of introduction to these thoughts for the day. The Bible is a book which speaks to men of different ages and backgrounds. Perhaps we should more accurately say, the Bible is a book through which, as through no other book, the Spirit of the living God speaks to men, under the widely varying conditions in which they find themselves. Coleridge used to say that it has a way of "finding" the devout reader of its pages. That is not a bad way of putting it.

So, in developing our theme, we shall take different circumstances in which man finds himself and in which the Bible has a relevant word to speak.

If I frequently illustrate what I have to say from human experience, that will not be surprising, for the simple reason that we have already noted, that the Bible is full of biographical material.

In Times of Crisis

There have been some, in days gone by, who have looked on the Bible rather as a book of charms, from which guidance can be extracted, by a kind of lucky dip system, in times of crisis, emergency, or uncertainty. They open the Bible at random and hope that, by a sort of supernatural good luck, their eye will light on a passage which will give them the direction they need.

Maybe God is good enough to overlook the immaturity of His servants and sometimes to answer their hopes in this way. For myself, I put little trust in it!

But how often we *do* need guidance! Has the Bible anything to say about how to get it? I think it has. I look at two people who have something to say on the matter.

The first was a king who lived in the Near East in the eighth century before Christ. His nation was a small one; his temporal power was not very great. Power lay in the hands of the great nations which lay to the north and east of his land of Israel—nations like Assyria. It was from Assyria that he received one day a letter couched in terms that would make any king tremble for the safety of his people and his throne. It was a mocking letter: "Don't start bragging about the power of your God to deliver you from my hand! Look at the other nations which I have subdued, and what has happened to them! Of what avail were their prayers to their gods? You had better learn your lesson—and submit, before I crush you."

It was a terrible ultimatum. Great issues were at stake. How Hezekiah needed the guidance of God!

This is what he did. He took the letter from the hand of the messengers who had brought it. He read it. He went up to the temple of the Lord and spread it out before the Lord, and poured his heart out in prayer.

The details of how God answered that prayer through the prophet Isaiah need not concern us now. But the action of Hezekiah certainly has got a lesson if we are trying to see how God guides on important occasions.

It would have been possible for him to rush into battle—in a fury at the cheek of the King of Assyria. It would have been possible for him to submit, or to flee from his post of responsibility. He did neither of these things. Quietly he laid the matter before God—and waited.

He did not wait in vain. No rush, no panic, but prayer. That is how the guidance came.

The second person who learned the way of divine guidance was Jesus Christ himself. There are indications in the Gospels that, before he made great decisions, he would withdraw from the bustle of the town and from the pressure of the crowds, and wait on God in the quiet of the country. He did this, for example, before he chose his twelve closest followers, the apostles. So much hung on this decision. He would not rush into it. He must seek the mind of his Father—unhurriedly. He must ask Him for His guidance in the intimacy of dialogue-prayer. These men were to be the leaders of His mission in the months and years ahead. "Father, show me Your mind."

As we read between the lines of the Gospels, we see a kind of rhythm in the life of Jesus. Nature has its rhythms of sleeping and waking; the rhythm of withdrawal and activity. So it seems to have been in the life of Jesus, planned with a kind of magisterial serenity—activity preceded by prayer; preaching, healing, teaching following quiet communion with His Father.

It was in this way, I believe, that Jesus may well have come to rely less and less on sudden revelations of guidance from God in times of emergency. By constantly repeated acts of communion with God, He had learnt the principles on which He runs His world and seeks to guide His children.

When the crisis came, He knew the way He must go.

In Times of Celebration

There is a strange idea about that the Bible is a sombre book. In the old days it used to be bound in black, and printed in small type; and that helped to convey this impression of gloom.

Of course, it does deal with the serious side of human experience—with sin and disease and death; with temptation and doubt and darkness. It would not be a very realistic book if it had not got much to say on these things. But, has it got anything to say to those for whom life is *good*? Can it be a "means of grace" at a time of joy and celebration?

The answer most certainly is "Yes, it can."

The central rite of Christian worship is the Eucharist. The word simply means "Thanksgiving". When the Church "does this in remembrance" of its crucified and risen Lord, it engages in a "celebration", a joyful feast. It uses wine—the symbol of gladness and warmth and cheer. Though that wine speaks of the blood of Christ out-poured in sacrificial giving, it also speaks of exuberant joy.

The story of the turning of the water into wine at the wedding feast in Cana of Galilee was the writer's way of saying that, when Jesus is present and His will is obeyed, there is festival, there is fun, there is something to sing about, something to celebrate!

There is evidence in the Gospels which leads us to think that Jesus had pondered a great deal on the book of Deuteronomy. Now that certainly isn't the first book which you would turn up if you wanted to understand the Bible and you went to it as a comparative beginner! But it has some very interesting things to say. For instance, if you were to open it at the fourteenth chapter, you would find a passage which might not interest you particularly—all about animals and birds that you may or may not eat; a sort of primitive list of health food laws. But that passage is followed by one which might be headed: "How to enjoy a celebration, a jollification". It is a description of a kind of super harvest festival, a grand feast or, if that were to prove impossible, a grand spending spree! No suggestion here that the people of God are spoil-sports, or dismal imbeciles, people ruled by negatives—"Thou shalt not, thou shalt not, thou shalt not." No, there seems to be a foretaste of what a New Testament writer was later to lay down as a kind of manifesto for positive Christian living: "God has given us richly all things to enjoy."

Here is a life-affirming principle which has not always been followed by the disciples of the One who sometimes seemed more at home, more comfortable, with the worldly types of His day than He did with religious, sour-faced rigorists.

If you look a bit more closely at that passage in Deuteronomy on how to enjoy a celebration, you will find two very interesting things about it. The first is that it is all done "before the Lord". That does not mean that God looks down with a disapproving eye when life is going well with us and we want to celebrate. Not at all. It simply means that we conduct our jollifications, as we seek to conduct all aspects of life (business, leisure, love, the lot), in such a way as he approves, or, to use the accepted religious phrase, "to His glory".

The other thing of interest about this passage is that strict instructions are given not to forget the under-privileged, the people less fortunate than themselves, the socially deprived. The equivalent today would be those who have slipped through the provisions made by the Welfare Services—and we always have such among us—and, looking further afield, the millions in the third world. While they are around, extravagance is obscene.

The Lord who entered into the joys of the wedding feast and made them infinitely greater by His presence and His action, loves to enter into our celebrations, to share with us when life is good and skies are blue. At the same time He reminds us of those for whom there is little joy in life, little to celebrate about. And He once told a story which illustrated the fact that a man *can* get so obsessed with celebrations, with wealth and all that goes with it, that the seed of eternal life gets choked. That is disaster beyond all telling.

In Times of Sickness

It is a pretty safe bet that, among those listening in this morning, there are a good many thousands of people who are ill, or who have in the past experienced illness—of mind or body. Very few of us get through life without some experience of sickness of some sort. The body—and even more the mind—is a wonderful and complicated machine. The surprise is that it doesn't get out of order more often than it does!

The Bible is a very down-to-earth book, and it has a lot to say about the body. The writers refuse to think of man as a soul (important) encased in a body (unimportant). They will not divide us up like that. They think of us as persons, our bodies being very much part of our "personalities". The body is a God-given part of us, not to be pampered, but to be treated with reverence as a temple of the Holy Spirit. That is why self-indulgence of any kind is blasphemous.

Speaking broadly, one can say that the God of the Bible is a God who is on the side of health, of wholeness. Quite a large part of the opening books of the Old Testament is given over to laws, including food-laws, which have to do with health, sanitation, sex-relationships, and so on. The body, and the happy relationship of mind and body, and the inter-relationships of people within the body corporate, *matter* to the God of the Bible.

But it is when we come to the Gospels that we see things more clearly, and so the Bible becomes a means of grace to us who suffer. Not that a reading of the Gospels clears up all the problems about suffering. It hasn't done that for me! But it has shed some rays of clear and penetrating light on the problem, and given me enough to go on with.

The Gospels show me our Lord as a fighter on behalf of health. How He wrestled with disease—curing the woman with the crooked back ("whom Satan has bound these eighteen years"); the paralytic on his stretcher-bed (whose paralysis seemed closely linked with his sinfulness); the mentally tortured man (whose nickname Legion spoke only too eloquently of his tormented disintegration).

Jesus lined Himself up with all those who are fighting for health; but He refused to deal only with the outward symptoms; He insisted on getting at the cause. He refused to say that suffering was always the direct result of the sufferer's sin—that would have been far too much of an over-simplification. But He recognised the interaction of evil and bodily and mental sickness, and allowed full scope for that in His healing work.

We never read that Jesus was ill. We read that He was tired, that strength went out of Him in the course of his work, and so on; but not that He was ill during the course of His ministry. Perhaps it was that He was in such close touch with the God of peace and health that God's wholeness became the wholeness of His Son. What we *do* read, however, is this; that, on the Cross, there came to Him such an experience of agony—physical, mental, spiritual agony—as has been the lot of no other. Here was a young man, at the height of His powers, nailed through feet and hands to a beam of wood, His dreams shattered round Him, forsaken, so it seemed, by His God and by His friends.

It was a bloody agony; all the misdeeds of the world seemed centred, that awful day, in that torn body. "My God, my God, why . . . ?"

He did not escape from suffering—nor do most of us! But He took it and made something wonderful of it. He transformed it; and through His wounds mankind is healed. His love in the midst of His suffering changed the meaning of events, made the ugly things beautiful and the hard things acceptable.

Two pieces of wood became the symbol of salvation; a crown of thorns a halo; Golgotha a throne of glory.

When suffering hits us, it is natural enough to ask the question "Why?" Jesus did. But it is more important to ask the question "How? How will God make this thing, which to me is so negative, into a plus in his hands? Is it possible that I am on my back, so that I may learn to look up?" That might be the most wonderful thing I could do!

An unknown soldier in the American Civil War wrote these words:

> I asked God for strength, that I might achieve,
> I was made weak, that I might learn humbly to obey.
> I asked for health, that I might do greater things,
> I was given infirmity, that I might do better things.
> I asked for power, that I might have the praise of men,
> I was given weakness, that I might face the need of God.

In Times when the World Seems to Have Gone Mad

Some centuries before Christ was born, a man looked out over his world. He had, of course, no radio or television as we have, no newspapers even, to bring that world into his livingroom and keep him informed from hour to hour of its goings-on. But such news as he got—through passing camel cavalcades, through couriers, through swiftly spreading rumours—convinced him that it was a mad, mad world. The very mountains seemed to shake and, as he put it, the waters seemed to rage and swell. It was like a volcanic eruption. The little land he lived in had proved in past history all too often to be the place over which the great powers fought. His people were a kind of pawn in the unscrupulous hands of competing nations round about! What could a man say? What could he do? Where could he find confidence in a world like *that*?

We do not know the name of the man we have been talking about, but from the poem he wrote we can deduce a good deal about him. He was very much a man of the world. He kept his eyes open and, as we say, "he knew a thing or two". But his vision was not confined to what his physical eyes saw about him. He was a man of faith. He had an answer to the question as to where his confidence could be found in a world gone mad. "*God* is our hope and strength," he said, "a very present help in time of trouble. Therefore will we not fear, though the earth be moved ..." So he kept quiet, and listened; and as he listened, strength began to take the place of fear. He heard God speaking: "Be still," He said, "and know that I am God."

Those unknown men who wrote the psalms breathe a superb confidence through their writings. "God reigns," they say again and again. God has not abdicated, even though men seem to have gone mad. God reigns. God loves. God cares.

Men like them, with their strong note of confidence, can become a "means of grace" to us who live in even more troubled days than were theirs; days which hold within them possibilities of disaster (nuclear and other) which they never dreamed of, and examples of human folly such as had never occurred to them.

There are many today who are appalled by human insanity and by man's inhumanity to man, and all the more appalled because they feel that they can do so little about it. They do not occupy the seats of power; their word avails little; they seem to be very small cogs in a vast impersonal machine. Perhaps this is especially true of the shut-ins, whose main life-work is behind them; who read the papers and find their stories depressing; who listen in and find the news to be little more than a series of disasters.

To all such people I want to say two things:

First: remember where the Psalmist put his trust. Remember that a greater than the Psalmist, Jesus Christ Himself, dared, in the face of all the terrors of His day, to call God Father and King—a Father who seeks the love of His children; a King who seeks their loyalty and obedience. He dared to hold, in life and in death, that God reigns; that He loves; that He cares.

Secondly: remember that God is not dependent on the big battalions to do His work. He has a way of working through minority groups, or even through individuals, undistinguished people, even through men and women who are unconscious of being agents of His power.

That means that *you*, far though you are from what most people conceive of as the corridors of power, can be a centre of serenity in a world that seems to have gone mad.

If the room where you live becomes a place of prayer, it may be more potent for good than the council-chambers of the nations' potentates.

Ministry

The Minister as a Man of God

I AM ADDRESSING those who will ere long be ministers, providing they can defeat the examiners and leap over whatever hurdles correspond in Methodism to Bishops, the Advisory Council of the Church's Ministry and all their works, in the Anglican set-up. I might have chosen many a different title beginning with the same three words—"The Minister as evangelist", "The Minister as counsellor", "The Minister as visitor", "The Minister as preacher", and so on. Any of these would have provided me with a good theme. But I wanted to get back of all these—behind them, beneath them.

How can a man be an evangelist, a counsellor, a visitor, a preacher, unless he be essentially a "man of God"? His evangelism will strike a hollow note; his counselling will be merely good advice (though perhaps flavoured with psychiatric phraseology or even the odd text of Scripture); his visiting will tend to deal only with the weather or the cricket score; his preaching will be mere talk, though maybe talk with expert techniques; unless the man himself be, in very fact, a man of God.

"But thou, O man of God." The words stared at me out of the passage from 1 Timothy 6:11 ff, as I prepared to come to you. What do those three monosyllables "Man of God" mean? They trip lightly off our tongue—"He's a man of God", we say. What is the meaning of the genitive?

I suppose that, primarily, it is a *possessive* genitive. This man is possessed by his God, and makes no bones about his allegiance. He is God's man. Others may have yielded to the claims of other

Wesley College, Leeds, Inaugural Service, 4th October, 1966.

masters, money, fame, pleasure, what have you. This man knows
the domination of One alone. He is God's, totally.

Or is it a genitive of *relationship*? If you know that splendid
*Greek Grammar of the New Testament & Other Early Christian
Literature*, by F. Blass and A. Debrunner, you may recall that
there is quite a section on the "Genitive of origin and relationship"
(p. 162). It is not irrelevant to the point we are considering. The
authors remark that the genitive is used "to identify a person by
his father", so the man of God is the man who knows the meaning
of the Fatherhood of God. The possession of slaves by a family
is indicated by putting the family into the genitive, as in Romans
16:10, 11—"the slaves of Aristobulus . . . of Narcissus . . ." The
man of God is the man who is content to be the slave, to be under
the domination of his God.

Do not take these words on your lips lightly.

Ponder that genitive.

1. *The Dedicated Man*

Perhaps we can do no better than begin at the passage from
1 Timothy. Its context is, at first sight, slightly forbidding—
forbidding because the verbs used immediately after our phrase
are such sweaty verbs, "flee" and "pursue". "Flee these things—
pursue these others . . ." The things to be "fled from" are lusts
and love of money, thorny griefs on which some have spiked
themselves (to quote the vivid language of the New English
Bible). The things to be "pursued" (I translate διώκω thus to
get its demanding, energetic sense across to you) are "justice,
piety, fidelity, love, fortitude and gentleness".

Here is a picture of the dedicated man. He sits loose to the
things which most men count dearest. If they come to him—
money, possessions, and the like—well, so be it; he must use them
responsibly. But their possession is neither here nor there. Indeed
it may be that they would be a snare if they came to him. Certainly
the *love* of them is a snare. His heart must "surely there be fixed
where true joys are to be found". In fact, there will be about the
man of God an element of ἄσκησις; after all, the word was used
in classical Greek literature for *training*, and the man of God is
simply one of God's athletes in training to be the best for Him.

Why should the word 'Puritan' always be used with a touch of
the cynical? Must there not be about any athlete a readiness to

say 'No' to the *soft* which will almost always be misunderstood
by the man of the world?

"But thou, O man of God . . ." Mark that "but". The discipline
of habits, of time, of appetites—all this is involved in being a
man of God.

Here is the razor-edge on which the life of the minister is
poised. It is the old problem of how to be a man of God in the
world, and yet out of the world. You will recall how our Lord,
in the seventeenth chapter of St John, speaks of His immediate
followers as the men whom God had given Him *"out of the
world"*. This does not mean that they are to contract out of their
worldly responsibilities into an other-worldly isolationism. This
world, out of which God has given these men of God to His Son,
is the world God so loved as to give His Son for its redemption.
Here is the paradox, the razor-edge. The man of God must be
in the world, but not of it; never blurring the line of demarcation
between Church and world; ever remembering that he follows
One who mixed with all strata of society, went to wedding-
parties, mixed with disreputables, died between two ruffians, and
yet was "separate from sinners" (Hebrews 7:26), undefiled, un-
touched by any breath of scandal, utterly pure.

"O man of God", you will need to keep very close to *the* Man
of God if you are going to live that kind of life!

2. The Authority of the Man of God

All this brings me to the second main point I want to make. I
refer to the *authority* of the man of God.

I am much impressed with a homely little story tucked away
in the fourth chapter of the Second Book of the Kings. It is about
Elisha at Shunem.

The ordinary course of his work brought him into contact with
a woman who got into the habit of giving him a meal whenever
he passed her way. But the character of the guest so impressed the
hostess that she could only describe him to her husband as "a
holy man of God, who is continually passing our way".

I am not concerned with the plans she made for his comfort—
a roof chamber equipped for his use. I am concerned with the fact
that it was his sheer holiness which struck the woman. He carried
his own authority about with him. It was a similar authority,
you will remember, which struck the people in the synagogue

when Jesus taught there soon after His baptism. He did not have to quote a long list of Rabbis' names, as did the scribes, to indicate the authority of His teaching. The authority was in the Christ Himself; it was the authority of His own holiness. "He taught them as one that had authority, and yet not as the scribes"—so says St Mark (1:22), reflecting the astonishment of our Lord's hearers.

There was nothing cock-sure or noisy about this authority of Jesus. There was in Him an astounding combination of authority and gentleness. He broke no bruised reed; He quenched no smoking flax. He was extraordinarily tender to the sinful. But His authority was unquestionable.

This problem of authority is to many an agonising one.[1] What right have I to stand before others and address them? Many of them, it may well be, are better educated than I am, more brilliant in mind, more holy in life, further on the road to heaven. The brashness of the newly ordained man, confident in the recent acquisition of a B.A. and perhaps in the newness of a B.D., marked by the collar which he wears, "full of wise saws and modern instances", is swept aside when he finds some illiterate parishioner who knows far more about God and the profound issues of life and death than he does. What right, what authority, has he to go to such as these?

The question is not patient of an easy answer. I believe there are several strands to the rope of the minister's authority. There is, for example, the authority which is inherent in the message which he preaches.

We believe that our God is the God who speaks. We believe that He has spoken, in a unique way, in the Person of His Son—not only in His teaching or in His example, but supremely in His mighty redeeming acts. When St Paul summarised the essential content of the message which he brought to the Corinthians—nervy in himself, but confidently assured about what he preached—he put it as I have indicated elsewhere in credal form—that "Christ died for our sins . . . that He was buried . . . that He was raised . . . that He was seen . . ." (1 Cor. 15:3 ff.). These are the mighty acts of God, to which nothing can be added, acts wrought out once and for all on the stage of human history. This is the

[1]It is dealt with at greater depth in Authority, Religion and the Church, pp. 157-169.

kerygma, the thing preached; this is the *paratheke*, the sacred treasure committed to us. It can only be expressed in a great series of indicative verbs—God loved, God gave, the Word was made flesh, Christ died for our sins, He was raised by the power of God.

These indicatives are the very stuff of which the Gospel is made. There is no good news without them. It is only in the light of them that we can ever face the imperatives of Christianity; but when we have grasped—or been grasped by—the indicatives, we find the imperatives to be not only possible but a joy to obey. There is authority inherent in the message itself, for it is a very word of God to *homo viator*.

Secondly, there is the authority of the experience of the Church down the centuries. As the centuries have passed, the members of Christ's Church have discovered that, when the word of God is faithfully and winsomely preached, men and women find newness of life.

When I ordain a man a priest in the Church of God, the only thing I hand him (as I have said elsewhere) is a Bible. I say to him: "Take thou *authority* to preach the Word of God and to minister the holy sacraments." When I consecrate a bishop in the Church of God, the only thing I hand him is a Bible. I say to him: "Think upon the things contained in this book. Be diligent in them." That is why we may not call it preaching when a man gives his own ideas and then, almost fortuitously, attaches a text to them!

It is the task of the preacher to be an exegete, but an exegete in a special sense. When he has wrestled with the ancient text, it is his responsibility to indicate its relevance to the people to whom he is sent. He is more than an exegete. He is a *hermeneut*— and you will realise that the word is derived from Hermes who was the *messenger* of the gods. As he fulfils that mighty function, he will find an authority far greater than his own. He is, as it were, the last link of a long chain which stretches back through the centuries of the Church's history to the Christ of God Himself.

Thirdly, there is the authority of the Holy Spirit. There is such a thing as *testimonium internum Spiritus Sancti*. Now here we are on dangerous ground—but then, all great theology is dangerous and open to great abuse! There are many who have believed them-

selves to have the authority, the inspiration, of the Holy Spirit—
and have been greatly deluded. History is strewn with examples.
As early as the first century, it was necessary to put out a warning
that the spirits had to be tested! But when all this has been said
and been heeded, we may, I believe, go this far: The man who,
so far as he is able, faithfully expounds and applies the treasure of
the Gospel entrusted to him; the man who realises that he is not
a lone voice stating his own views, but is a tiny part of that great
continuation of the word which has been committed to the
Church for all time; the man who brings meticulous care in study
and preparation to bear on his work; this man may, I believe,
quietly, humbly, confidently look for and expect to receive the
authority of the Holy Spirit in his preaching ministry.

Such authority, of course, will not always be recognised.
Jeremiah, despite all his questionings, had such authority—and
was rejected by his contemporaries; he was a man of sorrows.
Jesus, as we have seen, had it supremely. His contemporaries
glimpsed it. They saw He was unlike the scribes. They glimpsed
it and rejected Him.

The presence of the authority of the Holy Spirit does not mean
that my church will automatically be filled. It does mean, I think,
that, perhaps one by one and little by little, men and women in
need of God will find Him through my ministry of His word.

But all this, without the authority of *personal holiness* avails
little. There is no short cut here. This is the *sine qua non* of
ministry. Anyone can give a lecture, make a speech, address an
assembly. But it is not so with the fulfilment of a *ministry*. He
alone can minister who lives in the secret place of the Most High,
who has learnt to listen to the God Who speaks, who knows the
meaning of obedience, who can say not merely "I hold this view",
but "I am held, grasped, by this God." This is the final, quiet,
undeniable authority—the authority of holiness.

3. *The Man of Prayer*

Having said all this, I need hardly elaborate the assertion that
such authority can only be found when the man of God is a man
of prayer. That Christ was Himself a man of prayer is clear from
a study of the Gospels.

Let us look at a typical passage in the first chapter of St Mark.
The conflict of the forces of wholeness and light with the demonic

powers of darkness centred in the Person of Jesus (vv. 32-4). We see here no placid Galilean poet meditating amid flower-covered hills. We see, instead, God's "proper Man" doing battle with all that mars human life—and winning in the fray. Then St Mark sketches the story of the disciples going in pursuit of their Master, bringing Him the message that everybody was looking for Him (vv. 36-7). And he hints at the passion that burned within our Lord to preach throughout the length and breadth of Galilee in fulfilment of His mission (vv. 38-9). But between these two little accounts is a passage of the deepest significance: "Very early next morning" (i.e. after His healing work) "He got up and went out. He went away to a lonely spot and remained there in prayer" (v. 35, NEB).

"He got up"—no lying in bed beyond the time really necessary for bodily refreshment. "He went out"—out of the small house where every step would be heard—"to a lonely spot". He could not carry on a ministry of constant self-giving without such renewal. He knew *where* to find this—in the open country, alone with God. He knew *when* to find it—in the early morning, before the crowds were up and doing. With that behind Him, He could face anything.

Look at another passage in St Mark. In chapter 6, the evangelist gives the story of the feeding of the five thousand (vv. 33-44). Intense activity, considerable excitement, milling crowds again! Then the story of the storm on the lake, with the disciples terrified by the storm itself and by the appearance of One whom they took to be a ghost (vv. 47 ff.). How did the Lord keep His serenity in the midst of that? The answer is given in v. 46: "He bade them farewell, and then withdrew into the hills to pray" (E. V. Rieu's translation).

Withdrawal with God gave Him peace within and a serenity infectious to others. In the presence of God He held Himself still, and so had reserves of power which enabled Him to stretch out a firm hand to those who were finding life too much for them. At a time of intense activity, Martin Luther wrote: "I am so busy that I find I cannot do with less than four hours a day in the presence of God.

Thus there would seem to have been a kind of rhythm about the life of Jesus—withdrawal and work; withdrawal and work. It was a rhythm which He sought to teach to His apostles, as St Mark makes plain in this same chapter (6: 30 ff.). They had been out on their Master's errands, and now they came back to report to Him all they had done and taught. No comment of His is recorded, but simply the fact that He told them they must withdraw and rest. He went with them for that vital period of renewal which He needed; and if He, how much more they! and if they, how much more we!

4. *The Spiritual Life*

I have spoken so far of the element of discipline, of ἄσκησις, in the man of God; of the authority of holiness; of the ingredient of prayer. I want finally to speak of a quality called for in the man of God for which it is difficult to find the right word. St Paul speaks of a man being "rooted" in Christ (Col. 2:7). This phrase speaks to me of a depth of spiritual life which springs from a living relationship with Christ.

I have noticed the care which is given, in the first few years after a young tree has been planted, to the roots of this tree. The ground near it must be kept weeded. Rain must have free access to the roots. Only so will the tree be strong; only so will it be possible eventually to take away the stake which has supported the young stem. But *given this*, granted the rootedness, then there is flexibility, growth, development.

My garden has given me a reliable picture; it has provided me with a parable. Rooted in Christ, and then—no *rigidity*. Loyalty to Christ, and then freedom to think and develop. The very freedom will strengthen the growth; the flexibility will make for a larger beauty and maturity.

Let the roots go down deep in a great loyalty to and love for Christ, and you need not fear to look out and look up and to laugh as you labour!

Do you remember the closing pages of Morris West's *The Shoes of the Fisherman*?

The cardinals ask the newly elected Pope what he wants— *quid vobis videtur*?

He replies: "Men with fire in their hearts and wings to their feet." It is not a bad description of men of God.

The Ministry of Counselling

THIS IS ONE aspect of that ministry of evangelism to which every Christian is committed who takes his baptism and confirmation seriously. The text for our study might well be Isaiah 9:6. "Unto us a child is born; unto us a son is given: and the government shall be upon his shoulder: and his name shall be called Wonderful, Counsellor, The Mighty God, The everlasting Father. The Prince of Peace."

Isaiah had written the words long centuries before Christ was born in Bethlehem. Wistfully he had looked for the day when One would be born Who would bring peace and prosperity to the people, a Ruler of great power who would establish His Kingdom in righteousness. Christians have seen the fulfilment of the prophet's longing in the coming of Jesus Christ, for, with that coming, His kingly rule was established in the hearts of men, though we wait—sometimes impatiently—for its long-delayed consummation.

The passage in Isaiah 9 has been variously translated, for the original is patient of a variety of renderings. I select one phrase: "His name shall be called Wonderful, Counsellor." So the Authorised Version runs. The New English Bible renders it, "He shall be called in purpose wonderful"—a not very satisfactory phrase. Better, perhaps, is the Revised Standard Version which reads: "His name will be called Wonderful Counsellor." That is to say that one of the outstanding marks of this Ruler of the people would be such wisdom and insight as would make Him the One to whom people would come for counsel and advice, In coming, they would not be disappointed.

Certainly this was one of the outstanding characteristics of

Jesus. How else could He have trained the twelve if He had not been a "wonderful counsellor"? How else could He have healed the sick in body and mind if people had not felt free to bring Him their burdens and unload them at His feet? This almost every page of the Gospels makes plain. He bore men's griefs and carried their sorrows.

It is recorded by St John (2:24, 25) of our Lord that "He knew men so well, all of them, that He needed no evidence from others about a man for He Himself could tell what was in a man." There is insight into character without which there cannot be counselling in depth. There is the insight of holiness—an insight earnestly to be sought by all those who in turn would be counsellors.

We must take this thought further. Jesus, according to St John, told His disciples of Another who would be a wonderful counsellor when His own bodily presence was withdrawn (St John 14: 16). The Holy Spirit, the other self of Jesus, would guide the disciples into all truth. He was to be called the Paraclete. This word means much more than a comforter in trouble (though that is included). It means One who would stimulate mind and thought and resolve, One who would make and keep the disciples alert for new truth and new insights. The French have a word which gets very close to it—*Animateur*.

So it has proved down the centuries of the Church's life. It has been—and is—the experience of the followers of Christ that they are not left orphaned. On the contrary, there is with them, and in them, One who stimulates, incites, re-creates, renews, refreshes their thinking and their creative faculties. There is still in their midst, His power undiminished, a wonderful counsellor.

Let us take this one stage further still, for, in doing so, we come to my main point. It is of the very essence of the Church's mission that it should continue the work which Jesus did. The members of the Church are the limbs of His body, thus ensuring that the kind of things He did, the kind of person He proved to be among men, are continued and that His influence is extended throughout the world. That is the mission of the Church at home and abroad. That is your mission if you are a disciple of Jesus. That is my mission.

One of the areas of human life and experience where help is

most needed today is in the area of "counselling." I believe that there is a quite desperate need of counsellors, "wonderful counsellors" in our present day world.

Let me illustrate the kind of thing I have in mind.

In 1953, thanks to the compassion and genius of an Anglican clergyman by the name of Chad Varah, an organisation came into being called the Samaritans. It exists to help, through telephone and personal contact, those tempted to commit suicide, men and women distracted almost beyond endurance, people minded to end it all. In the big cities, especially, little bands of counsellors have been formed, and there are pretty clear indications that the drop in the rate of suicides in England in recent years may well be due, in part at least, to their existence. At the end of the telephone there is someone ready to listen, ready to counsel, ready to come to the rescue. Wonderful counsellors indeed. I want to see their number increased, multiplied many times—and not only in the Samaritan organisation.

In Oxford some time ago, the son of an old friend of mine committed suicide—a normal healthy young man who, so it would seem, had no worries above the average. When his father wrote to tell me the news, I wondered—would this tragedy have happened if there had been at hand, in the College, some young don who was prepared to set aside long hours of his time to be what so many undergraduates desperately need, a counsellor?

Sometime back, I returned to my old Cambridge College. There I was told that the chaplain's light burns late night after night. He is available. Men come to him. He knows that this work, costly as it is, snatched, it may be, from the research that he would like to do, is work of immense importance. He knows that to be a "wonderful counsellor" is to do his part as a limb of the body of Christ. It is to continue in Cambridge in the 1970s the work which Isaiah glimpsed, which Jesus fulfilled, and which the Holy Spirit continually makes possible.

Counsellors in the universities, counsellors in the schools, counsellors in those huge blocks of high-rise buildings, the dwellings (not to honour them with the title "homes") of some of the loneliest people in civilisation—in almost any area of our modern, highly-sophisticated life, men and women are needed who can be called on at any hour of day or night.

Now we come to the most important question. What is meant

by a "wonderful counsellor"? What are his or her qualifications?

One thinks, of course, of the experts, people who have graduated in medicine and specialised in psychiatry, those who know what psychology is about, particularly in its application to the problems of sociology. We need such experts—may their number increase! But they are not the people I have primarily in mind today. My thought reaches out to a far wider class, less specialised, less technically trained. I think of multitudes who could do this work without the special training of the psychiatrist or the sociologist. What qualities are called for in such cases, if a man is to be a *counsellor*?

He must be a *good listener*. If he cannot hold his tongue and listen patiently, he need not aspire to be a counsellor. Moreover, he must be totally *unshockable*. His knowledge of men and their ways must be such as to lead him never to express surprise at whatever is told him.

He might bear in mind the story of the man who had committed murder. He felt he should confess. He went to a Free Church minister who, on hearing his confession, fainted. He went to an Anglican clergyman who prepared to call the police. He went to an experienced old Roman Catholic priest who, on hearing that the penitent had committed murder, said quietly: "How many, my son?"

Knowledge of men, indeed knowledge of the secrets of his own heart and the perversities of his own personality, is a necessary part of the equipment of a counsellor.

But this must be added if the counselling is to go "deep enough" to be of any lasting avail. A counsellor who is to work in depth must know, not only himself, not only the men and women to whom he ministers, but he must know God. This is not said as a kind of pious addition to an address given to churchmen. It is the *sine qua non* if the work of counselling is to be permanent and solid. Man is made in the image of God. Man is restless till he finds his rest in God. Man is a wanderer till he finds his way back to God and to forgiveness and to reinstatement in the family of God. The *whole* man must be dealt with if the counsellor is to do a really "wonderful" work. This means that counselling must not only be remedial: it must be *redemptive*.

Such a counsellor as I envisage must, I say, at least have begun to know God—the God of the universe whose vastness is opening up before the explorations of science; the God of nature whose secrets are daily being disclosed to those who search for truth; the God of grace who has finally revealed Himself in the face of Jesus Christ. And the more he learns of such a God, the more he will learn of the true nature of those whom he is counselling, and the deeper and more solid will be the help that he can bring.

I delay on this matter of *knowing God*, for it is at the very heart of our subject of counselling. It is at the very heart of the Bible—indeed one might say that it is its main theme. Abraham because he has come to know God ventures out into the unknown (Gen. 12). Moses asks God so to disclose Himself that he may know Him and in the strength of that knowledge lead a rabble to the borders of the promised land (Exod. 33:13). Jeremiah exhorts his hearers not to boast in their wisdom, their valour or their riches but rather in their knowledge of God (9:23-4). Isaiah writes, "my witnesses, says the Lord, are you, my servants, you whom I have chosen to know me and put your faith in me ..." (43:10). Hosea writes, "Loyalty is my desire, not sacrifice, not whole offerings but the knowledge of God" (6:6). The word used in the Old Testament for knowing God is, as I have said before, the very same that is used when a man and woman "know" one another in the intimacy of a marriage relationship (we may compare the marital language of Israel as the bride of God and unfaithfulness to him being compared to adultery). What was glimpsed in the Old Testament became a vivid experience once the Church of the pre-Christian era had become the Spirit-filled Church of the New. God gave its members such a knowledge of Himself as provided them with insight into the mysteries of personality; and this somehow did not depend on such matters as mere intellectual equipment or academic training.

It has always been so. The brash young curate, confident in the recent acquisition of his degree, finds himself silenced and humbled before the wisdom and insight of an unlettered old woman who knows God. Who of us has not had some such experience as this? It is good indeed for our pride! It is only an up-to-date illustration of the point that we are making—know God and you will know the people He has made in His own image. Know Christ, of all counsellors the most wonderful, and in His mercy you will become a wonderful counsellor too.

All this means that the "counsellor" whom we are envisaging must be what the Bible calls a man of faith—a believer. This does not mean that he swallows hard and rattles off a creed, parrot-fashion, doing despite, as he says the words, to the intelligence with which God has endowed him. Far from it. I have spoken on another occasion of William Temple's saying: "I do not believe in any creed." Astonishing words, it may be thought again, to come from the lips of an Archbishop! But he went on to say that he used certain creeds to express, to deepen, to conserve the beliefs that he, together with the world-wide Church, held dear. The point he was making was that his faith was of a *personal* kind. He believed in God as He had revealed Himself in Jesus Christ. This belief, this faith, is based on certain facts, for Christianity claims to be an historic religion. It is not simply a religion of philosophical ideas, nor is it just a set of ethical propositions. It bases itself on the facts of the birth, ministry, death and resurrection of an historic Person, and on the giving of His Spirit to His Church. But it is more, far more, than intellectual assent to a proposition. It is the "Yes" of a man in the totality of his being to God's offer of succour and to God's demand of allegiance. Such a man, standing on the edge of the abyss of his own helplessness, takes the leap of faith and finds himself in the sustaining arms of God.

When Jesus, walking by the Lake of Galilee, saw two brothers, Simon and Andrew, and challenged them to follow Him, He received from them a personal response. "They left their nets and followed Him." They certainly did not know all there was to know about Him. Though they may have actually mixed with Him from boyhood, they had only begun to glimpse the significance of that astonishing young man who so imperiously, and yet so lovingly, summoned them. But they knew enough to venture, to respond, to follow, even though the way ahead was mysteriously dark. And when they said "Yes" to Him, responding with all that they knew of themselves to all that they knew of Him, they began a relationship with that supremely "wonderful counsellor" which was capable of almost infinite development. Their need was met by His mercy, their weakness by His strength, their ignorance by His wisdom. They began to know Him, "whom to know is life eternal".

When His bodily presence was withdrawn and physical contact had to give place to spiritual communion, they found that this knowledge did not cease, as they had feared it might. Rather, it increased and deepened. Within the fellowship which He had begun to create while living in their midst, they learnt that the discipleship which had begun as so personal a thing was in fact a highly corporate thing. They were members of Christ's Body, nourished by His Word and Sacraments, bonded together and growing into a holy temple in the Lord, building themselves up in love. Within that fellowship new insights into human personality developed; for as they increasingly knew God through Christ, they correspondingly knew men and women in the depths of their need and the heights of their potential development.

Have I pitched all this too high? I do not think so. God calls and equips those who are daring enough to respond and humble enough to receive the grace and the insight which He offers.

All that matters is that we become learners in His school.

The Ministry of Healing

THE FIRST FACET of evangelism which we have been considering is the ministry of counselling. The second is the ministry of healing. We shall tackle this now by studying the healing ministry of Jesus, always with an eye to its bearing on our ministry in the twentieth century.

We begin with the *name* of Jesus. "Thou shalt call His name *Jesus*, for He shall *save* His people from their sins." That was the message of God to Joseph before the birth of the Christ Child. Here was an idea whose roots went deep down into Jewish soil. Jesus—Joshua—deliverance *from* and *to* . . . The Name which is above every name is derived from a Hebrew root that denotes "to be spacious". Of this, Dr F. W. Dillistone writes: "He is Jesus, Saviour, because He brings men out into a new spaciousness in every sense of the term. He breaks through the false securities and shams and compensatory oppressions of human life in order that He may lead his new race out into the place of light and growth and expansion and enlargement. 'Salvation' means life at its highest level of experience. It means freedom from the cramping and confining limitations both of the world's prejudices and of our own timidities. The Hero-Saviour has won the decisive victory and thereby has brought near to man 'the glorious liberty of the children of God' " (*Jesus and His Cross*, p. 22).

This is germane to our subject. Jesus—deliverance—growth—enlargement—spaciousness. This can hardly be dismissed as irrelevant to an age terribly concerned with "repressions" and inhibitions and complexes. When Tyndale makes Christ say to Zacchaeus, "This day is *health* come to thy house" (where the

AV says 'salvation'—St Luke 19:9 σωτηρία), his translation spoke deeper than he knew, and made luminous the deep interest of Christ, for true health is impossible apart from God. At some such point as this, deep down in the Person and very Name of the Redeemer, must we make our beginning in any study of Christ's ministry to the sick.

Or again, we take the idea of *peace*, a word frequently on the lips of Jesus. True, "peace be to you" or "go in peace" were ordinary Eastern greetings in His day as in ours. But on His lips the greeting was more than a greeting. It was a potent benediction. When Jesus said to the woman who was a sinner (St Luke 7:50) "Thy faith has brought you liberation, health (σέσωχέ σε); "go into peace", He was not just saying "Goodbye". He was making a statement of fact, followed by a powerful command: "You may get out of this cramped life of sin and repressions and complexes; you are to get into the land of life and spaciousness, for I, the second Joshua, command you!"

"Peace" says Johs Pedersen (*Israel* 1-11, p. 311-13) "designates the fact of being whole", "consists in complete harmony", is "comprehensive and positive", "comprises all that the Israelite understands by 'good'". "It expresses every form of happiness and free expansion" (you will note here the proximity of the idea of *peace* to that of *salvation*). Now we see something of the meaning of the word on the lips of Jesus. "Peace" is not the absence of disturbance. It is the presence of the God who is Light and Life and Health.

The doctrine of *salvation*: the doctrine of *peace*. In both cases Jesus took up, and developed into fulfilment in His own Person, ideas which had been part of the very stuff of Judaism at its best. In regard to the *body*, Jesus showed Himself the heir of the Jewish tradition rather than of the Hellenic. He would never have subscribed to that Hellenic conception of man which "has been described as that of an angel in a slot machine, a soul (the invisible, spiritual, essential ego) incarcerated in a frame of matter, from which it trusts eventually to be liberated" (J. A. T. Robinson, *The Body*, p. 14). No σῶμα σῆμα for Jesus! No suggestion that the body is non-essential to the personality. Rather does He seem to have been motivated by the typically Hebrew concept of man as "flesh animated by the soul, the whole conceived as a psycho-physical unity" (Robinson, *op. cit.*, p. 14). "The body is the soul in its outward form" (J. Pedersen, *op. cit.*, 1-11, p. 171) "The spirit is the living body seen from within, and the body, the outward manifestation of the living spirit" (J. A. C. Murray, *Christian Psychotherapy*, pp. 149–150). If in this case, as in others, our Lord was the heir of the best thinking of His people and Himself gave His stamp of approval to their concept of the relation of body to soul, then we can understand the immense importance which He clearly attached to bodily health, and to the well-being of the *whole* man.

It is against some such Jewish background as this that we must come to the work and teaching of Jesus as recorded in the Gospels. Perhaps, for the sake of clarity, it will be well to make our points in a series of propositions.

1. *Jesus, when faced by physical and mental sickness, almost invariably showed Himself a fighter.* So far as we can judge from the Gospels, it would appear that for Jesus to be *con*fronted by disease was to be *af*fronted. The Oxford English Dictionary defines "to affront" as to "insult to the face . . . to put to the blush . . . to cause to feel ashamed". Out Lord meets a poor woman with a twisted body (St Luke 13:11 ff.). What does He do? Sigh, and pass by? No. Such a state of things He feels to be an affront to the plan of God, and an insult to His face. "This woman kept prisoner by Satan for eighteen long years", He heals her, and she finds her body not a hindrance to the service of God, but an expression of His glory.

Again, St Mark (1:40 ff.) gives us the story of the leper who came to Jesus. He records the compassion with which Jesus viewed the pitiable figure (v. 41). But in a well-known variant reading (common to *Codex Bezae*, the old Latin and Tatian's *Diatessaron*) no compassion is recorded but rather anger (ὀργισθείς for σπλαγχνισθείς). Judging by the canon of textual criticism which lays it down that *difficilior lectio potior*, the more probable reading is ὀργισθείς. This would fit in with the strange participle in v. 43 ἐμβριμησαμενος, for which the AV gives the doubtful rendering "straightly charged". This is a meaning "unknown to profane authorities" (as Grimm-Thayer puts it *s.v.*) and Moulton and Milligan (*The Vocabulary of the New Testament*) find that the papyri cast no fresh light on the meaning of the verb in the New Testament. In classical usage the word means "to snort" (of horses), "to be very angry, to be moved with indignation". We may well ask, then, at what or at whom was Jesus thus incensed? Not at the by-standers (as in the miracle of the healing of the man with the withered hand, St Mark 3:5) for no mention is made of them. Perhaps the anger of Jesus expressed the Divine anger against sin, of which leprosy, a living death, spoke. But is it not more likely that these participles, ὀργισθείς and ἐμβριμησάμενος, are the evangelist's attempts to express the re-action, the shame, which Jesus felt at the utter wrongness of the havoc wrought by sickness on the miracle which is a man's body?

We may further note, in the story of the raising of Lazarus, the extraordinary effort of the evangelist in St John 11:33 ff. to express the profound emotional disturbance of Jesus at the grave-side. Not only did He burst into tears (v. 35 ἐδάκρυσε and v. 34 ἐτάραξεν ἑαυτον—itself a strange phrase) but came to the tomb ἐμβριμώμενος (cp. v. 38 "snorting"). Again we ask "Why"? At the unbelief of the sisters and bystanders? Perhaps. Or was it at the tragedy of a life prematurely cut short by disease and death? Or perhaps it was *both*?

These instances—and there are others worthy of careful study—show us One Who, so far from showing any "resignation" to suffering and death, seems to have opposed them with all the power at His command. He was a fighter against those elements in life which detracted from man's fullness of life, from his full health, from his σωτηρία.

2. *Jesus struck a blow at the current doctrine which viewed suffering as invariably the consequence of sin.* The clearest case of this is the story of the man born blind (St John 9:1). Two subsidiary points may be made: (a) v. 2 would seem to imply some form of the re-incarnation idea; according to the disciples' question, if the man's blindness was due to his sin, it must presumably have been sin in a pre-incarnate state, for he was *born* blind. (b) The omission of the full stop at the end of v. 3 relieves us of the monstrous doctrine suggested by its insertion—that the man was born blind "in order that the works of God might be manifested in him" (some God!) But, these minor points apart, the main value of the story is the blow it strikes against the theory that "suffering is *invariably* the result of sin". Life makes it pretty obvious that

frequently that proposition is true (visit a VD clinic in any hospital!) but not invariably. If it be objected that that gives us no positive philosophy of evil and of suffering, it may be replied that nowhere in the recorded sayings of Jesus is such a philosophy to be found; but, negative though the blow be which the story strikes, it removes at one stroke much of the bitterness which the current theory caused (and, it may be added, still causes) in the minds of multitudes.

3. *Jesus refused to concentrate, in His healing work, solely upon the ills of the body.* A paralytic (St Mark 2:3) is brought on his mattress bed to Jesus. He looks expectantly to Him for physical healing. What must have been his surprise when Jesus said to him, *not* "your paralysis is cured" *but* "your sins are forgiven!" The great Physician diagnosed the trouble which underlay the outward manifestation of it which was the physical paralysis. He saw that if there was to be a complete and permanent cure, the *whole* man must be dealt with. First, his relationship to God and to his fellows must be put right (there had been *sin* of some sort); then his physical healing would follow and there would go to his house a man every whit whole.

Again, the story of the demon-possessed man, told as it is, no doubt, only in outline (St Mark 5:1-20) reminds us almost of a modern psychiatrist's approach to his patient. Jesus is apparently at considerable pains to get alongside the deranged man. He sympathetically questions him: "What is your name?" (v. 9) and elicits the significant answer of what sounds like a schizophrenic: "My name is Legion: there are so many of us." After the cure, Doctor and patient are together, presumably in close conclave (v. 15—"They came to Jesus and saw him that was possessed . . . sitting"). Mere expulsion of the demons was not enough. The man must feel that he was understood. He must be made whole in the totality of his personality.

The importance of this point can hardly be exaggerated. Any "healing movement" which simply goes out to cure physical sickness without reference to the well-being of the whole personality, will have results compared with which the efforts of a bull in a china shop will be pacific. For if, as we have seen, it is true that suffering is not *invariably* the consequence of sin, it is also equally true that, time and time again, suffering is the manifestation in the physical part of him of a man's maladjustment to God, to his environment, or to himself. To attempt to cure the symptom without dealing with the root of the problem is like putting on a new tile to the roof when the foundations of the building are totally inadequate!

When Jesus healed a man's body or mind, that healing was one of the ways, one of the most expressive and eloquent ways, in which the Love of God in Him went out to people in need. But the God who made man as a psychosomatic unity loves that man in his entirety, and, if we may say so reverently, is "all out" for his total restoration. "More and more," says Jung, "we turn our attention from the visible disease and direct it upon the man as a whole" (*Modern Man in Search of a Soul*, p. 222). Said a wise French clinician: "*Il n'y a pas de maladies, seulement des malades.*"

4. *Jesus viewed His healing work as part and parcel of His Messianic function.* Those of you who are familiar with Canon Alan Richardson's excellent book *The Miracle Stories of the Gospels* will recall how frequently he insists that the very language in which the evangelists record the healing miracles of Jesus is Old Testament language, and very often Old Testament *Messianic* language. This is intentionally so, as if the evangelists would say: "*This* which we saw happen is that of which we had read in our Scriptures. The Christ has come, and the signs (to use the word of which the Fourth Evangelist is particularly fond) of His coming are visible (for those who have eyes to see) in the works of physical and mental healing which accompany His Advent." "Your God will come and save you. Then the eyes of the blind shall be opened and the ears of the deaf shall be unstopped. Then shall the lame man leap as an hart, and the tongue of the dumb shall sing . . ." So Isaiah had written (35:4–6). The evidence of the Messianic Coming was to be seen in blind seeing, deaf hearing, lame walk- ing, as well as in poor being evangelised. In the Person of Jesus, the reign of God arrived with power. The evidence of its power was plentiful in the mighty acts of Jesus. The powers of the Age to Come were impinging on this Age. "*Si monumentum requiris*", the early eye-witnesses might have said (in anticipation of the in- scription on Wren's tomb!) "*circumspice*".

Perhaps this is the place to say a further word about the nature of the healing miracles, though it is not the place (nor indeed am I the person) to attempt a rationale of miracle in general or of the miracles of Jesus in particular. We may leave on one side the so-called "nature" miracles which have peculiar problems of their own, and which are, for our present purpose, strictly speaking, irrelevant.

H. E. W. Turner, in his book *Jesus, Master and Lord* (p. 176 ff.), has drawn our attention to St Augustine's singularly up-to-date treatment of the subject in his *The City of God* and other works. St Augustine draws a distinction between acts which are "beyond nature" (*praeter naturam*) or even "against what is known of nature" (*contra quod est notum naturae*) and acts which are "against nature" (*contra naturam*). Our Lord's miracles are best regarded as of the first type, that is to say *not* as against nature, but as beyond nature or perhaps against what is known of nature. This is in accord with much of the best modern thought. Science today is far less dogmatic than it was at the turn of the century. Its best exponents are far more prepared to admit the provisional nature of its conclusions than were their fathers or grandfathers. Where the grandfathers said: "Here is a clear breach of an unswerving law of nature," the grandsons prefer to say: "Here is a case which is not covered by our previous generalisations." They may even add: "With further knowledge this may well fit into our understanding of things." Turner is at pains to point out that this approach to miracle does not mean that we simply view our Lord as a practitioner of psychological medicine many centuries before His time. But it does mean that, in the recent advances of medical science, we have a background against which the healing miracles of Jesus can be most appropriately understood and satisfactorily set.

We may go further, I think. If we conceive of Jesus as doing his Messianic healing work not *contra naturam*, but *praeter naturam*, have we not here a strong hint that the Church, if she is entrusted with a healing function, should exercise that function, not against or at cross-purposes with the work of science but in closest liaison with it? But perhaps this is to anticipate what I shall refer to shortly.

5. Jesus' greatest contribution in the realm of suffering was not what He did in healing, nor what He taught by word, but what He was in His person.

The picture which the early documents give of Jesus is not of some superb Apollo, though it may be noted that we have no record of the sickness of Jesus, but have rather, the impression of One perfectly integrated and supremely at peace with God and with Himself. Rather do the documents stress the fact that He who was called Immanuel entered into our griefs with a terrible intimacy. St Matthew, after recording Christ's healing of a leper, of the centurion's servant, of Peter's mother-in-law, and of the demon-possessed, concludes the section by recalling the words of Isaiah and noting their fulfilment in our Lord: "He took away our illnesses and lifted our diseases from us" (St Matthew 8:17). He was indeed, as He Himself taught, the suffering Servant foreshadowed in the great Isaianic prophecies.

Dr Dillistone movingly pointed out in his book *Jesus and His Cross* (esp. pp. 114 ff.) that it is the function of the *servants* in society to carry the burdens, and to do the dirty work of mankind. He quotes Bushnell (*The Vicarious Sacrifice*): "Love is a principle essentially vicarious in its own nature, identifying the subject with others, so as to suffer their adversities and pains, and taking on itself the burden of their evils."

It remains to ask in the light of our study: What is the function of the Church, which is the Body of Christ, in a world which on any showing is desperately sick? The necessity for brevity may lay me open to the charge of dogmatism, but I will take the risk. The commission of St Mark 3:14, 15 has never been withdrawn. Jesus ordained twelve (1) that they might be with Him, (2) that He might send them forth to preach, (3) to have power to heal sicknesses and to cast out devils. To the early Church were committed gifts of healing (Rom. 12, 1 Cor. 12). Has the commission been divided, so that the third part is now irrelevant? Have the gifts of healing been withdrawn? Or has the Church fallen into a faithless torpor from which only now she is beginning to awaken? I think that the latter is more likely than the former. The phrase "The Church is the extension of the Incarnation" is non-biblical and open to misunderstanding. But there is enough truth in it to make us take seriously once again what St Paul meant by the Body of Christ, or what St Luke meant when He spoke of "all that Jesus *began* to do and to teach" (Acts 1:1).

Inasmuch as the message of the Church is precisely that of her

Master, that is to say, a message of salvation, of full health, for the whole man, body, mind and spirit, a message of peace, with God, with men, with oneself, a message of integration; in as much as the approach of the Church to body and mind must be that of her Master to those subjects, she must necessarily be committed to the task of healing those things which detract from the full health of the individual and of the body corporate. I submit that, we must not divide up the original commission of Jesus and fail to continue the healing work which He began. *It was part of His Gospel. It must be part of ours.*

To recur for a moment to my fourth "proposition" (that Jesus viewed His healing work as part and parcel of His Messianic function)—if we believe that, with the coming of Jesus, the reign of God was inaugurated in power, and if, further we believe that it is the function of the People of God to be that Body through which the powers of *that* New Age function in *this*, then surely we should expect the significant signs still to be evident. "These signs shall follow them that believe; In my Name shall they cast out devils . . . they shall lay hands on the sick and they shall recover" (St Mark 16:17, 18).

I fully realise that, for some (and those, very earnest good people) the healing of the body has become almost an end in itself. Such folk would do well to bear in mind my third "proposition", that Jesus refused to concentrate, in His healing work, solely upon the ills of the body. The only place in the world where the love of God can be understood and the forgiveness of sin be obtained is within the fellowship of the Church of the Living God. Unhindered fellowship with God—that is the first and last thing for which the Church exists. Its primary battle is with *sin;* its primary end is the glory of God; its message is health for the *whole* man. It may well question its own sensitiveness if, when faced with sickness, it does not "show fight" (see proposition 1—"Jesus, when faced by physical or mental sickness, almost invariably showed Himself a fighter"). But it will remember that the greatest insult to the majesty of Almighty God is sin. Deal with this and much sickness will fade away (though not all? See proposition 2).

Modern medical science would corroborate this. How many duodenal ulcers are due to the sin of worry? How much asthma is due to unresolved complexes or unhappy relationships? How many nervous breakdowns are the outcome of spiritual homelessness, and would have been averted if men had come to terms with God, and were living in the bracing warmth of a live Church fellowship?

I close with two points:

(1) One of the problems which I merely mentioned at the beginning of this paper was this: Can we simply say, "Given enough faith, we may expect healing"? I suggested that that was too facile an answer to a tantalising question. How many earnest people, possessed of a living faith, have pleaded with God for the removal of some physical illness. and been distressed that the illness persisted unrelieved! One such tells his story in 2 Corinthians 12. Does such persistence of disease mean failure on the part of God, or of the man concerned, or of the Church?

I suspect that *sometimes* it does indicate failure, for example, in the fellowship of prayer and faith in the local church, which is not strong enough to do for the patient what his four friends did for the paralytic in the Gospel story. But it does not always indicate failure. I do believe that God has lessons to teach which, for reasons not wholly known to us, can only be learnt in and through suffering. In the passage already alluded to (2 Cor. 12), God answered St Paul's prayer for the removal of his illness, and answered it with a clear "No". Why? Because God was not interested in a man's mere body? The whole thesis of this paper has been against that conclusion. It was because God had lessons to teach about overshadowing grace, and strength made perfect in weakness, which He could not teach apart from weakness. Because God wanted to teach the Apostle the hard lesson of Christian prepositions—that the predominant preposition is not "out of" but "through" and "in". "My strength is made perfect *in* weakness." "When thou passest *through* the waters, I will be with thee" (Isa. 43:2).

B. K. Cunningham prayed, and had the Laying on of Hands, for the removal of his deafness. It persisted, though he testified to great blessing received in the service. *But the deafness became a means of grace to him.* (See *B. K. Cunningham: a Memoir*, esp. pp. 57 and 156, by John R. H. Moorman).

(2) A final word must be said about the attitude of the Church to science and the medical profession.

I have already suggested that the nature of the healing miracles of Jesus hints at a close liaison between religion and science. The Church cannot but be ashamed of the suspicion, even opposition, with which in the past she has regarded new scientific discoveries, Was there not a sermon once preached, at a time when the discoveries of science clashed with the tenets of the Church, on "Ye men of Galileo, why stand ye gazing up into heaven . . .?" It is to be hoped that the worst of that discreditable epoch is over. There are signs that, with the coming of an age when science is less cock-sure and religion less bigoted than in days gone by, the two are beginning to work hand in hand for the welfare of the whole man.

Commenting on the fact that, as recently as 1919, the term "psychosomatic medicine" was unknown to the medical vocabulary, Miss Garlick writes: "The now current use of this compound word, describing the soul-body relationship, marks a far-reaching change in the attitude and approach of modern medicine towards the cause and treatment of disease" No small debt is owed to Carl Jung for his insistence that "a religious attitude is an element in psychic life whose importance can hardly be overrated" (*Modern Man in Search of a Soul*, p. 77). In a well-known passage he writes: "Among my patients in the second half of life—that is to say, over thirty-five—there has not been one whose problem in the last resort was not that of finding a religious outlook on life. It is safe to say that every one of them fell ill because he had lost that which the living religions of every age have given to their followers, and none of them has been really healed who did not regain his religious outlook" (*op. cit.*, p. 264). He comments: "It is indeed high time for the clergymen and the psychotherapists to join forces to meet this great spiritual task" (p. 265).

I would venture to suggest that, the more virile our doctrine of the Holy Ghost, the Lord, the Life-Giver, the more fully we realise that *all* truth is His gift to His world, whether it be truth about the Incarnation or about the atom, about the Atonement or about the constitution of man in his complex and wonderful make-up, so much the more shall we see that, as religion and science join hands, God's plan of salvation, of spaciousness, of full life for men will be worked out.

That will best happen, not in the rarefied atmosphere of high-up talks between scientists and theologians, but as Dr Jones and Rector Smith together consult (and, if may be, pray) about John Brown who is ill and whom God wants to be well.

IV GREAT PERSONALITIES

Peter Green—Parish Priest

MANCHESTER IN THE early thirties—and I mention it because it flowed into Salford, where Peter Green worked, as naturally as London flows into Southwark—was an interesting place. The Hallé orchestra flourished. C. P. Scott reigned over the *Manchester Guardian*. Walter Moberley was Vice-Chancellor of the University, Samuel Alexander (of *Time, Space and Deity* fame) was still around, looking like Moses *redivivus*. C. H. Dodd was about to take wings—he looked like a little bird— and fly to Cambridge as Norris-Hulse Professor of Divinity. L. B. Namier headed the distinguished school of history, a worthy heir to Tout, and Bragg was only one of a galaxy of brilliant scientists who lent distinction to the University. T. H. Pear explored the mysteries of psychology. William Temple had recently gone from Manchester to York, and Guy Warman was bishop of the diocese.

Hard by, in Salford, was Peter Green.

The only time that I can recall seeing him must have been over forty years ago, when I was in my early twenties and he in his early sixties; I, an assistant lecturer in the University of Manchester, he, one of the most respected parish priests in this country. I have a vision of him in grey flannel trousers and a brown coat, and I think it was in the University Union. The contact was slight, almost non-existent; but the vision of him has clarified with the passing of the years, partly through conversation with those who knew him intimately, partly through reading his books, and partly through studying his biography, written by the Reverend H. E. Sheen.[1]

Prideaux Lectures, Exeter University 1974.

[1]H. E. Sheen, *Canon Peter Green. A biography of a great parish priest* (1965).

Who was Peter Green, and what did he do? The questions must be asked, for men, even good men and prominent men, are soon forgotten. Further, he died more than twelve years go, and that at the age of ninety.

The bare facts can be quickly set out. He was born in 1871 and died in 1961. Educated at Cranleigh School and St John's College, Cambridge, he entered no theological college but was made deacon in 1894 and ordained priest the following year in Rochester Cathedral. Two curacies followed, one of four years at Walworth and another of four years at Leeds Parish Church, where he served in that nursery of Bishops, first under E. S. Talbot and then under E. C. S. Gibson, of *The Thirty-Nine Articles* fame. Eight years of service as a curate was nothing unusual in those days. Then followed nine years (1902–1911) as Rector of the Church of the Sacred Trinity, Salford, in the days when Bishop Moorhouse was chief shepherd of the diocese of Manchester. Then followed forty years, no less (1911–1951), as Rector of St Philip's, Salford. When he resigned that charge, he continued as Canon of Manchester.

As you will have seen, it is a very simple story. Honours came to Peter Green, of course: he was a Royal Chaplain, and the contact with the royal house brought him great joy. He was a Select Preacher at Oxford and Cambridge, and gave courses of lectures on pastoral theology at Cambridge and at King's College, London. He was a Freeman of the City of Salford, and an honorary Doctor of Divinity of Manchester University. But he would have been the first to acknowledge that, in so far as there was glory to his life, it lay, not in the acquisition of honours ecclesiastical or academic, but in being a parish priest of the Church of England for some fifty-six years. He refused four bishoprics.[2]

What sort of man was this? To answer that question is not so easy as to outline the main stages of his long life; but we must attempt the task. To be a nephew, on his mother's side, of Professor George Saintsbury, the authority on English literature, was on any reckoning an advantage. It may well have had something to do with the fact that, practically all his life, he was an omnivorous reader and a prolific writer. It served as a good background for the Presidency of the Cambridge Union and

[2]His entry in *Who's Who* included the words, "offered Bishopric of Lincoln, 1919, and refused".

for the First Class which he carried off in the Moral Science Tripos. Saintsbury, had he lived, would not have been ashamed of *Artifex*, the name Peter Green took when he wrote in the *Manchester Guardian* for over forty years. He could, if he had wished, have been a Fellow of St John's, but he refused. Intellectually gifted though he was, interested in the things of the mind as he continued to be, there were other calls, or, rather, there was one other call, the ordained ministry fulfilled where the shadows lay deepest.

He came of parents who were deeply religious. His father, a lawyer, was a member of the Clapton sect, a group of high Anglicans whose leader, Joshua Watson, lived at Clapton. His mother, born Elizabeth Sophia Saintsbury, was brought up under the influence of the Clapham sect, the evangelical counterpart, if such it may be called, of the Clapton sect. But early in her life, the Oxford Movement influenced her deeply and she remained a Tractarian for the rest of her days. Peter himself would have answered to the description of a high churchman throughout his ministry; but the background of his father and his mother can be seen in the openness of his mind and heart to Anglicans of all colours and to members of the Free Churches. What he did find hard to stomach was any kind of theological rigidity, and the ending of the episcopate of Bishop Knox and the advent of William Temple to Manchester came as a relief to his spirit. Politically he was a Liberal all his life, and he never totally despaired of the come-back of that party.

For a more intimate picture of the man, I am indebted to a conversation which I had, a little over a year ago, in Manchester Cathedral with Canon G. P. Morgan, who succeeded Green at St Philip's in 1951, and with Canon H. F. Woolnough (who died a few months after the interview), who was a colleague for many years. I pass on the impression which the conversation left with me, and I paint the portrait or, rather outline the sketch, "warts and all". He was, above all else, a man of God whose religious life centred in the daily celebration of the Holy Communion in his parish church. His life was hid with Christ in God. Though his teaching was little followed on this point, he, as a strong Tractarian, taught confession as a valued practice of the Church to be followed by the faithful. A bachelor, he had little time for women and girls—the curates could look after them: *How to deal with Lads* (1910) and *How to Deal with Men* (1911) was never followed by *How to deal with Girls* or *How to deal with Women*! He did not even know their names, though no doubt he sought to conceal the fact. He had nieces living in Southampton. Said he: "Southampton-Salford, Salford-Southampton—just about the right distance for relatives."

Never blessed with very robust health, and often suffering from severe sick headaches, it was a measure of his self-discipline that he achieved so much. A fervent teetotaller till near the end of his life, abstemious in all his habits, he would have two cups of coffee and the *Manchester Guardian* for breakfast, a poached egg for lunch, and a banana at a Rotarians' Feast. Near the end, before he was cared for for two years in Salford Hospital and for four years in a nursing home in Surrey, he nearly starved himself. "Just think of it," he said, pondering on a member of the Barclay family, "just think of it—sitting in your own bank, drinking your own beer!"

He was a man with an autocratic side to his nature, though in his methods of parish administration he was democratic to a fault— no alteration could take place without the agreement of his parochial church council. He could tear strips off people, though often his barbed remarks were accompanied by a twinkle in the eye. His biographer tells how a business tycoon who disliked Green tried to make a butt of him at a public dinner, only to have the laugh turned on himself. He wrote to Green complaining that he had made him look a fool. Green replied: "Dear Sir, You are mistaken. I merely called attention to the fact".

No one could say that he was a good judge of character. It has been claimed that in this matter he was worse than William Temple. He would get robbed and then go to great pains to get the man off next morning in Court. He was no administrator. He gave his furniture to his housekeeper—and then sold it; his books to the cathedral—and then sold them. To our great loss he destroyed practically all his papers, though we have the books which he wrote; of this, more later.

Though he was colour-blind and his house was barren of any signs of artistic taste, and though the country and things of beauty had little meaning for him, he nevertheless wrote a book on *The Problem of Art* (1937)! Of all men he was *the* town man. Mile End Road and Salford, a wet roof and a lamp-post—give him these and he was happy! It is true that, in his "London Sketches" in *Our Kid*, he is writing with his tongue in his cheek, but this passage tells us a good deal about its author: "There is a silly saying that God made the country, and man made the town. Not at all. God made the country, and made it lovely to the eye. And then He made the town, and made it beautiful to the spirit. The town, polis, home of politeness, home of man the political animal; the city, civitas, where civilisation is born, and civility reigns. Not for nothing have saints and sages, in all times since the days of the writer of the Apocalypse, loved to picture Heaven as a city, the heavenly Jerusalem".

Well, there is the man. No, there are some fleeting impressions of the man. What was it in him that enabled David Edwards to call him "the greatest parish priest in twentieth century England ... a saint of God"—a big claim from the pen of a skilled and judicious writer?[3] What was it that made *The Times* in its obituary notice write: "He was in the true succession of the great parish priests of the Church of England, and vast numbers who knew and loved him will thank God for his work and influence" (18th November, 1961)? We must assay an answer, if this lecture is to be more than a mere biographical sketch.

Perhaps the first clue to his greatness and to his influence in England during the first half of this century lay in the fact that he magnified the office of the parish priest. He used to say, "Had I nine lives like a cat, I should have been a parish priest every time". He would have made an able lawyer, or a university don, or a journalist. But having set his hand to the plough of the parish priest, he never looked back. Nor did he want to. "To the born priest," he said, "there is no other possibility open, and only the born priest is a happy one."

His pastoral lectures delivered at Durham University in 1935 and published under the title *The Man of God*, though, naturally, bearing the marks of their date and written in the simplest style, deserve to stand alongside such a book as Richard Baxter's *The Reformed Pastor*, which Hensley Henson described as the greatest book on pastoral theology in the English language. In these lectures, he speaks out of the heart of his own experience. Listen to this:

[3]D. L. Edwards, *Leaders of the Church of England 1828–1944* (1971), pp. 313–14.

I am sure that there is no life so rich in opportunities of service, nor any so happy, as that of the parish priest who really knows and loves his people. Given the bare necessities of life—food, clothes and a roof over one's head—there are only two things really needful for a happy life. They are, someone to love and someone to love you. And the life of the man who strives to be a true pastor is rich in both.

Or again, listen to this:

Nothing would do more for the conversion of England than for young men to regard the office of the parish priest as the highest and noblest to which they could aspire. When work in an English parish is looked on as being no less romantic, no less honourable, than work in the Mission-field, we may expect a converted England. But work at home cannot be as romantic and as honourable as work in Central Africa or in Melanesia unless we are willing to face it with an equal spirit of consecration and of self-sacrifice.

Here, in these two passages and in a score of others like them, we see a man who, like St Paul, magnified his office.[4]

One of the ways in which he did this was seen in his determination to remain in the parish he loved. Salford is no holiday resort. It has little beauty that we should desire it. But nothing would move him from it for forty long years, years which included two devastating world wars and a complete revolution in the social order. Such things as these did not move Peter Green. Rather, they made him determined to stay. In an age of movement and change, he would be a stabilising influence; he would remain, and people should know that, however much Salford might alter, the Rector was still there, in and out of their homes, available night and day.

He resisted the temptation, common to too many of us, to look over his shoulder—"I've been here five years; it is about time I moved on. Are my gifts being adequately used and sufficiently recognised? Are my feet on the ladder?" I believe it to be a fact that the value of many a clergyman's ministry—not all, by any

[4]Romans 11:13.

means, but many—is in inverse proportion to the length of his entry in *Crockford's Clerical Directory*. If, in the words of the funeral service, they "never continue in one stay", if they flit from one scene of activity to another like a bee among the flowers, they may get known to many, but it is to be doubted whether their work among them will go very deep.

If it is asked why he stayed so long in that unattractive place, the answer is simple: he *loved* the people. He loved his curates; they were often men of very humble social origin whom he had nursed along the road to ordination and whom now he trained in their first curacy. But he cared for them deeply and sought to instil in them the ideals of the ministry by which his own was shaped.

And he loved the ordinary people in the parish, not only those who attended his church but all those who lived within the bounds of his parish and who therefore were part of his *cure*, his responsibility before God. Such has been and is the vision of the duty of the parish priest which the Church of England has sought to hold before the attention of her clergy. Impossible of fulfilment it may sometimes be, in vast areas of dense housing and high-rise buildings. But the ideal is there, not to be lost sight of, if *Ecclesia Anglicana* is not to become a congregationalist church.

In 1920, Peter Green wrote a little book called *Our Kid: with other London and Lancashire Sketches*. It is dated, of course. Dedicated to that great newspaper editor, C. P. Scott of the *Manchester Guardian*, it talks of knickerbockers, and of a "mountainous woman in a mackintosh and a boy's cloth cap", and so on. What memories that brings back to *me* of parish work in London in the mid-thirties! It is highly humorous. It was intended to be—the sketches appeared as light little articles in the *Manchester Guardian*. You can call it sentimental in parts, if you will, and I would not quarrel with you for doing so. But throughout the book there shines a deep love of human nature with all its extraordinary quirks and foibles and a penetrating insight into the character which, often hidden behind a rough exterior, cried out for recognition and development.

When Peter Green's boys went to the wars, he would follow them with letters—and with his prayers. And when they came back, there he was to welcome them and remind them of the days when they served him at the altar or tried to harry him in the

Sunday School. *He was there*, a bit of the permanent in a world which seemed to be passing at an unbelievable rate.

I look again for an answer to the question as to where it was that Green's greatness lay. I find it in the combination which he somehow managed to achieve of constant and devoted parochial ministry with very considerable literary activity. It has been reckoned that he wrote some thirty-eight books. Let it be granted that some of them are very slight, a gathering together of articles written for the press or of sermons delivered in his parish pulpit. Some of them are marked more by imaginative flight than by detailed or accurate scholarship: I think of *Some Gospel Scenes and Characters* (1937), in which he lets a "devout imagination" play over the figures of the Blessed Virgin, the evangelists and others. Some of his books were written by way of protest against movements which he felt were disadvantageous to the church or contrary to the truth. *The Seven Golden Candlesticks* (1943) is a protest against the Modernism which he believed would, if followed, make shipwreck of the faith. Some of his books were occasioned by the particular needs of the hour. *The War—and After* bears the date 1915 and consists of six articles which he wrote for Northampton newspapers. A year later we find him contributing a chapter to a symposium edited by Bishop G. K. A. Bell and entitled *The War and the Kingdom of God*. His pamphlet *The Moral Condition of Great Britain Today* was written as the Second World War was nearing its close (1943), for Green was convinced that "there is an alarming deterioration today as compared with two generations ago". His *Devotional Use of the Bible* (1939) was one of the series of Biblical Handbooks edited by Bishop A. W. F. Blunt; though elementary, it is a very practical guide for the beginner.

No doubt, in these days of high printing costs, some of these books would never have seen the light of day. But there are others of greater weight and of more permanent value which would certainly have found a publisher today if Green had written them in the seventies of our century. His biblical expositions are still well worth reading, not for evidence of deep and detailed critical scholarship, but because they reveal a lively and devout mind at work on the text of the Bible, his findings illustrated from a rich experience of men and affairs. I instance his *Our Great High Priest: Thoughts on the Seventeenth Chapter of St John's Gospel* (1939) and

Good Friday Victory: Thoughts on the Seven last Words (1948).

Green had the layman constantly in view as he wrote. His *The Christian Man* (1937) is a companion volume for laymen to his *The Man of God* which was written for clergy, as was *The Town Parson* (1919). His *The Gospel Story: A Short Life of Christ* (1939) was written for use in mission schools abroad—he had taken a mission in South Africa and had refused the bishopric of New Guinea. We could multiply examples.

Peter Green's mind was always at work on Christian doctrine, as such books as *Our Lord and Saviour: A study in the Person and Doctrine of Jesus Christ* (1928) and *The Holy Ghost, the Comforter* (1933) show. This last book might well serve as an introduction to Green's writings for one who wanted to make a study of them. Written long before what we now know as the charismatic movement began to make its impact on the Church, there are passages in the book which might well have come from the pen of a charismatic leader. Listen to this, as an example:

> The difficulty is that even among our own congregations of regular churchgoers—and might I not add even among the clergy?—so many are still unconverted, and have never experienced the life-giving movements of the Holy Spirit in their souls. Or if not wholly unconverted many nominal Christians have not made a complete and whole-hearted surrender to the Spirit's guidance. Let me again assert my conviction that nothing but a re-baptism of the Church with the Holy Ghost, a second Day of Pentecost, can save the world from disaster (pp. 16–27).

He traces the activity of the Spirit in creation, regeneration and conversion, edification and sanctification, in the sacraments and in the Church; and excellent things he has to say on these subjects. He saw, in the course of his everyday work, the activity of the Spirit in the lives of many of his people; and he has little patience with those who say "that there is more of the 'neighbourliness which accepts people as they are' among the 'coarse oaths' of the public-house than in the parish church". "I wish people who repeat this silly cliché," he writes, "would adduce some evidence for what they say . . . I can only say that it corresponds with absolutely nothing in my experience. What does astonish me is that people who write like this do not seem conscious either of the harm they do to religion or of the extraordinary beauty of the lives of many simple Christians" (p. 6). A word well spoken to those churchmen who, in his generation or in ours, delight in denigrating the Church in the eyes of the world.

He sometimes makes extraordinary statements, as for example that there is "little in Holy Scripture about the Holy Spirit" (p. 21 —a strange remark from a man who used a lexicon!). But there are passages, and not least footnotes, which deserve reading and re-reading, as for example where he gives his view, though tentatively, that the gift at ordination to the priesthood is not the *power* to absolve and to consecrate the elements—that power belongs essentially to the whole body of Christ—but the *authority* to exercise the priestly office (p. 104).

If Green had been writing this book today, rather than forty years ago, he would, no doubt, have dealt with such a subject as the relation of the Spirit to the unity of the Church. But in the early thirties, the whole ecumenical movement had not reached the point where it was the outstanding theological subject of the day, nor had schemes of union throughout the world advanced or foundered as they have by now. Nor did Green see, with the clarity given to Bishop Lesslie Newbigin in 1953 when he wrote his seminal book *The Household of God*, that if one is to face the issues of the ecumenical Church with any measure of reality, one must take into consideration the charismatic element which is an authentic part of New Testament ecclesiology as well as the "catholic" and the "evangelical" elements.

Human conduct and the whole sphere of ethics had been a particular interest of Peter Green's, certainly from his under-graduate days at Cambridge when he changed over from reading mathematics to the Moral Science Tripos. "Had I not been a parson, I should have been a lawyer," he used to say. It is in this field that his most serious literary work was done, as is evidenced by such books as *The Problem of Evil* (1920) and *The Problem of Right Conduct* (1931), and among slighter writings *Personal Religion and Public Righteousness* (1923) and *Betting and Gambling* (1924).

In the *Problem of Evil*, Green sought to deal with some of the philosophical and theological questions involved. His argument, though not depending for its validity on the acceptance of the theory, includes a chapter on the idea of a pre-mundane Fall. This idea had interested him since 1896, and as late as 1944 he published a pamphlet under that title. We see him wrestling with the problem which faces every serious-minded Christian: is it possible to give intelligent content to St Paul's dictum that "all things work together for good to those who love God", in a world where, if it is true that "God's in His heaven", it is obviously false that "all's right with the world"? And Green wrote his book in 1920, just after the end of the First World War.

His book *The Problem of Right Conduct* was written to meet what he considered to be the lack of a text-book on Christian Ethics for candidates for Holy Orders, and because he wanted to work out the application of the basic principles of Christian ethics to practical problems. It is in this latter connection that the book is most "dated", for recent years have thrown up a host of ethical problems which in Green's day, if they had arisen at all, were only on the horizon and not at the centre of the subject. This book is one of the very few of Green's writings which has an index—strange that so systematic a man should omit so necessary a part of a serious work! In that index, the word "abortion" does not occur, though "ablution centres" does; "drugs" is absent, though "drunkenness" has six entries and "alcoholic drink" two; "homosexuality" is absent, though there is a small, and very unsatisfactory, passage on "unnatural vice" (pp. 223–225). The world of the early thirties differed greatly from that of the mid-seventies.

Nevertheless, there is much of abiding value in the book, and one can imagine how barbed a remark Green would have shot at the pundits of A.C.C.M. (or was it C.A.C.T.M.?) when that body passed through a period of its history in which it eliminated altogether from its General Ordination Examination a paper on ethics! Green at least had his eyes open to the basic necessity of giving a grounding to the clergy in right conduct, its theory and practice.

We have seen two answers to the question as to the reason for the greatness of Peter Green—his magnifying of the office of parish priest, and his combining of intense pastoral activity with considerable literary work. There is one further factor which must be taken into consideration if justice is to be done to him and perhaps it is the most important factor of all.

Though Peter Green's mind ranged out over a wide variety of problems, theological, philosophical and practical, and though he lived a long life of intense labour, he could be said to have been a man of one consuming passion. "This one thing I do" could have been his motto, as it was St Paul's.

> Who keeps one end in view
> Makes all things serve.

If this passion had to be summed up in one word, it would be the word "conversion", used in no narrow, party sense, but in the deep biblical sense of turning round and facing God in the immensity of His grace and in the intensity of His demands. It is what the Old Testament writers meant by *shubh*, turning and returning, "a deep and an ethical process, the breaking up of fallow ground . . . the seeking and waiting for Jehovah till Himself send the rain", as George Adam Smith put it,[5] what the New Testament writers meant by *metanoia*, a change of mind and heart leading to a radical change of life and action. This is what Green aimed at in pulpit, in pastoral work, in literary activity, and in the missions which he regularly took in different parts of the land.

The point is so important that I shall quote from his biography. "He was . . . a deeply converted man, with a passion for the conversion of others . . . He believed that every man must progress from a second-hand religion, an inherited religion, to one of his own."[6] Again, "the only kind of religion he considered worth having was a 'vital religion', the religion of first-hand experience".[7] And again, "he believed that there was a line everyone must cross if he was to gain a vital religion, and that involved full and deep personal conversion. In this sense his whole ministry was one of evangelism".[8]

Peter Green, as we have seen, was a Tractarian. He was devoted to the Book of Common Prayer: I wonder what he would have made of our attempts at liturgical revision? He stood for Catholic principles. He campaigned for national righteousness. He had a social gospel. Against this background, it is impressive to hear

[5]G. A. Smith, *The Book of The Twelve Prophets*, Vol. I (1897), p. 345.
[6]Sheen, p. 22.
[7]Sheen, p. 35.
[8]Sheen, p. 99.

him say: "Religion has social fruits, but religion is not itself social. True religion is an intensely personal thing. A revival of religion means an increase in the number of *converted individuals*".[9] Again, "it is not enough to get people to church. We need to get them to Christ. I fear there are congregations in which a very large percentage of the regular members have never really faced the question of entire surrender to Christ".[10]

It was this burning conviction which led him during most years of his ministry to leave his parish for three successive Sundays in order to take a mission, from which he always came back refreshed for the evangelistic task in his own parish. Again and again in his books he comes back to the importance of parochial missions. He has a chapter on them in *The Man of God* (pp. 165 ff.) and he wrote a book *Parochial Missions Today* (1928), to which Bishop Herbert of Blackburn contributed an Introduction.

Parochial missions as Peter Green understood them have gone out of fashion recently, with certain notable exceptions. It may be questioned whether we have found anything to take their place. Until we do, we should beware lest we are lapsing into a kind of general churchiness which does little to turn people to the repentance of which we spoke a moment ago. "Till you have got a man on his knees to pray, and on his feet to speak for Christ, you have done little or nothing for him spiritually"—this is not Billy Graham in Chicago; it is Peter Green in Salford.

"Only two things are really needful for a happy life—someone to love and someone to love you. The life of the man who strives to be a true pastor is rich in both." So he wrote. So he found. Peter Green was a happy man.

---

[9] *The Man of God* (1935), p. 128.
[10] *The Man of God*, p. 141. See further *The Holy Ghost, the Comforter* (1933), p. 57 ff.

Sir Winston Churchill—World Figure

1 Cor. 14:8

If the trumpet give an uncertain sound, who shall prepare himself to the battle?

THIS IS A house of God, not a lecture hall. This is a pulpit, not a public platform. And there is a difference. For a house of God is a place of worship where men turn from the temporal to the eternal; and a pulpit is the place where the Word of God is to be expounded and His ways made known.

It would be a misuse of the pulpit, for the preacher to engage in a long eulogy of the one whom we specially remember today. A brief word must suffice for that. History will ensure Sir Winston Churchill his rightful place, not only in the annals of these islands but in the perspective of the onward march of mankind. As a Church leader from Norway wrote to me last week: "He was not only *Britain's* great leader, he was *ours* also . . . His way of thinking, his speeches, but above all his way of acting have endeared him to all of us . . . We would like to thank God for him".

We thank God for him and for what the Almighty accomplished through a frail man, for the toughest of us is frail and his span of years is brief. So we rightly turn from the eulogy of a mortal to thanksgiving to the Immortal. That is a fitting activity for this time and place.

The task of the preacher is to make known the ways of God, to spell out the principles on which God works in history and in the affairs of men.

Memorial Service, York Minster, 31st January, 1965.

There are three things which I want to say about this, against the background of Sir Winston's life and work:

1. *God makes use of words*

There are those who think that words are weak things. "Give us deeds," they say, "not words." Churchill knew better. Words to him *were* deeds—they got things done. When he referred to Hitler as "that bad man", those three damning monosyllables were like three sword-thrusts at the heart of a monster. With words carefully chosen and skilfully aimed, he roused peoples from apathy and rallied nations to activity. "In the dark days and darker nights," said President Kennedy, "when England stood alone and most men save Englishmen despaired of England's life, he mobilised the English language and sent it into battle."

Churchill was not the first to realise the power of the spoken word. For centuries before him, poets, preachers and prophets had known the power of the word to divide and to heal, to condemn and to justify. And when at last God's revelation of Himself through the people of Israel reached its climax, the profoundest of the expositors of that revelation called Jesus the Word of God. The Word was God's mighty deed, was what God had to say to men, visible in human form, audible, tangible. "The Word was made flesh and dwelt among us."

Not the least of the lessons which Churchill taught us—and, if we will listen, would teach us still—was the lesson of the power of the spoken and the written word. Treat it with reverence, use it with responsibility, and it still can become a mighty medium of the truth of God.

The trumpet—the trumpet of the word—gave no uncertain sound.

2. *God makes use of men*

Many a time He does it when men are *unconscious* of being the instruments of His purpose—a Cyrus here as the rod of His anger, a Roman Emperor there, as an agent preparing the way of the Christ. Many a time He does it when men *consciously* put themselves at His disposal for the fulfilment of His will. Early in his career, Churchill records: "I prayed long and earnestly for help and guidance. My prayer, as it seems to me, was swiftly and wonderfully answered".

We do not need to commit ourselves to the view that all that Churchill did was right when we insist that, in the broad sweep of history, God used him as His agent in preserving that liberty without which life loses its meaning. I did not know him; but I was told by one who did that Churchill was conscious of having a part in God's providential ordering of the events of history. And he was conscious, too, of the fact that man, who "has conquered the wild beasts and ... even the insects and the microbes ... has only to conquer his last and worst enemy—himself". These are not the words of a moralising preacher but of Sir Winston, shrewd enough to see not only the potential nobility of man but also his potential self-destructiveness. These are insights which we do well to ponder.

Many of us believe—and I am one of them—that only in Christ can man learn to conquer himself.

> My power is weak and low,
> When by myself I stand;
> Imprison me within Thine arms,
> And strong shall be my hand.

To be, in however small a manner, an instrument in the purposes of God, is to achieve one's destiny. That can be the lot both of the man who makes his mark on the page of world history, and of the man who, in humbler sphere, serves Christ in home or office, in civic life or hidden calling.

"Thou shalt go to all that I shall send thee, and whatsoever I command thee thou shalt speak." In such fashion God spoke to prophets and seers in centuries gone by. But He has not ceased to summon and to send men and women to do His will. If we are deaf, we must not think that God is dumb.

"Speak, Lord, for Thy servant heareth."
"Send, Lord, for Thy servant would obey."
God makes use of men.

3. *God makes use of minorities*

It is likely that, in the long perspective of history, Churchill's greatest moments will be seen to have been those when he took his stand at the head of a small minority who had not bowed the knee to Baal. Europe was over-run. Britain was battered. Fear was abroad. Hearts were faint. But one man at least knew that to be right with a tiny minority was better than to be wrong with a multitude. And that knowledge gave him courage, and his courage proved infectious. Victory was born in that hour.

Is there any lesson which England needs more urgently to re-learn today than this? I doubt it. Do the forces of anti-Christ seem immeasurably greater than the forces of godliness, and the powers of evil seem to outweigh the powers of purity and light? What matters it? Rather be right with God and in a seemingly hopeless minority than run with the multitude against His will.

"Here I stand: I can do no other." To say that, if all the world is against you, is to have the secret of true greatness.

It is a lonely road.
It is the way of the Cross.
But the way of the Cross is the way of victory.
Through suffering comes glory, through death comes life.

Earl of Scarbrough—
Man of Affairs

Micah 6:8
God hath shown thee, O man, what is good;
and what doth the Lord require of thee, but to
do justly, and to love mercy, and to walk humbly
with thy God?

1. A modest man

"HE WAS A very modest man." Those words
were spoken to me last week by one who knew Lord Scarbrough
well, one whom he had served long and faithfully, Queen
Elizabeth, the Queen Mother.

She hit on the right word—"modest". There was nothing
brash, noisy or self-important about him.

He held some of the highest offices in the State. When honours
came to him as they did in abundance, he greeted them with
genuine surprise. He was a modest man.

It was this modesty which turned my mind to the text. "God
hath shown thee, O man, what is good; and what doth the Lord
require of thee, but to do justly, and to love mercy, and to walk
humbly with thy God?"

The last three words are probably the operative ones. When
we get some vision of the greatness of God, we also get a vision
of the littleness of man, ourselves included. Real, deep religion
helps us to get our sense of proportion right. God is in heaven:
we are on earth. God is the Creator: we the creatures. God is very
great: we are very small. God is all holy: we are sinners. It

*Memorial Service for Lawrence Roger Lumley, 11th Earl of Scarbrough, K.G., 17th
November, 1974.*

behoves us then to "walk humbly with our God". Perhaps it
was this which led Lord Scarbrough to give himself so generously
in the restoration of our Minster at York.

I recall the day when I asked if I might come and see him to
put to him the request that he would become High Steward of
the Minster. He replied that he would come to see me. I took him
up to my study. I put the proposition to him and without any
questioning he answered in the affirmative. Then he went on:
"I do not believe in letters. I believe in paying personal visits".
This is what he did.

His memorial is engraved for all time under the central tower
of the Minster.

2. A patriot

A second outstanding facet of his character was his love of his
country. He served it well. He loved his England.

"Patriotism" is an unfashionable word. I wish we could get it
back into circulation, if we know what we mean by it.[1] Patriotism
does not mean "my country right or wrong". Rather it is the
kind of patriotism of which we see instances in the Bible. The
prophets were brave men and true. Just because they loved their
country they dared to criticise it and to speak out against all that
marred and stained it. They spoke at great cost, sometimes of
imprisonment, sometimes of death.

The greatest of the patriots was Jesus Christ. "O Jerusalem,
Jerusalem, thou that killest the prophets and stonest them that
are sent unto thee, how often would I have gathered thy children,
even as a hen gathers her chicks under her wings, and ye would
not!" The fellow-countrymen of our Lord rejected the revelation
of God and so they stabbed their country at its heart. This it
was that broke His heart and sent Him to the Cross.

We in England need an infusion of men and women who, just
because they love and serve God, draw people back to His values,
to His love, to His Christ. Only so will the wounds of our nation
be healed. God make us patriots at that depth.

We think of Roger Lumley, a man of modesty, a man of
patriotism. We thank God for him, for his happy family life,
for his busy public life, for the service he gave, for the life he
lived, for the man he was.

[1]This theme is discussed at greater length in True Patriotism, pp. 53-57.

Alan Richardson—Scholar and Dean

St John 17:4
I have glorified Thee upon the earth; I have
finished the work which Thou gavest me to do.

ONE ONLY COULD ever dare to say those words.
To one alone could they ever apply. That one is Jesus Christ our
Lord. St John records that, as Jesus looked back on His life and
ministry and as He looked up into the face of the Father, He was
able to say: "I have glorified Thee upon the earth; I have finished
the work which Thou gavest me to do". So it was that on the
Cross, on that first God's Friday, He could cry with a shout of
triumph: "Finished! Accomplished! Completed!" "He made
there"—in the words of our Prayer Book—"... a full, perfect
and sufficient sacrifice". The actual offering of Himself on the
tree of Calvary was the consummation of an offering which
had been made daily, hourly, during His conscious life. Thanks
be to God for that wonderful obedience, for that mighty death,
and for that glorious resurrection which we celebrate week by
week and of which we shall be thinking, with special concentration, as Good Friday and Easter Day once again draw near.

There are others who, their earthly journey over, more nearly
approximate to the ideal sketched in these words than do most
of us. Alan Richardson was one of these. There was a singular
completeness to his earthly life-work which ended just over a
fortnight ago. God had given him a great work to do, and he

Memorial Service for Alan Richardson, Dean of York, York Minster, 11th March, 1975.

had done it—with distinction and dedication. We all of us hoped for more books from that fluent pen—yes, indeed. But the *great* work was done—and was offered up to the One who had endowed him with singular gifts of mind and personality—and, I doubt not, was accepted by the God whom he loved and served.

When the passage of time enables us to perceive things in their right perspective, we shall see more clearly than we can now the quality and the abiding effects of the work which Alan Richardson was enabled to do. That work was carried out mainly in two spheres, though it must not be forgotten that he had experience as a parish priest, both in a curacy in Liverpool and as a vicar in the diocese of Newcastle—an experience which enriched and deepened his work in the two spheres to which I now refer.

The first sphere is, of course, that of theological thinking, lecturing and writing. The importance of such work is not apparent at first sight to all, perhaps especially to the layman. But if we consider what in fact theology is—"God-talk"—and if we believe that right thinking about God and a right relationship to God matter more than anything else in time or in eternity, then the function of the theologian is seen for what it is in truth. This thinking Alan did with a skill granted to few others during the last four decades. He had a keen mind and a lovely lucidity of expression. He was an expert in his field and he wrote for experts. But he constantly bore in mind the clergy whose task is to expound the Christian faith week in week out in a highly sceptical age, and the intelligent laymen who need to be equipped to give a reason for the hope that is in them. Considerable anxiety is being expressed today—and rightly expressed—at the gap which yawns between the thinking of our academic theologians and the preaching in our parish pulpits. Alan Richardson was aware of this, and much of his thought was spent and his energy given in throwing a solid bridge across that gap. He did it by his writings. He did it, also, by his lectures in Durham, in Nottingham (where the school of theology is itself a memorial to eleven years of highly creative work), in York (where he lectured brilliantly right to the end), and in many parts of the world to which he went on theological missionary journeys.

A long row of distinguished books, some written for the learned only, some for the thinking wayfaring man, bear their witness to the dedication of a great theologian. And a big company of men and women, scattered throughout the world, can testify to the debt they owe to a man who enabled them to combine intellectual honesty with faith in the living God, and in their turn to do "God-talk" in terms which make sense in a scientific age. That alone would be an achievement big enough for most men. "He not only taught us sound theology, he showed us Christ"—so wrote one of his pupils. Who could want a more wonderful tribute than that?

The other sphere of his life-work is around us here today, for all to see. How well I remember the day when he and his wife came to discuss with us the possibility of coming to the deanery. I was anxious that the old tradition of scholarship in one of our greatest deaneries should be continued—and who better to fulfil that than Alan Richardson? We had no idea eleven years ago how desperate was the condition of the Minster—that was only discovered after he had taken up his work. But once the dread discovery was made, there was no looking back. The Minster must be saved. More than that—it must be cleaned. More than that—its surrounding area must be beautified to provide a fitting setting for York's greatest jewel. "If you seek his monument, look around you." "I have finished the work that Thou gavest me to do."

Of course—and he would be the first to grant this—this mighty operation was not the work of one man. It was the work of a very large team—a team in which a great number of laymen and women laboured alongside the Chapter and the architect. But a team, if it is to achieve anything, must have a leader. This team had just that—and at the side of the leader a helper who carried much of the load, provided much of the inspiration, and prolonged the life of her husband.

In this much loved place, I need not say more about the Minster. We have all had a hand in its restoration, but Alan led us, and for that leading we thank God.

Having spoken about the two main spheres in which his gifts were exercised, I must say a word about the man himself, as I knew him.

As I have thought back over the years of our friendship, I have been reminded of four Latin words in which St Augustine described God as he conceived him to be. I translate them in six

English words: "Always at work, always at rest". I venture to use them today as a fair description of God's servant whom we commemorate.

Alan was a mighty worker. Even in the years when the burden of the restoration of this great church lay heavy upon him, he managed, by dint of studying far into the night, to continue his writing work, to lecture, to travel, and to entertain in that ever hospitable deanery innumerable friends and people in need. "Always at work." Yes—but "always at rest". There were depths to his character which were not easily ruffled.

Alan was a gentle man. He did not cry, nor lift up his voice in the street. But in that very quietness lay his strength and the secret of the magnitude of his achievement.

So there can be no gloom about our service today—but, rather, *sympathy*, deep and sincere, for those who loved him well and especially for her who stood so closely beside him in all he did; and *thankfulness* for work well-rounded, by which he glorified the God who called him and enabled him.

V AN INSTITUTION SERMON

An Institution Sermon

St Matthew 13:43
"The man who has ears should use them"
(J. B. Phillips)

OF COURSE HE should. That is what his ears are there for. Of course. But does he?

"The man who has ears should use them"—this seems to have been a refrain in the teaching of Jesus. He would tell a story, one of His inimitable parables, sketching a scene or a life-situation with a few deft strokes, and then—"the man who has ears should use them"; and He would leave it at that.

The words were more than a refrain. They were a warning. For there is hearing *and* hearing. It is possible to hear with the physical ear but to be spiritually deaf. The word spoken does not register. If you oversleep one morning, it is possible that it was not that your alarm-clock had failed to go off; it might have been that you had become so accustomed to its clarion note that it failed to register on you. The fault lay not in the clock but in you. You had ears but you did not use them! That is a potentially dangerous situation.

Next Sunday's Gospel (the twelfth Sunday after Trinity) tells the story of a deaf man's contact with Jesus (St Mark 7:31 ff.). Both his hearing and his speech were affected. Jesus took the man aside from the noisy crowd, put His fingers into his ears, spat, touched his tongue, looked up to heaven, sighed, and said, "Open!" The wonder happened. The deaf man heard. His speech was clear. He was a new man.

313

1. *We clergy need this experience.* We must get away from the crowds and learn what it is to be with Jesus face to face, to feel His touch and experience His power.

"Take heed", says the bishop when deacons are presented to him for ordination to the priesthood, "take heed that the persons whom ye present unto us be apt and meet for their learning and godly conversation, to exercise their ministry duly . . ." That means both intellectual equipment and spiritual alertness. It implies that the men to be ordained are of such a kind as will always be using their ears, "alert and quick to hear each whisper of Thy call".

That is what Retreats are for. That is why the clergy do well to watch their use of the Daily Offices, their periods of meditation, of intercession, of steady study.

Do not expect your new vicar to be everlastingly "on the go". That is not the way he will best serve his twenty-five thousand people. He comes to you as a man of prayer, of study, of thought. He must withdraw to be with Jesus if he is to advance to serve his people.

2. *Your parochial church council and church workers need this experience.* The most important part of your P.C.C. meetings is that unhurried period of quiet thought and prayer which precedes the time you give to consideration of the agenda, when you wait on God to discover His mind and will for the parish.

It may well be that your new vicar will suggest a weekend away at some conference centre for the members of the P.C.C. That could well be a revolutionary experience. Deaf ears could be opened. Tied tongues could be loosed. Creative planning could be engaged in. The council could become a centre of spiritual power in the parish, if those who had ears used them. Why not?

3. *We all need this experience.* No wonder Jesus sighed as He looked at that pathetic figure before Him! The pity of it—a man with ears, but not hearing; with a tongue, but unable to utter! A man who hitherto had never heard the liberating word of Jesus! Perhaps he had not wanted to? Perhaps he had been afraid to? There are many of us like that—and Jesus, as He looks at us in His love, sighs.

At the heart of the Christian revelation is the belief that "God has spoken". He is not a silent God who never communicates with His children. "He has spoken—to us—in a Son", His supreme and authoritative Word. If we are deaf, we must not think that God is dumb. Perhaps we have ears but have failed to use them.

Patiently, and with infinite love, the Lord Christ waits to take us away from the noisy crowd, to confront us with Himself, to touch us with His healing hands, and to say: "Open!"

> Thy touch has still its ancient power,
> No word from Thee can fruitless fall.
> Speak in this solemn evening hour,
> And in Thy mercy heal us all.

VI AN ORDINATION CHARGE

An Ordination Charge

Your pre-ordination training is over. Your Retreat is nearly over. Tomorrow you will be ordained. You come to that great service in hope—and with trembling. To you, tomorrow, will come the solemn words: "Take thou authority . . ." To you will be addressed the questions: "Will you . . .? Will you . . .?" One day God will ask: "Did you . . .? Did you . . .?"

What can I say to you this evening, just before your ordination? I would draw your attention to two passages in the New Testament.

1. *Acts 20: 18-35*. St Paul has summoned the elders of the Church at Ephesus to meet him at the port of Miletus, so that he may speak to them before he sails to Jerusalem. He is in a retrospective mood. His mind goes back over his stay in the city—two long years in a city famous for its idolatrous worship and its wealth. No easy place this in which to plant the Gospel! There he had kept back nothing that was for the good of the people; he had delivered the message; he had taught, publicly and privately; he had insisted on repentance before God and trust in the Lord Jesus. Now, in serenity, he looks forward to finishing the race and completing the task assigned to him. What is his final word to be to the elders of the Church?

It is a word of *warning*—"Keep watch over yourselves and over all the flock . . ." You note the order—watch *yourselves* first, and only then your flock.

That word comes home to us this evening. For it often happens that after high spiritual experience comes severe testing; after the baptism, the temptation; after the mountain top, the descent to the plain and the wrestling with the demoniac.

The most tragic part of a bishop's life is that in which he has to deal with clergy who have *not* taken heed to themselves, when the bishop has perhaps to terminate a priest's ministry, or, almost equally tragically, to watch its formal continuance when the joy and power have gone from it, when prayer and sacrament and Bible study have died, and only the husk of the ministry remains. And all the time the bishop knows that this *could* happen to him.

"Keep watch over yourselves and over all the flock." It is a word of warning.

2. *St John 16:31–33*. Here is a word of infinite *encouragement*. Peace and courage in the midst of adversity—this is the theme of Jesus to His men on the eve of His crucifixion.

Do not expect your ministry to be easy. On the contrary, you will often be misunderstood. Your hours will be long and hard. The going will be very tough. But "be of good courage".

Right under the shadow of the Cross, Jesus gives to His disciples that rallying-cry which seems to have been part and parcel of His whole ministry: "Be of good courage! Fear not!" That cry sprang from His profound belief in God; from His close relationship to God; from His humble reliance on God. He was able to be "the Man for others" precisely because and only because He was the Man for God, the Man of God. At the end, there was trouble, the desperate, deadly trouble of the Cross. But He could be, and was, of good courage. He knew He had overcome the world.

With this, then, I leave you, with a word of *warning* ("take heed to yourselves...") and with a word of *encouragement* ("courage! the victory is mine; I have conquered the world"). You do not need more than that.

As you go to your rest tonight, on the eve of your ordination, think on these two passages. And as you humbly thank God for calling you to the ministry of His Church, recall the words of St Chrysostom pondering on his ministry in that same Church:

> "Oh the wonder of it!
> Oh the loving kindness of God to man!"

48909